A Broken Vow

Emerson Deline

THIS BOOK IS PUBLISHED AS IS

Forte Publishing

First Published in 2018 Published by:

FORTE Publications
#12 Ashmun Street
Snapper Hill
Monrovia, Liberia

FORTE Publishing
7202 Tavenner Lane
208 Alexandria
VA, 22306

FORTE Press
76 Sarasit Road
Ban Pong, 70110
Ratchaburi, Thailand

http://fortepublishing.wix.com/fppp

Printed in the United States of America

ISBN: 0648182347
ISBN-13: 978-0648182344

DEDICATION

In loving memory of the dearly depart,
especially my Grandmother, Eva C. Ross Deline,
William Francis Babyboy Deline, my dad, my
wonderful mother Amanda Julia Smith Anderson
my paternal [U]ncle Samuel Buster Deline,
and Wellington O. Deline.

.

Contents

Acknowledgement

It is not possible to mention all the people that came together to make this project work. Instead of trying the impossible, I'll just make a general notation of gratitude. You all know yourselves. So, in my Liberian voice, I say, "Thank you yah!"

However, mention must be made of few, whose roles were pivotal in this process. My family, who pushed me to the very end; my church family for giving me a reason to continue in the Lord's Vineyard and my parents for setting me along this journey unbeknowest to me. A special thanks to my editors and publisher, FORTE Publishing; Any error here in are entirely mine.

Preface

A *Broken Vow* is not a religious book. Nor is it a denominational handbook releasing perspectives of religious doctrines. It suggests that the individual believer's character is a compelling factor in their choices, especially, how they lead the Christian life. It is a book, which presents the Christian believer's will and desires with strong allusions to godly commands. It presupposes the individual believer's qualities within a unique volitional genre.

Ideally, it advocates the embracing of faith with openness, and encourages the development of the Christian believer's will towards godly happiness as an end purpose for living. The focus here is not just [any] living, but living in acceptance and appreciation of God's commands for productive and spontaneous growth.

A key purpose of this book is to discourage religious controls in any of its extremities. It purports the conscious apparatus for the discovery of the individual's inner convictions in life. It is an ideological focus of the inner self-confronting human realities as opposed to religious dogmas. It discloses the individual's emotions encroaching the imbalances of manmade rules for doctrines. Broken Vows splits the union of religious ideologues and fosters peaceful faith development. Additionally, it attempts to discourage, through the portrayal of the characters, the un-substantiating control mechanism leveled against sincere faith believers.

Throughout the pages, you shall find the subjugating sentiments of religious institutions. You shall also see how some Christian institutions deny the human factors in the development of personality and individualities.

Broken Vows is a book, which questions denial of God's command and thus replacing it which human conviction and assumptions. It is a path to seeing what God commands is what should to be idealized, and not replaced by the convictions of man

Introduction

These Broken Vows!

In life, we tend to find ourselves making vows- to ourselves, to our loved ones, to others and even to the Most High God. Yet, despite our best intentions, we often break them not because we are necessarily bad. However, with human interplay, other challenges in life and because of man's imperfections, things go south or get out of hand and we end up breaking the best-intended vows.

Human relationships can be contemptuous, distrusting and disappointing. It is adjustable. In life, a person can be true to him or herself, often committed to self and responsible to others. And then, when these possibilities are achieved, responding to ideal relationships with others can be better managed with greater spiritual balance. Being young and enthusiastic is like fuel in jet engines; it keeps the youthful individuals wondering, planning and projective; sometimes with without full convictions.

These stories are about the actual lives of people, yet we doused them with fictional characters for anonymity. They are an indication the many paths pursued through the socializing processes of growth and the pains associated with such phenomenon. It also explores the vulnerabilities surrounding individual attempts to resurrect their pasts, [in life]-a serious mistake which on the surface seems okay, but, is plagued with darkness orchestrated by spiritual forces. They enslave these lives to prisons of secrecies and pains.

The book also presents scriptural resolves for problematic situations in relationships, commitment to oneself and relationship to God and man. Preferably, everyone would wishes to have all possibilities come through with ease or free of trials and struggles. However, no successful point in a person's life is without challenges.

Seemingly, any good and inspiring functional condition is worth the price paid. As is depicted in the story, Melinda Yates and Bobby Ross encountered the obvious and they indirectly learned valuable lessons through their various life experiences. Melinda and Bobby would have never experience the true meaning of life, if it wasn't love at first sight and the blending of the truthful content of real love, inspired by commitment and subjections to spiritual scrutiny by faith. They utilized their skills and serving with quality realness to others.

A person can get lost but the sentiment of love finds the broken heart and reunites. *Broken Vows* is a saga of intense motivation and determination in the lives of its host of characters. This book discloses the aspects of Scriptures alluding to the substantiating relevance in which the bliss of the Kingdom of heaven is not about food, drinks and other satisfactions; rather it is idealized into the bliss of the Holy Spirt in righteousness, and by this our services to Christ in this manner is approved by God and man (*Romans 14:14-15*).

Please enjoy the read and be mindful of the exhilarating cadences, for you just might find yourself, or whole chunks of you, within one of these characters.

Chapter 1

Melinda Yates and Bobby Ross

Melinda Yates grew up in West Africa, and her early days of schooling were strictly catholic. Melinda was dark and beautiful, extremely formal, eloquent and entirely committed to celibacy. She knew that she would dedicate her life to that of sisterhood at the convent.

She attended mass throughout the week and on Sundays. Melinda sang on the choir and lead devotions early on Sunday mornings; her voice was exquisitely melodious. When she sang, the sound was that of angel calmly descending from the heavens on wings as a host of doves. The congregants were move and inspired at the sound of her voice. Pleasantry was almost automatic when it came to her deportment and composure; it was Melinda and nothing could be compared to her honesty and caring for others. She was the epitome of humility and kindness. She knew that her call in life was a dedication to ministry and total serenity. She attended the University of Liberia and obtained her BS degree in applied Nursing and Psychology. Her composure kept her exquisitely calm and attractive. Melinda was also skilled in all sorts of fine arts and was compulsively interactive with everyone.

Bobby Ross was friendly, cooperative sharing and a great person to know. Nothing was too little for him to do; once it came to helping others. He was a social scientist and love life. He was single and available, but very reserved. He had a PhD in Philosophy with emphasis in family dynamics. He worked as director of corporate culture at a known corporation. He organized the industrialized international plans and was responsible for managing change processes.

Melinda and her family migrated from Liberia, West Africa. They settled in Jersey City, New Jersey. Bobby's parents were from England and Sierra Leone. He was a bi-racial handsome young man and exquisitely intelligent as well. When questioned about his ethnic makeup, he noted that the Master is colorblind and loves all men from the shade of the color of red. He only sees red – the plasma proteins in the human race.

By the way he; responded this is the proliferation of relationships within this society; because racial integration has made many strides; it has come a long way; not where it should be, but there are visible changes. The American society is not reflective of a hundred percent racially integrated society, but evidences are seen everywhere that efforts are forth coming to this end. We have today in the White House a bi-racial president; we have governors from Indian background, and more so universities show greater signs of racially structured enrollments. We see that publicly racial couples can walk the streets freely without disdained, and this is the epitome of selfless and genuine love. Answering the question about racially integrated society; it is not so simple but more accuracies are evidentially clear by the way people interact today within those states, which were intensely racially segregated. Do we see changes and efforts geared toward a substantial change?

Yes off course, there are restaurants, clubs, water fountains, sport arenas, which in times past, were not integrated, but are today. The changing of time, the turn of a new era is ushering a coalition of people who are totally color blind, and increasingly societies are becoming more acceptable to humanity because of character validating meaningful human reciprocity. Prophetically, the great Dr. Martin Luther King spoke about his little children, blacks and whites hands together singing the Negro spiritual "Free at last! Free at last! Thank God almighty! Free at Last!" Listen, I am part white and in love with a black woman. You know something, love has no boundaries, and love has no color. When love finds its target, it engulfs the heart and paints the color of the spectrum. You think about it, love brings the heart together and releases a sentiment which is like the core of the apple that brings all the juicy flavors; I am in love and I am committing to love; I shall get the desire of heart "Melinda!". I am determined and focus I understand that nothing is impossible with God. I am going after my desire. I am trusting God for this miracle; I know it is not Melinda's desire but the God I serve is able to change the situation in her life and make us one. This I know and I am waiting on His time for my quest!

The Meet?

It was on a raining Sunday afternoon when Melinda ran across the street to find shelter underneath the shades of an ice cream parlor. There Bobby saw this earthly angel. He had a glance at this stunning beautiful young woman; and from a distance, he became affixed on her and consciously concluded with all the fiber of his being that this is the woman on earth for him. He knew it, but his imagination and convictions expose him to a gaseous alluvium and he was enchanted beyond measured.

Not understanding the conditional formative moments of this saga, he approached her as a bold suitor ready for what it takes to get to the next level. Sometimes things seem unfair, but life's preparation takes on all forms, and no one can tell what his trials are the next moment when he steps outside of his controlled environment. It is only by chance that we can oppose the glaring realities and take sensible chances for happiness. When the time comes, it comes with a kind of stupor, which arrests the heart and brings the faculties into submission.

Real human connection is the controlling factor, which brings satisfaction beyond the natural with rest from the spiritual domain. If I may digress; Bobby tried to gain her attention and offered her a seat as she entered the shop; she understood his outstanding qualities, and accepted his offer as he kept the door opened for her. The rain was intense, like they say, "It was raining cats and dogs"; she sat with him and accepted his offer.

When Melinda sat down; Bobby was confused and thought to himself; "what have I gotten myself into?" The ambiance had glowing and tasteful sentiment; it was the pleasantry of Melinda. Her presence spoke volume and many people drawn to her stunning and angelic look. She was admired, and confused and more confused was Bobby.

The young man didn't know where to begin. He introduced himself and she gladly reciprocated the gesture; oh my God; it was love at first sight; oh well more evident by bobby's action! However, he questioned her about where she lived because she seemed new in the neighborhood, but Melinda was from the neighborhood; she only live in seclusion and with complete divinely appropriations.

Her complete focus was ministry and school. Bobby found himself out of place and when the rain stopped; she asked to be excused. Bobby offered to walk Melinda half the way home, but she refused for fear that she would be mistakenly confused. She thought to remain in seclusion and celibate. Her father did not support her life style; her mother knowing that Melinda a younger daughter should get married and have children encouraged her constantly to do just that; for she could be committed to God, and not prevent the spiritual continuity of their family's heritage. Melinda mother told her that procreation was also a part of God's blessings, and denying the opportunity for others to come into the world was also not a part of God's plan.

The situation was intense, the mother was consistent, and then; Melinda explained to her mother that she wanted to serve God and that her body was for God. Mrs. Yates argued that her body can still be for God but she can serve humanity by aiding in populating God's creation. She also argued that Melinda was chosen to bear blessed and beautiful children. Mrs. Yates exclaimed my child just look at you; just look at your beauty. Don't' you know that you can be a beautiful wife and a wonderful mother? Mrs. Yates once again said Melinda you have all the qualities of a spectacular woman who can mean so much to her children and the rest of the world. The young euphemistically exclaimed that she would live a life of sacrifice and be faithful to God almighty and the Church.

Immediately after the argument, Melinda decided to be successful and to live up to expectations. She went to post graduate school and with good aptitude; was awarded many scholarships and other meritorious grants. She played sports, ran track and played successfully on the girls' basketball team at church. One evening Melinda walked into her locker; saw a dozen roses and the card which read from Bobby Ross with all my love; and she smiled and took the roses to the sacrament hall and left it for the Widows' social gathering; that night. Melinda's activities confused many, her fierce competitive involvement with sports and academics; had many guessing her sexuality and some were assuming that she was hiding behind Catholicism. I just want to drop this descriptive view of Melinda and when she wore jeans pants; she was the sight to see, and she was well compacted and totally shaped as a beautiful woman. She never refuted any assumptions about her sexuality; but instead focused on serving in the Church and commitment to family and the community services; with the youth and widows. Everyone wanted to know "who was this young woman; who never exhibit any frown; carried around the world greatest smile and could not get involve with a man?" Many questions about Melinda sexuality came about but to no avail.

One afternoon Bobby ran into Melinda and asked about her where about; she replied right here in town; he replied for real; she replied yes. He asked her out to the movie; she looked at him and smiled, and later said okay no problem. She pondered if this was the best thing to do; she knew that she had to grant a favor; since the young man was so kind to her sometimes ago. She went home spoke to her mother about the date; her mother was delighted; replied that young man is a fine Young man with a great smirk on her face and I know his family very well; Mrs. Yates seemed cautiously delighted and hoped that a relationship develops.

She then repeated the same "Melinda that young man is a fine young man". Melinda smiled and told her mother that she knew who he was and it was the only reason she was going out with him in the first place; she said mom I know

Bobby is educated and single; looking for miss right and I am hoping that he finds her, but me! She thought to herself that this guy could make a woman happy and I hope he finds her. Bobby had already discovered Miss. Right, the only set back here was he had to compete with time and Melinda's spirituality. Melinda conducted herself well; she knew and understood her ambitions and they were completely aligned with her goals. While at the movie; Bobby rested his arms over Melinda's seat; she was uncomfortable with it; nevertheless, she tolerated it. It seemed good after a while. A turning point came and it came in a fashion when the inner part of Bobby's palm touched her neck; she then moved forward; and softly he said I am sorry. She replied it is okay; this was an unusual event for her; she had never been touched like that before, and this was too close; how could this guy get so close. The touch on the back of her neck meant something, but Bobby was not aware of the impact; she had never been touched in that manner before, Bobby's action was not intentional at all. I guess like the woman in the Bible who touched Jesus at the hem of His garment.

He knew that it wasn't an ordinary touch. This was a plus for Bobby, but he had a hill of a mountain to climb. At the theater some friends from church ran into them; Molly asked Melinda; what was she doing at the movie? She replied just hanging with Bobby the family's friend. They later left and decided to take a stroll, and strolling back home; some associates of Bobby walked by; pulled him to the side and asked "did you get her? Are you going out with her?" Bobby smiled and they took the insinuating silence to be truthful and spread a misconception around. The situation kind of pulled Melinda back into her shell and she started the secluded life.

The Priest?

The priest Father John the patriarch heard about Melinda's situation and summonsed her to his office for a talk. Father spoke with Melinda, explained to her that many are the afflictions of the righteous and that throughout her life she would come across many mistaken situations but she needed to be strongly focused and not angry. She and the patriarch later strolled around in the garden at the convent and they prayed and recited the rosary together.

After that evening's devotion and meditating, she grew stronger, more open still introverted but associative. She called Bobby, and because of his silence, he was afraid to answer his phone; she tried many times but he rejected all of her calls. She went home inquired Bobby's address; her mother was astonished at the request and hastily called out to her husband Frank; Melinda's father.

Frank knew his daughter's desire for ministry and did not bulge about the inquisition. Evangeline; Melinda mother then provided the address to Bobby's house and Melinda gladly accepted it. She asked her father for some change and told him that she was going to see Bobby; Frank never asked why he knew that Melinda wanted to set things straight with the young man! Bobby for days did not leave his house he was locked in and told no one why! He thought he had messed up and that he would never get an opportunity to speak with Melinda no longer.

As the young man struggled with his inner feelings; succumbed by a depressive malady; over taken by his fears; suddenly his doorbell ranged. Who is it? He yelled! Who is it? The doorbell ranged again and he replied who is it? As Melinda started for home; Bobby looked through the windows and caught a glimpse of her from the rear; he thought it was an illusion or an apparition. It seemed ghostly and he quickly yelled hello! Hello! Melinda; she turned with tears coming down her face; walked over to Bobby's house.

An instant euphoria got a hold of him; she went in crying; the tears were streaming down her beautiful face and her lovely innocence calmed him with a strong and arresting concern. He exclaimed, "Melinda what is the matter? What is going on?"

"I am sorry I should have conducted myself appropriately." She replied "Bobby nothing is wrong; I have never felt strongly about my faith as I do now I understand that it took lots of nerves to talk to me and I appreciated your company; you were respectful and I like that about you, there is something you need to know about me!

The first confronting thing for Bobby was that he thought this woman was about to tell him off; and he knew she was too good a woman for him; as he thought, but at least he tried. Bobby in his mind ponders if Melinda is gay or maybe she is just stuck up and overly confident about her stunning beauty. None of his thoughts was accurate. Bobby sat quietly; Melinda said Bobby you are a good person I don't want to lead you on, and sadly I had to come to inform you about my goals in life.

First, I must admit that I like your company, but frankly, I don't want to be involved with you in any other way than a family friend or brother! I love all humanity and wish them the best of God's love and that is as far as it can get with you and me!"

Bobby said. "Wait a minute are you gay?

She replied, "No!"

"Then what are you or who are you?" Melinda saw that Bobby was becoming agitated she asked to be excused!

Bobby said, "Okay, you came all the way across town to say nothing Melinda? Please tell me the truth about you! She spoke quietly with a pleasant voice to Bobby, and it seemed as if an angel was speaking; he admired her beauty and her lovely white teeth.

"I am serious; I have been accepted in seminary to study as a worker for the cross of Christ and to live a celibate life!"

"What?"

"Yes," with tears running down her beautiful face; Bobby stood astonished lost for words and completely stoic.

Heartbroken and defenseless and submerged as if a ghostly present had overtaken him; he was speechless and broken as a toothless lion in the jungle of the great marched land in Mali. She said strangely Bobby I feel connected to you somehow; I feel you in my heart but my choice is to serve God in full dedication. He sat down thought for a while and inquired about her travel time; she replied in a year's time! Instantly he saw this as a moment in which he could get her to change her position about ministry. As she was about to leave; he insisted to drive her home, and once again she accepted and they left. It was late that night; the family sat together in the living room for an evening of family chatters, Frank was concern about his daughter's trip; asked how that went, thinking her father was a bit intrusive; she quickly responded; alright dad.

She walked to the windows in deep penitence and poignantly contrived about her new feelings. Things seemed glaring at the time, but her first love was the church and now a fear had interplayed with the possibility of not making it to convent. Melinda was beginning to develop an inner conflict. Judge the truthfulness of her thoughts; the very first man she allowed to get closer to her had so much impact on her emotionally. She tried to figure out what it would take if another experience came about; she thought she was fragile.

No she wasn't she knew that this was no ordinary a person in Bobby and it impacted her wholesome being. Frank understanding his daughter; walked over to her extended his arms to her, and said my child you really need a hug; come and hug your father. She calmly reached over and rested her head on her father's shoulder and whispered; dad I don't know what got over me, but I felt a strange feeling going through my body when I looked into the eyes of Bobby, I saw so much rest and peacefulness deep into his soul. I am confused about things. Strangely, her mother understood the situation from a woman's perspectives. Realizing that whatever Melinda might have been predisposed to, was now in a conflicting condition. It was a struggle and it was making the choice remain celibate or become a faithful and loving wife! Mrs. Evangeline Yates automatically thanked God for Bobby! Oh, mine this as a battle with greater forces from within.

Instantly the telephone rang and it was Sister Carolina from the convent; she called that night to informed Melinda of her appointments for the next day's chores at the pariah; it interrupted this moment and the family excused themselves and went to bed. Sister Carolina was also an influencing factor in Melinda's life and more so her mentor at church. Encouragingly she cautioned Melinda about temptations; she spoke about her commitment to the work of the ministry. Melinda informed the sister that all was well. The young woman hopes were built on traveling the next year for studies and to make her vow; live a celibate life and serve the church and humanity. This was necessarily primary for Melinda, she had confessed this to everyone but she was extremely close to turning back.

She never understood the realities of life nor what came along with the processes. The next day, Bobby was struggling with his inner feelings growing in him for a real woman- a woman whom he might never have as his wife. He saw no other woman as he saw Melinda, and nothing on earth could change that for him; he felt that Melinda is the only woman, which could bring peace into his life; he saw greater possibilities with her; only if they could fall in love. He realized that some matters in life may seem unfair, but the end also justifies the means when there are clarity and understanding of certain realities. He appreciated Melinda and her dedication to her faith, but selfishly he thought her service still could be given to the church, but not to deny him of the joy of living with Melinda.

On Tuesday afternoon, Melinda was walking to the church around the corner; on her way to confession, she decided to walk in the rose bush garden at the pariah.

The birds were whistling in the trees, the wind calmly blew and she sat on the bench, looked up into the sky and commenced praying and thanking God for the splendor of His beautiful handy work. Softly she sang "here we are all together as we sing our song joyfully; here we are as we pray we shall always be" Father heard her sing and walked over to her; he told Melinda that she seemed trouble;

she replied no Father! No! I am not. The real troubling thing was that Melinda burned deeply on the inside for the love of Bobby.

She felt a special care emanating from his person; she hope to, be kissed and caressed, but she struggle with a combustible flame and it seemed twofold. Her first love for faith and now for another; how to handle her real feelings seemed unpretending and undyingly consuming. After the priest left her, she walked quietly into the corridors of the pariah with this pressing joy but poignantly confused. The mother superior called her while in the entrance of the sacrament hall, sat her down and told her the truth about life. Melinda was an educated young woman, smart and has been awarded a scholarship to attend Harvard University a year from now; after seminary. The Priest told her about a poem called the

The up-Hill Climber

If your mountainside climb is rough, pray that it is not smoother from the beginning, the tougher your climb; the sweeter the trophy at the end; just don't get distracted by the way side climbers they will interfere with your arrival at the end. Keep the climb steady; stay focus on the joy ahead and be steadfast for your view at the top! Some-things you just cannot change therefore if the road up hill is tough get tougher for there's a just reward for the uphill climber! Just be persistent and endure the pain; set your eyes like a flint and go on! Your victory is at the next round. Remember your victory is at the next round for each round goes higher; so look to the hills above and be a good climber! Remember help is at the next round!"

Father John purpose was to encourage the young woman so that she remained committed. Oh well such is life everyone can be an up-hill climber provider that person commits to the task ahead. The goal is to determine and be steadfast so much that you can taste success without seeing it visibly.

When anyone puts in time and greater dexterity, time rolls on and along with fruitful platforms for the future. We can all be the up-hill climber; once we are goal focused. No matter what the circumstances are in life, we all have to keep the climb steadily going, because the higher we can climb the clearer we would see the path whether up-hill or downhill. A clearer path takes into consideration all of the glaring realities and unfold a systematic prospect. Therefore, never give up trying; never give up climbing for the end results shall take you higher into positions; than when you first started. I must admit that throughout there would be encounters with two kinds of individuals and they are conditional and unconditional folks and these are some things to look out for as I tell you my experience with them and my faith just listen.

Chapter 2

My conditional friends vs. Unconditional Friends

was down at one point in my life and I walked with some friends; with whom all along; I was dependent because of my imprisoned past; I thought they liked me. I expressed my deepest heart secrets to them and they had pity on me conditionally; I believed them. I remained a loyal prisoner by the words of my expressions to them, but I was disillusioned by the temporary protective pretense.

I was submissive until I met a man who told me that he could be my friend (Jesus) without conditions. I decided to become independent by freeing myself from the bandage of my conditional friends. I give my hands to my unconditional friend (Jesus), and as soon as I did; I felt the inner joy and peace of freedom. I was free and independently sober; not walking under the pretense of my so-called friends who were my closest friends.

One day, I refused to accept the abuses and took chances with the new unconditional friend. I said to myself the longer I keep silent and accept abuses because of protecting my previous expressions, the more I would always be a prisoner to my circumstances. I broke free and one day questioned the sincerity of my relationship. As soon as I did, I became the scum of the Earth with so much hidden baggage as per my conditional friends. I was confused. I was called unrighteous, fake and a hypocrite and one who is rejected by God. I said to myself, "How could they?"

Then the words of David came to me (Psalm 49:8-10 "A wicked thing is poured out upon him, That when he lies down, he will not rise up again.

9 Even my close friend in whom I trusted, who ate my bread, has lifted up his heel against me"

Then I understood that this was character building and that going back to the portal house meant remaking the person in me. Oh well I was marred by the words of my friends who I trusted and disclosed my thoughts to; it was the natural thing to do as per the scripture, but then I realized that some people are not mature enough to handle any matter concerning anyone not even themselves. I did this as per "James 5:16 confess your faults one to another, and pray one for another, that ye may be healed. The effectual fervent prayer of a righteous man availeth much." Oh well I thought they were the righteous ones (my conditional friends). I did my part; I found God; I was renewed, but my past became their taunting apparatus for their fiery darts at me, I would feel the hurt but I said to myself who is more the child of God? The one who confessed his faults to his conditional friend, got forgiven by God or the one who uses his past friend faults as leverages for taunting? Then I found the answer within which promptly told me that everyone has to hold on to the end, because God never stops remaking His children "Jeremiah 18:1-4 Arise and go down to the potter's house, and there I will announce My words to you." 3 Then I went down to the potter's house, and there he was, making something on the wheel. 4 But the vessel that he was making of clay was spoiled in the hand of the potter; so he remade it into another vessel, as it pleased the potter to make...." We can become new and well-furnished for the Master's use don't let anyone put you down. God cares more than you can imagine!

Melinda we have to pray David's pray every day; for guidance! "Psalm 49:10 But You, O LORD, be gracious to me and raise me up, "That I may repay them...." If you or anyone who is going through this experience don't feel God is able to bring you through, remember the words of Jesus. (Matthew 5:44-45: 44) But I say unto you, Love your enemies, bless them that curse you, do good to them that hate you, and pray for them which despitefully use you, and persecute you. 45 That ye may be the children of your Father which is in heaven: for He makes his sun to rise on the evil and on the good, and sends rain on the just and on the unjust". Melinda you must persist on the good for your best shall come in God's time stay put; follow your conviction and hold on to your faith.

△ △ △

The Separations

Melinda continued her work with the church recited the Hail Mary so many times and remains committed to church work, Bobby continued with his quests but they seemed meaningless. He finally decided to get involve with work and volunteer at Melinda's pariah. On occasions they met for lunch and went to various Christian gospel concerts; they grew closer and he supported Melinda's choice. One day Bobby invited Melinda over to his house after work; she came over and they watched some clippings from the catholic mission school in West Africa -Liberia.

The clip was about the mission work, and it fascinated Bobby and he was enlightened by its spectacular; he kept quiet and thought to himself if I can see this place and work in the mission field; then I shall find fulfillment in myself. He thought life was over since he could not start one with Melinda. As he sat motionless; she noticed him; saw his convictions and she was delighted and hinted that:

In the quests for a desirable goal, pressing forward is actually creating paths towards developmental opportunities. No one can actually conceive his path, but following one's own heart and convictions ushers the beginning of a journey with the first great successful step. There is always that moment when the heart profusely conjures a unique solitude in pondering reality. It's for certain that no one knows the mind of Jehovah God, but everyone can prepare himself to be in position of service.

At the end of her hinted moment; Bobby realized that his and knowing Melinda was a turning point and it meant giving back to humanity what has been freely given. The campus in Africa was going to be a hideaway for Bobby, realizing that he could not stop the call on Melinda' life; he decided to take time off from his six figures pay job to one of servitude and serene.

△ △ △

Two Months Later

Two months later Bobby met with father John at the pariah and told him about his convictions; he felt that he was called to devote two years to service in Liberia and this was to be kept secret from Melinda. In the main time Melinda was about to accept her training for Sisterhood; the night prior to leaving; she cried all night; asking God why did she had to meet Bobby? Why did she had to develop such inner caring for a man? Oh she cried and cried but she could not negate her call. She had a few months left and decided to move into the convent; hoping to avoid Bobby's advances.

At the convent

Visitors were allowed and after mass Bobby would often sit in the rose garden pray for Melinda and he also asked God why did He had to bring Melinda into his life? what was the real reason if he could not hold on to the desire of his heart; he was upset and profusely confounded; he asked God why can't he (Bobby) be left alone in his misery?

He also prayed that Melinda would commit to the church, and become his wife; this would set him free from the jolt of love bondage; thus releasing him from solitude, because solitarily; he was confined.

He strolled glancing at the building as if it was a wall of defense, which he would one day tear down, and rescue his wife to be. He saw the entire ambiance as an iron blanket snatching the life out of his heart; it was Melinda after all, under lock down. He felt a part of him was incarcerated; he pondered why was life so cold to him; that his happiness was extracted, and he spoke as if the building had ears and could understand the conditions of his fated saga.

He cried out "I am hurting! I am hurting, but I cannot compete with the masterful Creator." Consistently, He visited the rose garden and positioned himself in locations where he believed Melinda would see and maybe notice him. He was right because, she would always come to the east end of the building hoping that he shows up. She struggled with the commitment to the church and the life, which she might never have, here was this pleasant man putting everything about himself clamped down just to have a glance of her presence.

She was haunted by his daily presence in the rose garden. Melinda was calculated. She knew the time of the day Bobby would show up, like clockwork, he was on time. Whenever he entered the garden, she said, "Forgave me father for this sin haunts me. It seems as if I am engulfed by the sentiment of the love of a real man.

Father I know that you are real but I am questioning the thoughts of my mother, the approvals of my father and my own desires now; oh my God it is so confusing; I am caught within the realities of my imagination and my faith; I love my faith but previously I had not a struggle until I met Bobby Ross, is this a test or are these just feelings which make me feel wanted and special? Are these also tests of my faith and commitment to sisterhood?

Oh, my God, I am in a situation; she looked and there was Bobby standing and steering directly at her but it was not known to him that she was in the exact position. He couldn't see her because it was a one way transparent window glass- you could only see from the inside out and not the outside in. Melinda's heart burned from the inside out and she stood motionless as the tears rolled down her lovely face. She then placed the palm of her hands on the windows as if to say, Bobby I love you deeply, and as he turned the corner; she walked slowly to her room; dropped across the bed and wept bitterly. Soon the call was made that all of the new sisters should report. This for her; was the safe by the bell call; immediately she composed herself; walked to the rest room and watched her face and piously walked down the stairs as if an angel was upon her with a special halo above her head.

This woman was the breath of Bobby Ross and in his heart, the radiance was real, thinking about her made him comfortable; he was determined to see her again; how? He had no a clue, he then condescended to a life of vassalage, and it was love at first sight which concocted this moderate servitude. Was this fictional, fictitious or an imaginary malady by which this man was stricken by; was this the realities of the knowing heart discerning an inept fallacy of love? No this was real and it was accompanying by the heartbeats of true love, real love and a beautiful life. Yes, Bobby knew all too well this woman wasn't an ordinary woman; she was made to bring peace to the world and that included him and for him; this was special and a personal quest!

One evening while Bobby was strolling in the rose garden; a ball of paper dropped from one of the windows; Bobby looked and saw a glimpse of Melinda face; she waved and immediately went back to her quarters. Bobby picked up the ball of paper, opened it out and there he saw a picture of Melinda with an inscription which read, "If it was meant to be and if it his will; then we shall meet no matter how long it takes if it is his will our paths shall meet again. I love you Bobby and be blessed." After reading the note Bobby sat down and sobbed and asked how if you are already been sent for confirmation? He looked up and said, "God let your way be my will and let it be done! Bobby glanced at the windows threw a kiss and moved on!

The Parting ways

Melinda got sent to Italy for confirmation; while Father John made contact with the African pariah; thy agreed to accept Bobby as a brother of religious work for two years; conducting family therapy and marriage counseling. Melinda became overwhelmed with mix feelings while at the airport; she wondered what would become of Bobby; she toiled with the possibilities of a broken vow and what it would mean if such occurred. She was drained and betwixt by factors of emotional maladies; her heart loved the work she contemplated but it was now competing with the words of her mother, And the thoughts of Bobby and the chances that they might never meet again. It was love; definitely real love it was beyond the flabbergasted state; it was real, she was in love her entire composure spelled out what she felt on the inside. It was love real love for a man and the possible opportunity of disavowing.

Astonishingly; the feeling was real. Humanly we can decide on many prospects and commit to them, but the truth lies within our conscious convictions. A person's religious convictions should not isolate him/her from their God's given potentials and human relationships they must collaborate for the best results. If we from some persuasive presuppositions; construed the obvious appropriation to be a predicate for our life choices; we might experience dilemma which could compete with the ideal goal. It is not religiously correct to be convicts of drawn up assumptions; thus construing the same as God's divine purpose for life. It is however; necessary to commit to life experiences and understand the readiness for a hard and purposeful decision. Limiting your human ideals for the unknown can also be risky and rambunctious; more so when you have not heard the voice committing you to your relevance; don't be hasty in deciding a role. With Melinda; faith was great!

Her spiritual self was correct, but her human connections and alignments were not! You would see as we progress through the rest of this book that at one point I was Amos; I wanted to live a life avoiding the pleasure of being a father and raising children. I was convinced that almighty God was calling me to be celibate; it was a choice, which by external convictions arrested my heart. I wanted to avoid all sexual connections and just be entirely sacrificial.

I was convicted to this end; it became my ideal end until I met Brother Bobby Ross who told me about his experience with Melinda. Thanks to the God of Brother Bobby Ross; I would have missed the choice of living out my human obligations and live in pretense of my inner feelings and desires; which I could not have suppress. Read on you would see what I am talking about; just look at the case of Melinda's cousin Starr!

Chapter 3

Starr Melinda' Cousin

The Twist of Tales

Starr Wilmot an introvert and a serious businesswoman, extremely attractive and a graduate of Adelphi University; had a passion for life and was mentally attracted to women of her caliber; strong and assertive as she was. She concluded that her career was her first love and vowed never to have children nor get marry. She wanted life and was determined to be the best at what she did. Starr lived in Manhattan; after graduation and worked in New York City. She partied and was independent. Determined not to return to Africa; she connected with her peers.

Franklin Phil-more a lawyer handsome and seeks Miss Right. He is well mannered and has life ahead of him. He decided to find the right woman in his quest for a successful family with great passion and determination. Bobby later said this is how this story went: One afternoon Ms. Wilmot walked across the street into a Starbucks joint for a cup of coffee and free Wi-Fi as she approached the cashier; she saw an old acquaintance of her; Jenny Cash by name. They embraced and kissed on the cheeks, and later went into chatters and caught up with old times.

At the end of the last sip of coffee, Starr decided that it was time to leave but desired to hook up with Jenny later. They shared contact information and went in different directions. Jenny was petite very eloquent and vivacious, she walked with a glide and had the smile of ferry just from the enclosure of the Blue Nile. She was understandably a loving mother and well connected. She was not an ordinary woman, but controlled the glamour of Wall Street.

She was a mercantile specialist and understood the puts and calls of the business, and a good friend to Melinda's family. Later that afternoon Starr's sister; Christiana had to be rushed to Mount Sinai hospital where she went into labor and had twin's girls. Starr thought this was the most adorable thing that could happen to a woman, but with her career and with other things in the balance; this wasn't a life for her as she supposed; said Bobby! Starr hid well her flirts with women; she struggled with her sexuality and wasn't sure of what she was.

To keep a balance she only hung mainly with her married friends who would not want to go the next level. She admired their marriages and seemed more interested in those who had wonderful lives with children as well; now you can understand why she connected well with Jenney Cash. Starr desire was the pleasure and work. It was in late May of 2011 Franklin travelled on a lawyers symposium at the onset of the event he was to present the concept of constitutional resolutions to dysfunctional social programs. Bobby said, "Personally I knew Franklin and I understood his plight, Like him; I too am with many struggles trying to find Ms. Right.

Starr seemed to be the wrong choice for him, but nothing comes easy in life I understood this too well from my experience of love and her grip on a person's heart; everyone has to persevere; the best things are worth seeking with diligence and determination.

Starr was attractive as her cousin Melinda; she was irreligious and unlike Melinda attracted to strong women not sexual but flirtatiously. In the main time as the story goes, Bobby had to make a decision about his conviction and sabbatical.

Bobby's Decisions

Soon Bobby decided that there was no way that he could live without Melinda, slowly he contemplated seminary as well. He decided to research becoming a priest; in this case he could live similar life as Melinda. This decision was a result birth out of frustration. Ultimately most people act out of frustration, and pretentiously punish themselves in ways not suitable to themselves and others.

The human nature is naturally structured with spiritual links beyond the natural realm. Acting proportionally to the upsets of life within scope of self-sacrifice as means of appeasing disappointments; is strictly not the order of the day. Father John knew all too well the situation and he therefore encouraged Bobby to become just a missionary; relegating to priesthood was not a joke. This didn't take Bobby long, and he accepted the suggestion and he believed that when a person's finds the right partner; the heart gets to know and understands that you wouldn't need anyone telling you otherwise. Bobby was in love and because of love he decided to live as Melinda just in case; she changes her mind about life and a family of her own. Melinda cousin Starr; Ms. Stuck up ran into Bobby and they chatted for a little while. Starr wanted to know why Bobby a once all around dude was seemingly perturbed and bewildered. He never looked the way he did; no not ever but it was love at first sight pulling courage away from within.

Starr said man you look sick and in love. He noted that things were complicated, I was doing fine until I met this lady; who for years lived in this community!

For years, I prayed to find a woman of her caliber. I dreamed about her and wondered when she would come. A picture of her was always in my memory. I ate and slept with thoughts of her in my heart, and when I woke up, a special kind of joy filled my heart just knowing that she is alive and living on the same planet as I. I have searched all over towns after towns; couldn't find anyone like her. I have become bewitched, the air she breathes enchants me and my entire outlook surrounds her now; mine oh mine she came by, but she has no feelings for me nor anyone else! Her commitment is to church and community services. The good thing about this she doesn't want another person; Starr later said what? You said what? She wants to be a nun and by next year this time; she would be in the convent?

Tell you the truth I have never said anything to her but she is for me and if she would be celibate then by all means; I shall be as well until she is no more and I am not any more as well! Starr stood up! Sat down and stood up again; she wonder if Bobby was out of his mind becoming something just out of sheer despondency. She thought to herself that this could be noble and she wondered who the woman might be! Melinda is the woman! What are you talking about Bobby? Yes, Melinda is the woman! Oh my God, I really don't believe that; I never knew that was her plan, but Bobby if she said that; then I don't know what to tell you, because she never goes back over her words. If she says it and works towards it, you might as well count it out. The women from our family never go back over our words. We are not vows breakers; we keep vows with man and to the Supreme Creator.

I am sorry this is the case. Now I understand why you are doing what you want to do. I am clear that love is actually alive and that it seeks the right individuals who are selfless and driven by the relevance of the purpose. My Dear Bobby my cousin is my cousin and for real; don't throw your life away! Bobby later said, "Could a man throw his heart away? Can a man lose his heart and stop trying. He said "every effort in this life worth something, and every chance has life within" I don't know where this is going to lead but right now I am going to subject myself to a life of sacrifice and help someone get somewhere with his own predicament. I am confident that our path shall cross again; I can feel it and I can taste it; I shall see her again! I have an unction that life can come up with twists to bring about changes and I know all these are possible with belief and determination. For now, I am going to commit to service in the mission field. Melinda indirectly cautioned Bobby about consideration of life in the mission.

She had become pretentiously involved with her work, and with second thoughts; embellished the chance of living with children; this was not known to Bobby, but they dwelled in the thoughts of Melinda. You see it is easy to say things about today when pieces of the future are not present. The moment a full consideration of the inner you surfaces in contrast to your myopic choice, second thoughts arise and there you are in between choices. It is a good thing to be committed to ones' faith, but it is not good that one's faith disavowed them of life's realities.

Every human has an intended purpose and was created with this fulfillment in mind; negating such importance of a call; conflicts with the real inner desires. Life is a construct, and set in motion so that within its confines, the idealistic you are possible. An unfounded; deliberate and denial of human interactions and involvement can leads to a substantial disavowing of sacramental obligations; thus making violable the inviolable. The real sentiment is to ravage the truthfulness of the heart; once the heart is fixed a certain end would not be disturbed in pretense. Melinda mother knew this all too well and been a matured individual saw these confusing moments ahead of time.

Starr and Bobby's Conversation Interrupted!

As Starr and Bobby continued their conversation; Franklin Phil-more walked up to the two of them; spoke and proceeded to talk to Starr; she wouldn't give him the time of the day; she thought he was a jerk who didn't understand her at all. Bobby asked how things were doing with him and the family, he responded very well! He asked about Bobby's work and relationship. Starr stood steering at him as if to say "what rude a pompous character is this?" I wonder who in the world does he thinks he is; she walked up to the both of them and told him that she was in a conversation with Bobby and why was Franklin so rude? Franklin later excused himself and asked for a pardon. Starr said so Bobby what are you going to do; are you going to follow your heart; he replied yes off course; it is now my mandate for life! Franklin quickly interrupted them and said wait a minute; what is going on here? Starr looked at Franklin and then turned her back to him and said oh well wish you all the best and keep up your faith. Franklin once again interrupted what is this and faith man what is going on. Franklin didn't have a clue of the situation, and was actually confused.

The Burden of Service to others

Bobby then said, "Man, I have become a missionary due to circumstances in my life and I am going away for a short while. This is good for me. There are some African people in need of professional counseling and I can provide a quality service to help someone. I mean I need to make a real impact with tangible improvements to make life worth the while and this is a mandate for me.

Franklin stood motionless and said, "Man this is noble of you, and tell me if there is something which I can do to make your trip successful. Bobby later said oh no! Oh no! It is all taken care of and my flight is next week. Thanks Frank. Starr later walked across the street to meet one of her friends. While talking, Franklin said, "Pardon me my Dear Starr; could I join you all; the other lady?"

Molly said, "Sure why not, you seem to be a wonderful man. He thanked her and said I am Franklin Phil-more from Phil-more and Associates; the law firm across town.

At this point Molly felt compelled to know Franklin, she felt the allegiance and truthfulness of this genuine man. She related this in spirit that this man; is a gentlemen. It wasn't her doing it was the Spirit of the Lord interceding in Franklin's stead. The will of God was present for service to individuals loved by God. God's good Spirit possessed the good spirit of love for service to others.

Starr listened and stared deeply into the eyes of her friend and then she spoke; Molly what is wrong with you? I called you for a talk and now you are engaged in conversation with a total stranger; Molly responded Starr what is your problem and what is this all? This guy is just trying to be a friend and you are getting all upset about nothing! Oh well hope you aren't sweet on this good looking man; Molly! What did you just say? Getting sweet on who Mr. Lawyer and rude man? Oh please spear me the chase; you know me. Franklin laughed. Knowing within himself he loved her; he was completely stoic at the hearing as if he was in court and mentally facts finding.

He walked over to Starr and said; I heard you and understood the sentiment, but I would like to see you some other time. Molly said wow; just like that, man, you are completely direct, he knowingly understood what the situation had spelled out for him, but he had nothing to lose and therefore went for the prize. Starr quickly called the meeting to an end and proceeded to go home. Franklin walked to her while she was leaving; called out to her; Starr you are going to be my wife, and I am coming after you. She laughed and kept on walking. In her mind; said she to herself there is no way that I am giving into a man; that is my mandate. Look the fact of the matter is that we can project and declared, but when life is reaching a turning point, there is nothing we can do once the prize is right and the efforts are pleasant. Molly then spoke to Starr and cautioned her about her attitude. Molly insisted that if you want excellent quality; then recognized it once it comes knocking at your doorstep.

Open up your mind and stop this educated smarts' nonsense, Miss! Independent nonsense and understand who you are; for there are many women of your status out there seeking the right man and now you have an opportunity and rejecting it.

The fact is you are very confused. You don't really know what you want- to be gay or straight- you just don't know. So woman make up your mind, before I start communicating with Philmore; I need a husband; I am a single mom and trust me I can really use the help of a profound lawyer; I think he is the right man, but if you are really up to the what I am oblivious; kindly inform me because I am interested. Starr stood back; looked at Molly; walked up to her and said woman! Girl you made some sense but let me think about it and for now, I don't know what to say! I just want to know which is best single motherhood or the traditional family or nor no family. Molly said I love to oblige you on this one "Single Parenting"

Chapter 4

Molly's Confessions

Single Parenting as Per Molly

B eing a single parent is an overwhelming task, nevertheless it yields greater benefits; with persistence and dedication. A strong bond is developed between the parent and the child/ children. It is a desired and heartbeat of everyone to have a traditional family; wherein both the mother and father are fully involved in the lives of their children. In this way, all different roles at various levels of responsibilities are equally proportioned. There are times when as a single parent; one encounters difficult moments; when performing tasks which should be handled by both parents especially those pertaining to gender.

Being a single parent is not an easy task; from experiences of mine, a single mother with a 10-year-old son; validates my point of views relative to my assertions. It is a stressful situation trying to balance work, school, being a parent to my son, supervising his homework, projects and other things which come along with being a mother and father at the same time.

You can just imagine the energy, which I exert daily. My experience with school full time; working full time without support of any kind; makes the joy of being a parent more strenuous. As this confession conveys a personal experience; it shall substantiates the role of being a single parent; is not quite clearly a joyful one, but rather there are glaring realities which make the role a more difficult one as oppose to a joyful relationship. It shall demonstrate that it is better to have two committed parents equally involved in a child's life, and it also provides many justifications in support of a single parent relationship if it has to be. More so when life goes on with/ or without the other parent. In this case, it is better to raise your children alone or with two parents who are mutually involved.

A person cannot really tell the appropriate way to tackle certain issues nor even communicate it to the child appropriately without the help of another experienced individual and this is difficult; everyone needs help in this direction; however, a single parent can be very strong, attentive to every detail in the child's life. It can be motivating, and I have gained unique camaraderie that is fostered by the allegiance of the parent, and thus empowering the parent to serve as a role model. Notwithstanding; I believe in the values of the traditional family, and I consider this the best, because it creates a corporative balance in the home where there are children of other genders. Single parenting can be categorized differently as they come about.

A couple who separates after marriage and one of the other spouse gains custody of the child/ children. A common question here is what difference does it make when both parents are together and not committed? I had to answer this when my son's father walked out on us! Sometimes you do have parents who are very abusive to the point of anarchy in the home. When fathers are abusive to their wives in the presence of their children, the result or outcome can become traumatic for the children. Now; would it be safe to say, "it is better to have a single parent family with peaceful home or an abusive home? I choose a single home with all the peace and good healthy relationship with the child/children then to live in hell on earth, and this is a travesty and vexation of spirit!

You see Starr I conducted a research on this topic and it has been reported that it is difficult to estimate the number of parents becoming single today; yet the number is increasing daily. Statistically it was documented by the 2010 Census bureau that the number of single parent has doubled compared to 1960. An analysis by the Washington Times for all 50 States; revealed that with the increase of household with children; 160 two parent families shows a decline by 1.2 million. Out of a total number of 15 million children are raised without father and only five million without mother. These were the analytical findings and Starr yet I am not afraid of a relationship; if I had the opportunity as you do I shall reconsider my decision and fall in love.

Forget about your vowed choices; become the person for which you are intended to be. Starr despite all of the bad experiences; I cannot polarize nor stereotype men; do I have the reason to? Yes off course I do! Listen my ex-husband was a mess; I mean a total cheat and cheap snake! Starr, the man was a wreck; I mean he was a wicked man; I became bitter because of him and I, at one point, despised men. I vowed never to love again; never to allow a man to touch my body nor be a wife; I thought it was okay not to trust men in general, and that they are insensitive; however, there are men who are very loving; and some are even single parents themselves.

A friend of mine is a single parent; he was abused by his wife, kicked out of his home and left broke, he gained custody of his daughter; raised her and they have had normal relationship as father and daughter, as a matter of fact; they are like friends. This guy comes home before his daughter does; cook and cleans up the house; she loves her father and the young woman has a better relationship with her father then with her mother. So Starr there are other men with great caring and loving nature. Now if you had met the slick of a man I had, and contrast his nature with that of Phil-more; you would think Phil-more came directly from heaven. I know great men when I see one.

You see in my house, my little niece lived with me. This criminal took advantage of her and thus insulted me. He hid well all evidence of their relationship in my home. I was cleaning up one day and discovered that he had divorced me. He addressed the proceeding to my address while I was away at work. He stayed home, forged my signature and the divorce decree was approved; I lived with this character for years; until my discovery.

I called the police and had him locked up; he stayed 200 hundred days in jail; got him released because of my son. He came back to the house I let him in; days later he left the house with a note which stated "today I walk out of your life please drop my name". I obliged him, but my son carries that name; I have tried not to envision him through my son and the first thing which I did was to forgave him in my heart and by this I could live with my son!

Starr I am not bitter at all; I have no hatred; I am a human; Melinda helped me over the years to find in my heart forgivingness. I have learn to be long-suffering and live so that my joy can invigorate my son; that he is galvanized from the traits of his dad. I am glad that I have a positive friend whom my son emulates.

This man has shown me that love is not lost and when someone walks out of your life; it creates greater opportunities for rejuvenating for a better you. If someone walks away from you; then so be it; once there is a pulse or a heartbeat; there is always hope; but I refused to walk around been bitter. I want to love again and enjoy the peace of knowing that I am appreciated; so Starr I am watching you Starr and don't take long to make up your mind; you hear me girl! Starr turned and glanced at Molly as if she (Starr) was just struck with an avalanche of collective data for a pragmatic concaved paradigm. Molly continued with this assertion; we have to make others good others around us. We have to improve so that we can be the best.

$$\triangle \ \triangle \ \triangle$$

Iron Sharpens Iron

Listen Starr; the scripture in Proverb 27:17 says "Iron sharpens iron, and one man sharpens another." and it is about the effectiveness of us making the other person as good as we are. Starr you can make him as good as you are; it is to my understanding that the word of God is true; it takes the same quality material to shape the other, this I know and if you carefully focus; you shall see an opportunity, which awaits you. You see Starr; you are educated, but the facts about you are also hidden in the word of God. The Bible is a deep source of comforts and resolves. Just refocus and see the hands of God which is about to mold your life.

This is what Melinda taught me, "Starr you might become upset because someone robbed you the wrong way? You might be going through a struggle, and this is no fault of yours. It is because of someone else's actions. Oh well my beloved sister; forgive. (Matthews 18:21) It is our responsibility to exercise forgiveness. We may not humanly like to, but it is our God given responsibilities.

Notice I said responsibilities; this is due to the multiple times in our lives which we have to display this God given virtue and quality. Your victory comes after performance of this act. So; If someone hurts you; lets you down for God's sake; you become the better person and let it go. Forgive, Jesus died so that this quality is successfully active in our lives. My Dear friend please let it go; no need to grudge Jesus is in control after all. Love again so that you can become loved and be blessed in Jesus's name."

Two days later

Bobby travelled to the mission field and arrived safely. Chants were echoing from the windows of the church "Hail Mary mother of God the Lord is with thee pray us sinners; holy Mary mother of God pray for us; Blessed are thou amongst women and blessed is the fruit of thou womb Jesus". The sound was Melodious, and Bobby then glanced through the front window of the Church; there he saw Father Peter; standing in front of the church telling of the new Missionary coming to help with the social programs. Father Peter told the church that Bobby would come and go straight to work, therefore everyone should welcome him with open arms. Oh well his work was cut out for him immediately upon his arrival.

Bobby's Counseling- Mission Work in Africa

Bobby's first assignment was a troubled couple; not marry but love each other; were real friends prior to having children and moving in together. They were highly suspicious of one another and kept constant watch to ascertained trust and family emotional sustenance. They were not in the divine will of God, and were mere participants of the permissive will, God's common grace which allows all man to live and work totally on their own volition.

Bobby understood at first hand their major problems. Lack of trust and no good Christian reciprocity; no honor in the relationship, but they felt a bond through the birth of their children and commonality on the bases of an assumed commitment granted by the definition of a loose and irresponsible boundary.

First Case Problem

Jacqueline and Jimmy two lovers almost inseparable, but could not find common grounds for trust. As lovers, they were totally suspicious of the other. They kept a closed ended relationship and with great pretense lived together as the best of friends. Jimmy had about two extra relationships and kept a tight lip about them. Jacqueline had an ongoing affair on the job and did as Jimmy did. They had four sons while eloping together as lovers. They somehow managed to provoke the best to secrecy that surpassed the suspicions of their children. It was on a Sunday afternoon and the day was sunny and fair.

Jimmy happened to be on the phone and Jacqueline walked in on his conversation. She heard him telling someone on the phone to, "Hold on and that everything would be just okay." Jacqueline then waited until Jimmy got off the phone. When he did get off the phone, she asked him "Who was that"

Jimmy kept quiet for some time and later responded "Oh it was Lucy Cousin Henry's daughter" he responded

She later said "Oh! I see, but why is she calling you?"

"Just to tell me that cousin Henry is sick". She walked into the bedroom and then returned with a steer on her face as if to say; I have gotten you now! She later said to him "then come on and let us pay them a visit" Jimmy being a quick thinker said "but tonight is family night; what would the children say?" Jacqueline later said "we can all go over together"; Jimmy knowing well that this situation resembles an entrapment; walked over to Jacqueline and commenced massaging her on the neck in a way to throw the conversation of the topic. Insistently; Jacqueline continued with the subject and follow the line of questioning. In the main time while she insisted continuance of the discussion; her cell phone range and unknowing to her; the speaker was activated. A male voice from the other end sounded "hello my dear!

Hello!" Jimmy saw the opening as a relief from his entrapment; moved in and commenced a rage in pretense of his anger. He responded, "Who the hell is that? Why is he calling you my Dear?" she instantly shuts of the phone and said "no one it was only Bob from the job!" Jimmy later said "Job my foot; on a Sunday afternoon" "come on baby! This is crazy"

Jacqueline knowing that she was caught; tried also to be evasive; changed the topic and later said "honey you something ?" he said "what?" She said, "Today is Sunday afternoon and it is family day." Jimmy ceased this moment and perceived a perfect way out; walked over to her and calmed the situation. He continued massaging and stroking her neck and they both walked towards their bedroom and pulled the curtains as the light went dimmed. All was well, but the residual distrust remained. The next day they visited the church and decided to speak with the family therapist; Bobby Ross who has just arrived. Mr. Ross walked into the office and was then introduced to the couple. He asked if they would like to meet with him.

Chapter 5

They decided to see Missionary Bobby Ross for counseling

They met Bobby for the first time and he was glad to have met them; he told them that he would be glad to listen to them and if he could be of any help; he also assure them that they were the children of God and that He had the cure for their souls for improving their lives. Bobby assured them that they are wonderful and that they should expect great changes for their lives. He promised to provide them with the best of services for fixing their situations in the most amicably way.

They decided to meet with the missionary for counseling. He informed them that they had to be open with him in answering questions and doing assigned home work for the progress of the sessions; they agreed. They kept their hands locked together; a bit nervous they massaged the top of each hands as if to say be comfortable with me I am in love with you. You see life is about giving and taking not just taking; it is all about trying not to always be on the receiving end, but more on the side of cooperation and great reciprocation. He later said I would talk about myself and it shall be the means by which I make you appreciate what you have.

For starters always appreciate what you have because once it leaves you; it might not return. So hold on to what you have. I can see the real persons in between the two of you and they are your inner thoughts and feelings; they are genuine and honest, but you are not honest to your relationship and the children. You all need to know that love has integrity, respect and dignity, therefore if the both of you appreciate one another; then you should impact the quality of your relationship via mutual honesty. Allow yourselves to be emptied of the extra wasted time, and spent quality time one with another, include the children. If you are willing encourage yourselves by reconciling your true feeling with yourselves and the children.

I would like to ask if there is an explanation; why you have not considered marriage as a means of been of responsible one to the other as true commitment. Jimmy quickly responded, "That is my fear and this is why I do what I do! I am afraid that she would get cold on the relationship if we shall get married; this is my fear" I understand; but the both of you have to respect yourselves; honor your selves and contemplate your true affections after having four children! Anyway see you all tomorrow; remember we shall talk about the following topics listed. Brother Ross later turned to Jacqueline; asked do you have anything to say?

She replied, "Brother Ross, I have not been sexual with this guy on the job, but I needed someone to talk to. I am a woman and I have needs even if it is not sexual, I need to be appreciated, I need to be told that I am loved after having four children; not marry, not even an engagement ring; it puzzled me and therefore evoked the possibilities in me. I was trying to figure out what Jimmy didn't see in me; after four children; it hurts and I have been holding all these emotional stains within; Brother Ross I am a woman and I need to be told that I am appreciated; the little things means so much to me, but Jimmy takes me for granted and remains unfaithful. This guy on the job I am sorry; Brother Ross but he is a gap filler. I love my friend Jimmy and after four sons; I want to be his wife and not a piece of tool. He tells me that he loves me but it is hard to believe. Please Brother Ross help us we need directions.

Second Case Problems

While the first couple was leaving, another couple came in with the husband's fighting words echoing across the corridors of the parsonage. They bore the contents of deceptions; the husband was in great rage complaining about his immodesty fussing with a female friend, which he knew in past times; she needed help; he helped her but she wanted a relationship and he did not and she therefore spewed her wrath upon him. The man was entirely nervous and thought he was losing his family. Mr. Ross the counselor had his hands filled with problems. A Person had inflicted upon the other so much stress that the family had to come and see the new marital counselor Bobby Ross; he stood there and listened as they went on; continuously here is the fight as it happened! The wife was hurting feeling betrayed and not loved. She came home late because she thought it was meaningless rushing home to a nagging man; grumpy and secretly confined.

The Fight

The husband; Larry Moses was on the phone fussing and said listen; just do me a favor and I do not want this back and forth I have to get my life together as I need to face my future. Thanks for the help you can keep all of my email submit it anywhere; do whatever is good for your satisfaction. I need to put behind me as I look towards bringing my home and myself in order. Oh by the way, if you need my wife's email address I can send that to you too and maybe you can forward her all of my mail. This too would help to fix my situation because I am tired of hiding I need this out in the open; I have to get this right, and this shall stop you from stalking me.

The voice on the other end said, "What? Stalking what? This is not stalking. This is what is happening because of your little trickery. The woman said. So God bless you and may He continue to be our judge and trust me I would be just fine. Just as you believe in Christ I do too and He shall be our judge; the woman said what irony a sinner calls on the name of a holy man; why are you so confused Mr. slick willy. Stay bless, and have a wonderful day. No more mail please. What did I lie to you about? How did I stalk you? You tell me because I have every email you sent and that I sent you too. What did I ever lie to you about? How did I stalk you? I need you to tell me because I'm completely baffled and shocked!

Larry at this point had become overwhelmed with the stress and said; "No problem but life goes on and if it breaks it is still good for me. I never painted you as anything! Larry said oh well; you know if I have been so evil to you then let God be our judge and let life continues.

So please let everything stop now. Thanks for the help. Bobby interrupted and said listen Mr. Moses your wife is here do you want to continue with this session today; he replied yes, but I need to rid myself of this evil which I have resurrected in my life. Bobby told Larry I am that you acknowledged this one fact, because once the past is gone; just don't go back and resurrected it. The person you knew then is not necessarily the one you are meeting again. It doesn't matter how much good you intended to do; she did not see it as such; you lead her to think she had something with you; she was looking at the possibilities of having you and not what you were given she wanted you for herself. This was your error Mr. Moses; he nodded I agree with you Sir. Just kindly hold my wife at bay so that I settle things with this woman.

Bobby told Mr. Moses that he has to take responsibilities for his actions! You see no one can just become reckless and take others for granted; your marriage is meaningful and once you open the doors to others many; would come attempting to cross the thresholds of your life to make you responsible to them instead of your spouse. Once failures are in the lives of others; don't seek to be joined with that because you could become the victim of your own circumstance.

Larry stop picking up the loose ends of others because they are not yours; Isolate your selfless attitude to your marriage and keep your wife appreciated and loved; listen my friend we need to talk!

~The fight Continued~

Bobby interrupted by saying Larry! Larry! I cannot get involve with this matter but your best now is to quit this conversation and let us take this matter up right now! First; your wife is impenitently awaiting your presence in my office what do you want to do Sir?

Larry asked that Bobby keeps his wife focused on some other things for about fifteen minutes. While talking she disclosed that she had her sibling living on the campus and that their grandmother had just passed away. She said I know for Amos this is taking a toll on him, because she was the only mother parent he had.

Please look after them. Amos wants to be a priest. Bobby asked why? She replied that it was the request of their grandmother and that Amos was working up to it.

Bobby was cautious and said okay; I shall look into that for you. He later walked outside and this time; Larry was wrapping up his call and said, "Please I don't need any of your sarcasm as a response. I'm just trying to make things right so that one day we will be able to all get together and talk like nothing's wrong. Larry said okay; and started walking towards Bobby's office; instantly his phone rang again; and this time.

Bobby said don't pick it up because you are inviting her more into your life. Bobby said to Larry do you want to see mean; just messed with the feelings of a woman and don't follow through. Listen Larry don't open the flow of water and expect not a splash; you have gotten a splash and man pray that God help this situation, because more is coming. The woman said who is that talking to you Larry while I am talking to you is that your Pastor? He said no it is the new Missionary in town Bobby Ross the marriage counselor to help my family overcome you.

She said Larry I was extremely sincere when I told that this was not good but you want to talk. Brother Moses it seems like you encourage this and now you both are going crazy; your wife is in my office hurting and you are fighting on this phone; what is your goal now? I've been trying to get you to leave this situation alone for some time now so we can begin the session, so don't try to make it seems that there are so much evil now.

Somebody wants to get you; I heard you say "because I talked to you on the phone and help you make it through Is that the secret? Please for God sake kindly stop all of this; to be frank I don't know what you expect to gain." What she wants to gain is to get you to pay for her emotions! If you are married don't seek to be what you cannot be or else circumstance would uncover the conditions of your attitudes. Larry you have to understand that you cannot be what you are not. You are in deep wrong and it is a problem; by the way, we can fix this!

Larry tells her now these words "Ok I agree I wrong and did you all of the wrong. Can we please put this in the past; I don't want this anymore. I admit that I am wrong and ask that you accept my apology. I quit. Please in the name of God, kindly let us drop this. I beg. Why the hatred you all? Both of you have caused things to escalate and it has damaged me. My family is upset with me. I don't know what to do right now. So please I am sorry! I just need to move on now! What I may or may not have said, I said because you were my friend.

I didn't know that you would later use them to destroy me. So please I am sorry kindly let me move on. For the Name of God If I have wrong you I am sorry kindly let it stop. Please consider and let me go. I am sorry and sorry for all of the wrong that I have caused you. Just leave me with what little that is left of my dignity. Larry walked with him to his office, and this time Bobby asked to put the phone on speakers; he was no longer interested in Larry's little secrets; his wife needed to hear everything for healing to begin. The phone was place on the desk, the speaker turned on, and this was said, "Okay don't blame me it was you searching me out on the internet until you got my phone number. Bobby on the issue emphatically told Mr. Larry that everyone has to be true to himself; never take advantage of any situation when it is comfortable to vent. Never assumed that everyone is listening to you because s/he wants to help. It is always good to understand your sense of discernment, unapologetically stick with your faculty, and soundly protect your privacy. Look at what went on and see what you bitterly said; I knew you were a mistake in the first place when you demanded so much giving the situation.

~Larry Seeks Forgivingness~

Larry turned to his wife and said honey I am sorry that I let you down; I was only been kind because it was a mother in need of help and I reached out to her. The fact of the matter is I am in the wrong I should not have permitted myself to have been drawn back into my past when it was already over Bobby!

Bobby said Larry! Oh yes that is the truth and the good thing is she got the anger; just do me a favor never and I mean never make contact with that woman again, because she is hurt and needs time to heal and move on. I would like to caution all of you, never take anything and I mean no one or anybody for granted. Moreover, if you want to be kind, find the Red Cross, the Salvation Army or maybe the school in Amos jurisdiction and help, but reaching out to someone you were involved with can be extremely risky and many people get hurt in the process. Folks please govern yourselves and be wise, let the past stay buried and have no thought for looking back. The cautious you are; the less shame and embarrassment would knock on your doorsteps!

Just look at the embarrassment of Larry; read his conversations over the phone; see what he had to deal with and these are his own confused confessions:" Woman you a fool and don't know what love is even if it jumps up and bits you." Bobby looked at Mrs. Moses and said you have to be strong; you have to be open to this question; do you want to continue with Mr. Larry Moses as your husband? Do you want to say something to him right now?

She responded "my heart is aching; I feel faint and broken on the inside but for some reason I want to listen to him" Mr. Moses got on his knees and asked for forgivingness; he begged to be forgiven. Bobby encouraged Larry to look at his wife and tell her what he is feeling.

Larry said, "I am feeling as if I have opened a flood gate and the well is running dry. I need my wife. She is my friend, she is my help, and I need her to understand that it was my fault. Honestly, I was driven by my humanity. I tried to help an old friend; I admit my wrong and seek recompense for my wrong and repentance for the wrong; I am sorry, and I need another chance.

Larry turned to Brother Ross and asked about the elements of unconditional love; Brother Ross said Larry unconditional love starts with friendship and appreciation. If you can appreciate what you have and form an unpretending relationship with your heart; then you would have all the elements of a mature individual in love.

Real love never fails; real love has no boundary, real love seeks peace and reunification most of all it is totally appreciated. Larry when a man's wife is his friend; she is his confidant and support. Unconditional love has no reason to be involve it is sacrificial and without merits. Larry if you can only show some sensitivity, a little more remorse and appreciations, you would gain the heart of your wife. I am going to call this session to a close for today. Remember you all must talk about this at home and we shall see tomorrow.

Acts of true love and forgivingness~

While going home Mr. Larry Moses kept his head bide down to the floor, sweats started flowing down his face, combined with great drops of tears and his body overwhelmed with shakes; he held the left side of his chest and complained about the shortness of breath. He managed to pull the car over to the other side of the street. Mrs. Moses jumped into motion. She knew that her husband was having a heart attack and she helped him to get out of the car; laid him down on the side of the road and commenced chest compression maneuvers; she breathed into his mouth and he started breathing on his own. When he could talk; he thanked her and caught a tight grip of her and whispered in her ears; "Ma I love you; I was stupid please forgave me"

She cried and said Larry I have forgiven you!

Yet we have to see the Missionary tomorrow! You know folks; life can have greater twists most of the times, circumstances can inflame the courage to live again after a bad situation. Everyone can show some appreciations for the one s/he loves beyond conditions. Sometimes it is the little things, which matter the most. People in relationships must understand that courtesy brings satisfaction and it echoes that thankful moment. If a spouse is going through difficult times, move closer and show some concern, it helps to bring them through from a dying position. Love and kindness awaken the stubborn and relentless heart; so keep on trying!

Chapter 6

Larry's confession prior to the next session; he discovered the power of deliverance and said

~Larry's Prayer~

I am a child of God; birth by the blood of Jesus' Christ; by whom death on the cross my sins and shame were taken away. I am the child of God, joint heir with Jesus Christ because of adoption and a family of God. I am empowered by the spirit of Christ to release into my life peace, love and good Christian reciprocity. I am the Child of God; follow daily by Grace and Mercy. I am not afraid to take chances with God; I am saved, I depend and trust only on the Name of Jesus. I do not trust the will of man nor their hope for me; for they are insincerely designed filled with letdowns. For the word of God declares, "Thus says the LORD, Cursed is the man who trusts in mankind and makes flesh his strength, and whose heart turns away from the LORD (Jeremiah 17:5)." I know in my heart that no weapon formed against me can prosper;

I know in my heart that every tongue, which comes up against me, shall be condemned in judgment. I do not have any regrets of who I am and whose I am. I am walking in the fulfillment of my destiny; I renounce daily the hidden works of darkness; I am not afraid of the shadow of death, for God is with me (Psalm 23). I am filled with joy and desire daily the steadfast love of God for me it is New every morning. In Jesus name, my enemies shall come in one way and run out in seven different ways. I declare as the word of God says; the Weapons of my warfare are not carnal but mighty through God for the pulling down of strongholds. I pull down evil every plan of darkness against my life; my family life, my Church family, and return every curse visible or invisible to the sender or senders! So shall this be in Jesus' Name I surrounded to God". I am changed and on my way to counseling.

The Next Day joint session

Brother Ross seeks to restore hope and bring about change.

~Marriage and Couples Therapy ~

Listen out everyone; it is great that you are all here today and this is evident of your willingness to accept the responsibilities for your actions and make the necessary change. I am Brother Bobby Ross and you all have met me already. I am hoping that you all shall accept me as a friend, willing to help you all. I understand your plights and believe in you all. Secondly, right is right and wrong is wrong. I have listened to your problems; I have witnessed firsthand some of the problems.

Consider me a person who is here to help. I respect you and I expect you all to be reciprocal. It is important that we do everything possible to save marriages to the extent that we can refute the statistic, which demonstrated that marriage rates are on a decline. It is also stated that 50 percent of first marriages end in divorce, and this is considered true all over the world; so even in civil Africa, this supposedly is true. I want to refute this by making a difference over here. Divorce rates also vary with the partners' level of education, religious beliefs, and other factors. I like to use a different word for "Change"

AMELIORATION:-

It denotes improving the conditions that is presently obtained, and the addition of the "Immediate", and. It is effective beginning now! (Improve, Upgrade, Amend, Better the situation now!) Ameliorate! Rather than been postponed to the future, actions now can better provide positions for the future. No action now, means there are no starts for the future. The current conditions obtained has to change, consequently the positive actions now is to address the results for tomorrow.

Nothing postponed for the future is effective, unless you start now with an effective approach doing something positive that segues positively into the future;

therefore ameliorate now! For starters, Jimmy, why are you apprehensive about marriage? What is your fear? Jacqueline loves you; she cherishes you and has done so by giving you four sons! She deserves to be value as a wife; is this your intention? Jimmy then folded his hands; stood up, glanced at Brother Ross as if to say; "Man you are too direct!"

Nevertheless, he walked over to Jacqueline; steer her down and looked up to the ceiling with a kind of stupor resembling a lost messenger seeking heavenly directives, but for some reason he was short circuit. The room got quiet; Brother Ross waited for a response; yet Jimmy was stoic as if he was struck by a jolt of elucidating-bolt. Brother Ross then asked if everything was okay; Jimmy nodded his head in the affirmative. Brother Ross then asked Jimmy to sit down; asked him if he needed a drink of water. In the main time, Mr. Larry Moses asked Brother Ross if it was okay that the session is exclusive; he thought Jimmy wasn't comfortable with the group session. The

Missionary thought the group session could help both couples concurrently; he wanted a convergence resolution. Jimmy wanted an exclusive session; he relegated to the points of Mr. Moses; and the Moses walked into the adjacent office. Brother Ross disclosed that the real enemy is fear, and fear dwells in the heart and soul of man; if only a person can believe in his plans and spiritual aspirations; follow his conscience; then taking chances would be without internal apprehensive monologues. Jimmy later opened up; told the Missionary that he was apprehensive and the reason was fear; and this derived from Jacqueline's rejections of him; she does not have the same fire as before; she always on the phone late at night, pretentiously using the rest room for hours.

I decided to live the rest of my life with her; but if marriage is involve; she would waxed even colder or probably leave my children and me alone. It hurts to live pretentiously; I want to be truthful, but at what cost. I flirt with other women; I have not had any physical contact with them because of my relationship with my friend and partner. Jimmy while standing sips on a class of cold water rested; he sat back and pointed to the missionary this is it! Brother Ross later went over the words of Jimmy; stated Jimmy you said she has gotten colder and that she rejects you; if this is true Jacqueline; you are not acting in accordance with what held you all together in the first place.

No one married or not should use the pleasure of their relationship as means to abate a situation. It is necessary to communicate and ask questions and get the appropriate answers as opposed to acting on assumptions. The problem here is that both of you have been victims of your assumptions and foolishly created a blockade. I shall advise you all to break down the bearers; stop flirting and embrace your past; the foundations upon which your attractions kept you this far.

Jacqueline is it your plans to leave Jimmy if he marries you? No! Brother Ross no! I love Jimmy. I would never want another man on earth other than Jimmy; we have been lovers from high school; I have known no other man; Jimmy was my first and has continued to be until now.

Jimmy leaped out of his chair; drops to his knees; took Jacqueline by the hands; hugs her and whispered in her ears; honey I am sorry; I am so sorry; I need you in my life; I want you in my life, and my world is incomplete without you. I love you so much and I need you to forgive me. Jacqueline what do you have to say; she looked with tears rolling down her face; almost blinded by her drenched hair soaked with tears; lifted up her hands with arms wide apart as to welcome her prodigal lover; it was as if to say honey I always left the doors ajar for your return.

Jimmy walked over to her; kissed her, and told her never shall you be kept out of my heart; there is so many room in my heart for you. We shall workout this situation after therapy! Jacqueline said which situation Jimmy; I want to be your wife; make me your wife; be there for me; take me by the hand and make me yours; I want to have dignity as a wife with four sons. At this moment the young Jimmy was energized; inspired by her words; he was moved by the reciprocating spiritual conduits which linked him with the realities of love; he extinguished convincingly the apprehensive veneer; hugs Jacqueline and said honey would you marry me?

The missionary stood up and ask the couple to take the time off and talk to one another on issues of their hearts, and to put the past behind them; he encouraged them to always be open and truthful. Marriage is a matter of the heart and it works well by individuals in love solemnizing vows by reasons of attributing dignity to a relationship. The importance of this rite is functional when the parties involved are correctly advised; instructed, encouraged to be cooperative and selfless. The altruistic values of this union is dauntless; propelling when there are greater self –sacrifices; mutual understandings and fearless opportunities for a broader communicative genre. I shall encourage you all to accentuate your positive emotions, rid yourselves of the negatives and be truthful to your children and then to yourselves. The day was far spent and Brother Ross was emotionally drained; he therefore call the Moses family in and decide to see them the next day. Jimmy later went home with hands locked together with Jacqueline and this was significant of the impacts of reconciliation and forgivingness.

A BROKEN VOW

~The Acts of Reconciliation and forgivingness~

Larry money is not everything, money cannot buy health; it cannot provide genuine relationship; only seasonal friendship based conditional merits; Larry your thoughts were atrocious, frightful and appalling your money could not resolve the woman's problem, your actions were self-destructive and selfish; your behaviors produced all of the raging moments.

You convinced yourself that you were acting appropriately in line with your good nature true but at the same interval; you were been unfaithful, deranged and disillusioned. Haven't you heard that the dead must bury the dead? Who promoted you with resurrecting qualities? You were wrong and caused your family great grief; you almost lost your life in the process as well! This hidden shame almost killed you after it came to the light!

I am hoping that you have forgiven yourself from the self-destructive nature of yours. Mr. Moses later hung his head towards the flow seemingly seeking to search-out his position, but as nature would have it; he could not see the ugliness of his image as reflected; the concrete could not contain such; it lacks the reflecting qualities as Larry behavior. He sobbed and accepted the fact that his impropriety caused him the shame and embarrassment; on his knees, he sobbed and extended his hands upwardly. He had this propelling demean fueled by shame and disdain.

His supporting wife walked over to him as a redeeming angel; rescuing him from the miry clay; a condition which he had created for fear of his health she stroked his head and comforted him. This case had worked itself out - nature had resolved this situation. Larry was genuinely remorseful and repentant.

His wife believed him and therefore helped him out of this malady. Brother Ross did not hide the truth; he brought the wrong out in the open. He was keen on the facts and pointed out what Larry Moses could not see. He delivered the message to Mr. Moses, "thou are the man"; it is imperative to point out the wrong and state the truth in the light of fairness, with concern and empathy. Brother Ross had a relationship with Mr. Moses and this opened out the windows through which he could peek into and deliver the goods. The truth always set free the repentant heart. If folks cannot see nor hear the truth; then we cannot usher them in the direction for embracing the delivery of the freedom message. The liberating messages are always welcome by the repentant heart in the process of reconciliation and forgivingness. Mr. Larry Moses was taken by the hand and he woke up from his stupor. He rededicated himself to a self-less relationship with his wife; in the presence of Brother Bobby reached out for the hands of his wife; hugged her and said thanks for giving me another chance; he knew that he deserved it, although at times his wife drove him crazy; he relegated to accepting the faults and to rekindle his relationship. Brother Ross sat down and pondered about Melinda; he saw the acts of love at its best and he wished for the same. He saw the power of love he could taste it and desired it closely! Mrs. Moses then inquired of him if all was well; he nodded yes and that he was having a moment of his own. He later told the couples to return for the final instructions. Larry you have to break vows with your past, that circle of your life has to die. You have to pray so that the power of Jesus; help you to renounce and destroy that linage to your past. You saw the many pains, which it caused you.

You almost lost your life and your home. I recommend that you severe the past and make sure that you support the social works within you home. Remember you cannot care for the entire world, but you can for your loves ones and the house hold of faith. Here are some recommended help and instructions for rekindling and moving along.

Brother Bobby Ross's instructions to the Couples

Bobby articulated some psychosocial plans for solidifying the results of the therapy. He called the session to order; encouraged the couples to participate collaboration; this time around and that the instructions were simultaneous and not specific to any particular couple. They agreed and assembled in the auditorium. He commenced by saying let me emphasize the following

Self-destructive behaviors are often an attempt to hurt you as individuals by overpowering you with awful bitter feelings and these are directly spiritual and from the devil as a tool to destroy godly relationships; it leads to additional shame and disgrace, avoid this destructive path it has no good intention, but to lead you into areas of degradation. Commit in relationship and be truthful to it.

Secrecy out-of-control; causes shame and embarrassments; avoid them and be truthful to yourselves; don't be controlled by mundane innuendos, leave your past alone and hold on to what you have now. Remember, shame makes people want to hide and not to be found. Even in the good book, it was documented that Adam and Eve realized that they were naked and so hid themselves because they positioned themselves in that situation and they were shame. Therefore, avoid the awfulness of this condition. Avoid the secret scenarios; cleaved to the good, which brings about respect, honor and dignity. I am glad that we avoided divorce and accepted the path of reconciliation and forgiveness. The realities of divorces are dreadfully complicated with hate and scorns. It makes life stressful and uncertain.

Avoid the self-fulfilling prophetic things which you proposed as fate; they are not; they are setups to sabotage your relationships; if the past is gone; leave it alone and live as if you are always refreshed in your caring for one another.

Contrast the quality of the relevant you from the monotonous you. Seek to take a hold of love, I mean unconditional love without merits. Validate that it is your heart in love and not the satisfaction of a desire. Get a hold of the real you and pass it along with your greatest intent for a lasting relationship based on friendship and total spiritual agreement aligned with the fittest camaraderie.

~Session Interruption~

As Bobby spoke; his phone rang; he excused himself and it was Melinda on the phone; she told him that she was back in Jersey City and that she was booked for a speaking engagement on guns control. He knew that this was an interest of hers. She had worked on it while living in the community. He later returned to his clients and adjourned the session for the day. Melinda had to speak the following day.

Chapter 7

~Melinda Returned to Jersey City –Speaking Engagement~

Shortly after Sister Melinda return from Italy; she was invited to speak at the St. Patrick pariah in Jersey City on the issue of gun control amidst citizen of Jersey City; the auditorium was jammed packed; victims' families were present from all over the town, advocates came from the adjoining towns to lend their voices in this worthy cry. They were conscious about their objectives. Melinda walked in dressed down to her toes in garments reflective of the Reverent Sister; she was entirely beautiful and as she walked towards to podium; she had an expression on her face as that of a saint.

Her exquisite posture dominated the entire ambiance and you could sense that a good quality of an individual was present to bring about decorum of joy and peace. There was a qualitative serene of a mood and the characters of the individuals present were absolutely confined. The priest introduced Melinda and the community of activists responded in the affirmative, she approached the podium and smiled. Oh, you could see such elegance of beauty as spread across a rose garden and the gaping end of a waterfall gushing at the site of pleasantry. Melinda's movement was the resemblance of such pleasantry. As she smiled, the arousal of decorum stood still and the people stood with an overwhelming applause. The boisterous sound was in such unison that welcoming gestures placarded itself beyond the walls. Oh yes Melinda; Sister Yates had such commanding presence; everyone sat back in motions as if to say tells us your view; and then she said, "Gun control matter is an argument, and it is a valid one; deeply rooted in the conscience of civil societies.

There are many unnecessary deaths, which are the direct cause of illegal guns and misuses of out of control legal guns. The ease or lackadaisical controls of handguns are directly related to the amount of deaths caused by handguns across the nation. No one can impede the rights of citizens who are legally seeking to protect their lives and properties.

The right to bear arms for the legal ramifications; are the absolute cause for possessing a fire-arm, but equally so this privilege cannot be the green light for out of controls possessions. It is documented that in every inner city most of the deaths are caused by and ease of possession handguns. If the situations were certain and more approaches were deployed so that responsible people become owners of handguns; many unnecessary deaths would be deterred.

However, unlawful possessions of these deadly devices are the main culprits for the out-of-controlled situations as we have it today. If the stringent methods for controlling gun possession were in place, many lives would be saved and legal guns ownership would be in the hands of more psychologically mature individuals. Assault weapons should be restricted to the jungles and other areas, but not within the inner cities limits. How many deer do you find running at Times Square? On a serious note; regulating guns ownership might not eradicate the deaths caused by guns, but it is certain that regulating guns ownerships; just might save lives, and that could me someone close by or the nearer relatives; just think about it.

Melinda Calls Bobby Ross

The people applauded and cheered Melinda; the speech was wonderful, but she suddenly felt lonely and decided to call Bobby again; she dialed his number; the phone rang and the voice came on hello; this is Bobby Ross! She said, "Hello Brother Ross, this is Sister Yates. In the main time, she decided to tell him about her struggles and how she felt. She said, "Hi Bobby, you mean so much to me; sometimes ago, a special treasure came into my life, one of the best treasure that life could bring and the special treasure is you; you are one of the best treasure that one could desire.

You are wrapped and packaged in a wonderful person, and you hold a special place in my heart I know that I have found what I have been looking for all these years, and that is why I loved you this much. I am however struggling with the fact that I might have to break my vows to my faith in pursuit of my real life and self-worth. Bobby I can still love and remain dedicated to my faith and become a part of God's life cycle or I could end that process with me, and obliterate this great command "Be fruitful and multiple". This I believe is obstructive to the plan of God, and I want therefore to present myself to God in being truthful to love another person such as you, but I have taken a vow. I want to be your wife Bobby! I want to have your children Bobby! I have made a vow! I am a nun struggling with my human nature.

~Bobby's Reply and laments~

Hello Melinda

In all my life I have not forgotten about you and the sentiment of your kindness, as the woman I first fell in love with, and could not spent the rest of my life with. I just cannot get this out of my mind. I knew that God is a just God and not having you would have been an injustice to humanity. You were or are everything I wanted, and even till now I just cannot get you out of my system. I don't know why but it been that way. Maybe you were ashamed of me while growing up; but your work for the church was more important! I might have done something to you as I thought, but your life for ministry meant the most. I really still don't know and even you don't know what happened, but commitment to God's work was in the short list. However, I always think the world of you. I am just sorry that life did not allow us the opportunity to really share our lives together. This is my email address <u>Bobby.Ross@Peace.ORG</u>

Please feel free to contact me anytime whenever you like to. I will always return your mail. To me you will always be special. It is only that my life style now has prevented me from pursuing you as I would like to. I remember when I first saw you I said to myself this is my wife, but I was young and didn't know then how to keep you from leaving me. What I am telling you now; I have been waiting to tell you all my life. I said maybe because she is what God has chosen, and the friend of my siblings, but it really didn't face me like that. What I felt inside was truthful and I sometimes prayed that it materialized, but it didn't. My Dear please don't think that I am trying to make you feel guilty, I have just been holding all of this stuff inside of me. Sometimes when in Liberia I tried so hard to get away from the group just to call you on the phone, but I have not been successful at that.

Let me just ask you a question, did you at sometimes consider me someone you could have loved and still love? I don't know but you made me feel like I just couldn't have you. Any way Let me just forget this old pursuit, because I am kind of becoming sentimental on this issue, knowing that our lives would have been even more productive if we had the opportunity of staying together as a family.

Melinda I loved you and will always be your friend, and you will be the love that got away from me. How are your works over there; are they okay? Moreover, how are you; are you okay too? I am hoping that the people are treating you well.

Sometimes I wonder what attracted you to the work and that I lacked but have realized that I couldn't compete with God. Oh, my God there I go again back to the same issue. Yes and truthfully, no one competes with God, however man can contend with God on matters for a greater good.

In the scripture Jacob did; he know that the next steps to his posterity predicated upon God's actions and guidance throughout his journey; therefore as per **(Genesis 32:22-31)** in the realm of the Spirit; Jacob struggled all night and he would not let the Angel of the Lord to go when it was time. No matter what circumstance you find yourself, a grasp of your goals and objectives must always be predicated upon God's intervention. No matter what drives you, God must approve the desires of the heart. He holds the keys to all areas of our lives; in this case our success are within His will; God's will and this is why we seek His approval in everything we do. You see what you did to me. Oh well just forget about it. I will always be your Bobby. Bye and talk to you when you reply. Bless you. Bobby!

Bobby; said Melinda; guess what I have a speaking engagement tonight; the folks at my mothers' church wants me to speak over there, I don't know why? I am a catholic and they are Baptists! Bobby was silent for a while; spoke later and said this is okay just do your best; it doesn't matter where you talk about your faith just be on point. She responded all right! Just before she hung up, she said Bobby do you have faith? Do you believe that God can provide the needs of the just and positively provide the desired justified benefits for the just man? Bobby if you believe in prayers then; commits with your faith and heart desires; God is in control!

He paused and pondered the thoughts and meaning of her words. Bobby, she said it is our persistence, which ushers the daybreak fight and thus manifest the visible victory; therefore, persisting and remaining focus brings about opportunities for receiving the desired prize. Stop the crying and wait your time in God's plan. Understand that God has made every event and actions significant in His time He later felt a jolt of lighting after she spoke and decided that he felt some hope in place. He later told her to put her good foot forward as she does all the times during her speeches.

~Melinda at the Frist Central Baptist Church~

Hello everyone I am Sister Yates; a member of St. Patrick Catholic Church, as you can see I am a Catholic nun; originally I am from West Africa by way of Liberia. It is my pleasure speaking to you all today. I shall speak today on the Glory of Jesus.

As she commenced to speak, the audience was captivated by the eloquence of her speech! She said "The Glory of Jesus-Amongst man (St. John 1:1-21)

December 24, 2005

On this glorious day many have come to worship, and wonder about the awesomeness of the most High God in the person of His son Jesus Christ; Today we shall explore His Glory through the eyes of some of His Disciples. First of all the meaning of Glory: magnificence, splendor, beauty, wonder, grandeur, the brilliance, praise and admiration.

The delight of our Lord and Savior Jesus Christ is all over the world. His presence in our lives has caused changes that we cannot imagine. His disciples or the First century Christian Church were more focused on the spreading the good news of His Glory, and explained the process by which many of them paid high prices with their lives. They saw His sacrifices along with the effect of his earthly Ministry; that many of them were convinced that He was God amongst man. Even as the century commenced to unfold, Hebrews settlers,

Pharisees, Scribes and other devout men were aware that the Messiah would come and that he would be a liberator. The Old Testament saints were aware, but how; they did not know.

The manner in which he came was totally out of character for the typical Jewish family, it caused shame and embarrassment for Joseph. Joseph was deeply concerned; privately he would attempt to put Mary away, but the Supernatural would intervene and somehow persuaded Joseph to accept the situation, because the situation was no impropriety on the part of Mary, but rather the working of the Holy Spirit. The unfolding message was about God, and that He was to be with man. Matthew the Jewish writer and a Disciple wrote that He was Immanuel-meaning God with man. He wrote that, He was and is the Messiah, the Anointed One amongst man.

The statement made many Jewish religious leaders upset and refuted the pronouncement of such deity. They could not accept the miracle the entire thing seemed untrue and not possible; yet with God, all things are possible; many of faith about this glorious birth accepted the concept, and believed on the name of the savior. I cannot tell anyone how to live his life, but I can encourage many how to make choices; in selecting his or her spiritual connection so that communication between the spiritual purviews is realized.

For us who are Christians, we believe on the name of Jesus Christ and the Virgin birth." Sister Yates ended her speech and sat down; in that moment the people stood up and applauded her for the speech. She was delighted and encouraged to be living the chosen path for her life. As all these moments were moving along, she in pretense and not free of thoughts about Bobby; struggled every minute with thoughts for him, she had such emptiness to the point that it became an unquenched exuberance. She became the more troubled and sometimes questioned her commitment to ministry. She immensely struggled with the thoughts of Bobby at the same time maintaining her devotion to sisterhood.

She had butterflies in her stomach whenever the mention of Bobby's name came about. It was a roller coaster life for her, she had to pretend about her celibacy; she was still a virgin, her sexuality wasn't the matter; she had that under control. This aspect of her was in subjection, but what was out of control was a genuine feeling of completion. Real love is like a seed once it falls into good soul and properly nurtured; growth is extremely rapid to full propensity. She wanted to be love by her friend Bobby; she yearned to be in his presence, but distance, and her faith were the blockades. She loved the church and the work, but she felt special in remembering the palm of Bobby's around her neck at the movie. She never forgot that special and exhilarating experience she had; the tenderness, the calmness and the warmth of the inner touched of a man around her neck.

Yes, it was not an ordinary man, but an extraordinary man. It was Bobby's impact; burning deep in the heart of Melinda, and oh she yearns and desired to see him, but her faith and distance kept them apart. She became even more afraid as she struggled with the thoughts of what might occur; if and she shall see the missionary Bobby Ross.

Love is exhilarating and stupendously sagacious. It is like a flint of a gun and aims directly into the inner person. True love never fails it prophetically envelopes and unfolds into its proper genre. No man can stop true love; true love might be suppressed for a moment and that is it. Once the prospected are in close proximity; love stands as a liberated prisoner of war just released from a moment's suppression. In many events of suppressive saga; were persons and people are forced to deny the unfolding process of this inner yearning; they find themselves victims of circumstances. Melinda might have love the convent but her heart had its solace in the Land of Bobby Ross.

Over in Africa Bobby continues His Lecture on Group therapy

Positive Emotions and things to do!

The Counseling things to do were listed and cautiously explained:

• *Communicate more effectively*

When you effectively communicate, it is interpersonal and shared historical values are then the basis for your connection. In this, you are able to understand where the other person is coming from. It is always good to communicate all of the day's events and by this, you can solidify your proactive strategies for your lives. Communicate your true feelings and desires.

Tell what you expect of the other person involve in a relationship with you. It doesn't matter; whether it is a professional, romantic or fellowship relationship; it is always a positive addition to communicate your thoughts and desires. Clearing the air makes a refreshing inner you without second guesses and suspicions.

Rebuild and maintain your emotional connection, love, and respect

Most people forget about where it all begun, and they relegate to the mundane. The more you treat one or the other with respect and dignity; then you would fully realize the importance of the both of you. Therefore, go out revisit the old spots where it all started and fall in love repeatedly.

Rekindle the fire and let it emerge as newer than ever before. This exercise must be repeated all the time and trust me; you would appreciate the worth of the each of you. Please don't neglect this; it is important. This is house cleaning and all excess baggage must be emptied of all hidden un-necessaries.

$$\triangle \ \triangle \ \triangle$$

Improve the quality of sex, romance, and passion between you and your partner or spouse

Listen people it is necessary to work on some other things and appreciate your sexuality. Your passion cannot die because that you have children and that you are old, or too engaged with other activities, which interfere with your "due benevolence" as per the Apostle Paul in his version of the importance of sex in the marriage (1st. Corinthians 6). You cannot be too holy to share your erratic joys with your partner.

You must keep the fire sparking at all times. Help one another in the process and communicate your real fantasy, be intuitive and forth coming after all it is your lives and your home; therefore be true to yourselves and be proactive. Most of all hear this; when love is no longer a factor of the heart, it becomes conditional, unnatural and erratically influenced.

At this level, doubts and feelings of despondency are invigorated by disgust and confusion so improve your sex life. Sometimes couples wondered why this and why that? The only real and truthful answer; is relegated to the foundation or on the premise of the love relationship which is heart driven. When real legitimate sexual love; I mean real love which is heart driven is present; the needs to feel Secured and belonging to are met and realized. In this case, people feel the impact directly from the heart enveloped with greater sentimental expressions of a realized discovery of a soul mate.

Identify your relationship vision

You all are given roles and you have to assume those qualities with greater responsibilities. Always ask the question what is the worth of my relationship and where do you want to see it. Understand the propensity of growth you have from within and become certain that you care for one another as Christ would care for you. Therefore, it is necessary that you identify the relationship and where do you want to see it; be objective.

•Reduce the risk factors build lasting trust

Stop attempting to go back in time trying to relive the past. You are not graves diggers therefore what is dead let it remain dead; it is risky going back to the past.

Leave well alone and do not discuss past relationships with your spouse. It is risky and self -trapping. Build trust on what you have now! Let the joy of an unconditional friend resonate with you. Keep your faith ahead of you and build your hopes on the love of God and the fellowship of your family life with Christ.

At this point one of the counselee asked, "Was it this way with you and Melinda?

Chapter 8

Anyway about Melinda; We Are Not Close Anymore

Bobby spoke of Melinda, "We are not close anymore, I am in Africa she is in the United States of America; she resides at the St. Patrick Parish in Jersey City, New Jersey. Father Peter understanding Bobby's desires and mission; decides to share a Prayer with them from his I-phone.

Heavenly Father;
We come to you as
Humble as I Know
How. We Confess our Sins,
Those Known and Unknown.
Lord, you know we are
Not perfect and we fall
Short everyday of our lives.
Father, We just want to take this time out to
Say thank you. Thank you for Bobby and thanks for Sister Yates. Thanks for your Mercy. We have more hills to climb and trials than money and freedom, but thank you for shelter, Life, and everything we do have. We understand that these lives which we are living are filled with trials and tribulations, but thank you for not making them unbearable on us. We understand that we must go through the Storm to Appreciate the Sunshine!

Father whatever is slated for Melinda and Bobby; make it a properly fitted condition for their lives according to your good will and pleasure. We understand that everyone is tested to for definition of a quality relationship with you Father, and if this is the case then Father may your way be done in Heaven as it is on earth. We bless your Name; Amen!

Bobby tells a story about hard work and determination

Brother Bobby later said my friends I have a story to tell and it was written by a young man which I have known for some time now. The brother asked the couple to sit and he said the title of the story is the "Life you choose to live" and it went as this: Bobby's play written by Bobby Ross!

THE LIFE YOU CHOOSE; IS YOURS TO LIVE; he later said I am hoping this story would help you all

Introduction:

Life is for people who fight and struggle to live the intended lives that extensively produce fruits way into the future. The path a person chooses to follow throughout his/her life determines the future outcome. The Bible states, "There is a way that seems right to a man but the end is the way of destructions". A destructive path is chosen by those who would rather trace life in the fast lane. The fast lane lives are only short lived, flashy and attractive without any sense of fortitude for future plans. Confusion only awaits a person who isn't prepared to face the future. Anyone who chooses to walk with Christ is guaranteed a place with God and hope for the future. At present that person lives a quiet and peaceable life, and is rewarded opportunities for living on earth. Choosing your life style is necessary for determining who you are and what your outcome shall be. In the story "The Life you choose; is yours to live" The characters Clearance Henry, Marylou Crawford, Timothy Olu, and others were all interested in lives that reflected or spelled success.

These West African men and women migrated to the big City in America, New York City that is. To their likings; they accepted to live in the most affluent State, and that is New York, and mainly New York City. Their past lives in Africa were humble, peaceful, slow and with honor. Back in Africa they loved the Church and occasionally visited friends and families parties. They lived a subsistence life and always looked out for one another. In the meantime Clearance happened to be the most intelligent one of them all. He was an honor student, made the dean's list regularly and love helping out at Church.

He was mostly described as an introvert, and stayed mostly to himself. Marylou Crawford was **the** daughter of a preacher and got Clearance interested in attending Church and mostly accepted Christ as his personal Savior. Timothy Olu was rich and the son of Mr. Onanuga Olu. Mr. Olu made most of his money in shipping cargo on the West African coast. Clearance was poor but loved God. Olu was rich believer, but did not practice his faith. He always chooses his friends based on their status. Clearance could not roam in Olu's inner-circle because he was an unfortunate; a have not.

The Story:

On Sunny afternoon in Africa; people gathered themselves together to prepare for the Christmas holiday. Clearance was heartbroken because every time Christmas came around; it reminded him of his never present father and mother. Living with relatives made Christmas sentimentally controlled an event for Clearance. He could not make a list for Christmas, because within his world Santa

Claus was not answering his calls. Keeping up with others he constantly looked for emptied beer bottles and sold them. While others were having fun and looking rich, Clearance was selling bottles to prepare for Christmas. Oh yes there were the smell of the smoke from the Christmas light which children with parents could light and throw up into the air. Once up in the air they cheered and jumped with joy counting the days before Christmas. Although these were melodious sounds Clearance only contemplation was what would happen if December 25th came and he could not be in the crowd.

During his hours of pondering Marylou Crawford would shout Clearance come on man, you are always quiet and you know if you are not here the fun would die. Even though Marylou was a friend; she could not understand the quietness of Clearance. One morning while talking with Marylou Timothy Olu came by, and he stepped out of his father newly bought Toyota Taxi cab. As he entered the location where Clearance stood conversing with his friend; Timothy presence became intimidating that it rendered Clearance almost inadequate to stand face to face with the most beautiful Marylou who was to be captivated by the appearance of Mr. Olu. Clearance became more withdrawn and more cautious about how he shall intertwined with others. He felt a kind of betrayal that only he could understand.

Marylou liked the appearance of Olu, but she was not an admiral of the young and rich fellow. The fellow was interested in her, but she was committed to her church work.

Clearance's commitment to church and schoolwork always kept his mind off the things he could not have. He later would become a Sunday school teacher and Church Sexton. Faithfully he cleaned the church and prepared the place for Sunday morning services. Whenever Mr. Crawford would come in,

Clearance would stand at the door and say "welcome in Pastor" and the Pastor would respond Clearance you know "One day the Lord will deliver you and set you up; you will be the head and not the tail; remember that okay; remember that". For some reason Clearance considered this blessing something that would eventually come to pass and for this cause he always stayed around after the cleaning of the Church to hear the Pastor bless him constantly.

Pastor Crawford knew that the young Clearance loved the blessing and so he consistently blessed him using the same blessing phrase. Clarence knew that when the blessing came from an elder of the Church; the Lord would honor it. For the Scripture says "what-ever you loose on earth would be loose in heaven and whatever you bound on earth will also be bound in heaven" Clearance knew that God was real and choose to continue working for God, irrespective of his poor condition. Trusting whatever you do for the Lord will always last. He also remembered that Hebrews 6 tells us that God will always remember everyone for all the good deeds they wrought for God. The Bible promises that God is not slack concerning His promises. Knowing all of this Clearance stayed closer to God and did not compromise his position because he knew that his labor was not in vain.

One afternoon while at Church, and everyone was praising the Lord Marylou Crawford announced that she was going on a Student exchange program, but was not sure that she would return after the program was over, because the family sponsoring her; had already made provision for her to attend the State University at Albany. Clearance at this juncture knew that he was about to lose his friend and it meant more loneliness.

His faith could not afford to let him feel the void even-though Marylou was still around; he commenced making the adjustment for living without her. For this cause he decided to intensify his communication with God. He prayed that God make a way for him, and that God blesses Marylou for her kindness towards him. While the entire saga unfolded, Timothy Olu was graduating from high school and his father the merchant had decided to send him to the state university at Albany.

Many others commenced their migration to the United States, some laughed at the fact that Clearance that they would come back and find him still cleaning Pastor Crawford's Church. Some even reminded him that Marylou was also leaving and that he would get nothing because the Pastor had nothing to offer. Being a younger man and greatly trusted God, he also felt some faithless moments. He started to think that maybe God was slow like Santa Claus during his younger days who could never answer his calls. All those who were travelling did so successfully all that had to travel made the trip, and adjusted just find.

While in New York, Timothy Olu started hanging out with some of the other rich kids, which he knew from Africa. He was not an over achiever but was an average student. He loved the limelight and wanted to maintain his standard of living that he had in Africa. His father could only provide him his college tuition and monthly allowance for up keep. He hung out mostly on the weekends, traveling from state to state. While in Rhode Island he ran into Marylou who was spending the week-end with some friends. She was happy to have met him, and he was too.

They met each other and spent some time together reminiscing about the old days. Clearance name came about and Marylou said, "Yes he is still back home and working with my father in the church"

Timothy said to himself, "I knew that that Church stuff was a waste of time. Look at Clearance when will he ever get out of that place. He said to Marylou I thought you liked him?"

She said, "Yes and still do. I believe that there is something special about him, though poor yet life is in him.

As time would have it, a black BMW rode up and the windows rolled down, the yell came from within "come on man leave that preacher daughter alone; in America she is still talking about Church". Come on let us go we have to make it to North Carolina. Marylou held her peace as Timothy said to her girl "do you want to come along" almost tempted she started to go inside the house to get her coat for it was a cold winter night and the streets were covered by some residual snow from the previous fall. As she attempted to leave the house she remembered that prior to her departure from Africa, Clearance said to her that "Where ever you may go, where ever you may find yourself remember the opportunity that God has granted you. Make the best use of it" at this quick juncture she said to herself no I am not going I am here for a purpose. She later yelled out to Timothy no I am not interested in going. I lived in Albany and I'm on a visit to my friends in Rhode Island what am I doing in North Carolina. Timothy said okay that just find preacher's daughter. She pondered to herself that it is always good to look back to where you are from and not to let anything change the person that you are. Two months later

While in Africa. Pastor Crawford understood Clearance's commitment to the Lord's work and decided to contact some Missionary from the Church of God in Christ he had met some years ago while they were in Liberia. They told him that whenever he needed their help he should not hesitate. Therefore, he decided to utilize his chance by calling on the Missionaries. He asked if they remember Clearance who was so generous to them while they were in Africa. Mr. Spellman quickly said yes "Young man, there is something about him and I would like to be a blessing to Him" Pastor Crawford quickly yelled, "Yes God is real! Yes, God is real! Mr. Spellman quickly asked, "What is the matter Pastor Crawford?"

Pastor Crawford replied, "Sir I have just call to have you help me get Clearance over to the States for studies on some scholarship, but hear that you were anticipating the same because the Lord had laid it on your heart to assist the young man. MR. Spellman quickly replied yes, as the matter of fact I have secured a place for him at the Church, and we would be glad to have him work for the church over here in New York. Will be in touch with you please inform me if the young man is accepting my offer by tomorrow!

Pastor Crawford quickly placed the phone down and ran to the pulpit and cried and praised God, because God never forget those who work for Him (God) He is always rewarding and remembering

His promises. He said to himself look at this poor boy, yet so poor and yet so rich in God. God is about to reward him. He ran to Clearance while Clearance was in the Church teaching Bible studies and said my man! My man! I do not know what to tell you, but there is good news from a far off country! Proverb 25:25 states that "as cold water to a thirsty soul, so is good news from a far off country". Pastor Crawford insisted that no matter what a person's circumstances are once they choose to follow God and choose the right life style they can determine what the future brings their way. He later said, "Trusting in God and really makes you better and richer in this world and the next world."

He waited in his office for Clearance. Clearance knew that Pastor always leave early during the week's services because he trusted him to shut the church and open up the next day. However, this day Pastor was late and praising God, and yelling Clearance! Clearance! You are truly a child of the living God! Guess what!

"Guess What!" Clearance yelled, Pastor you making me scare, while you alone enjoying all of the joy.

Pastor Crawford later said to Clearance sit down here and I need your answer right away too! He said, "What Pastor don't you know it is getting late and that you have to travel to New Georgia. Pastor said, "Son I do not care, but I am happy. He said do you remember Mr. Spellman the missionary that you helped. The missionary who clothes you always washed, and wiped the sweat off his face when he was praying for people here? Clearance he requested that I ask you if you would like to move to New York and work with him in the Church over there! He wants an answer from you tonight, and I have to call him tomorrow. What do you say?"

The Young man (Clearance) could not believe it, but he knew that Pastor Crawford was an honorable man and that he does not play with people emotions. Therefore, quickly he replied, but Pastor who will help you when I am gone. The Pastor said the Lord will send me another Clearance, because with God there is always another Clearance. Pastor Crawford later said but Clearance this is good news and you asking what would happen to me. The Pastor later said that is why you are blessed because you care. He later said I take it that it is a yes! Knowing that Clearance was living with relatives, he said I know thing s would be just find; I am calling Spellman.

The next day Pastor called Spellman, and the Local Church prepared and escorted Clearance to the airport. In the main time, Marylou was in college still praising God and studying Nursing. Timothy and the other rich kids were running back and forth forgetting the training of their parents. Timothy father took sick and business in Africa became bad, he could not send Tim money as before. Some of the other rich kids saw Tim situation and kept him along with them hoping things would improve. Later Clearance arrived in New York and started work in the Church. They sent him to school, and he graduate and started working. Marylou decided to visit the local Church in New York and met him. It was like love never left their hearts. While traveling together in Manhattan on Broadway they saw Timothy looking depressed. He was broke. His friends had left him and the fighting damaged his father's business.

Timothy ran to Marylou, not remembering the looks of Clearance and he totally ignored the man walking with Marylou, as if to say the man didn't really matter at all. His total interest was in the woman who at once captivated him and thought she had the same feelings for him, but he was wrong! Marylou later encouraged Timothy to look at the guy and to guess who the fellow was. In the heart of Timothy, this person appeared familiar but could not place his imagination anywhere closer to Clearance.

Nevertheless, Marylou with her insightful character later relief Timothy of his embarrassment She informed him that it was Clearance, and that he was a computer consultant; consulting for IBM. She later stated that their families were coming over to conduct a traditional wedding at Pastor Spellman's Church. Clearance also insisted that Timothy takes his business card and that he could work out some thing for him. He later reminded him not to forget the wedding and to keep in touch.

Chapter 9

The Wedding!

nvitations were sent all over, invitees were coming from Nigeria, Liberia, Sierra Leon, Senegal and Ghana. Everyone was informed that the wedding is traditional, and that the proper attires were African garments. Anyone who was out of the traditional garments was requested to sit in the rear of the reception hall. There were delegations arranged for meeting all of the guests. The local church was also getting ready for the wedding of the year and no one wanted to be left out. Many persons in the church were organizing to make just the right garment for the occasion. So many discussions were going on. Sister Hussy and others were planning to cash in on the festival by selling garments.

As the people were getting themselves together, the African cultural dancers were getting ready and preparing to perform at the wedding reception. Rev. Crawford and Pastor Spellman were overly joyous. They could not stop talking about what fine a young man Mr. Clearance had turned out to be.

Impressed by the transition which Clearance had experience, Rev. Crawford yelled "God can do anything but fail" he paused and later said " who would have known that guy would be what he is now" He said " for truth when a person submits to God; God can do the impossible" while speaking Rev. Spellman said "Rev. Crawford! I knew that the young man was special and knew that God was on his side, and what has happen for him; no one could have done it but God! Spellman later said, "We were the channels through which God was blessing that young man.

As they spoke Clearance walked up and said hello Revs. "How is everything and have you all eaten; I would like to arrange to take you all for dinner tonight and maybe Marylou can come along with us.

Meanwhile as they were discussing preparation were going on for the wedding and the guests were still arriving. Mr. Spellman asked "Why a traditional wedding Clearance?" and while all those guests and dancers. Rev. Crawford later said just let me answer for my son Spellman! You see we want this occasion to be special, and we want to identify all and everyone who is actually ready for the wedding. We want to separate the real invitees from the crushers. We would like to treat the invited guests with the outmost respect and prepare a place for them. You see Rev. when Christ comes only the ready guests would make the marriage.

As they conversed more preparation were going on. The church folks were discussing how the reception would look like and what should be accepted in the hall. Sometimes sister hussy would complicate everything by suggesting different dimensions to the organizers. The organizers were also busy discussing what color everyone should wear and how their formation would be at the wedding.

They finally decided that the dancers would come in dancing before the bridal party is ushered in. Sister hussy remained fussy and insisted that it would be necessary to have the bridal party come in before the dancers. Anyway, as usual church folks never forgot the democratic process and decided to vote on the issue. As the vote was conducted, the group agreed to have the dancers come in before the bridal party. Timothy latter decided to attend the wedding and turned in his invitation. He also sent home a letter telling Mr. Onanuga about his experience with how life is funny and most of all that he has seen from firsthand how God can make the first last and the last first. He requested that his father sent him an Ibadan suit for the wedding, because he had to attend the wedding. Timothy because of his encounter with Clearance became a Christian. He realized that God can change anyone's life if that person waits on God's time. His confession in his letter was "that only the patient who wait on God gets God's blessings" .He read his open letter before he dropped it in the mail. His testimony was that the present condition of a man does not determine his end. He expressed that it is only by determination that success can come in the name of the Most High God. He later ended by telling his father that if he could come to the wedding his life would be changed. Timothy later prayed for his father, and as he was praying on the phone his father commence to experience a change. Mr. Olu said son what has come over you something is happening. I am feeling well. Oh, son you have just prayed one of the best pray and I am healed! Mr. Olu later said son I am coming to that wedding and would like to see the young man who has had such impact on you.

The Organizers hastily commenced telling everyone that the bridal party would be in a traditional rainbow fashion. That there would be colors matching, the men would match the woman they are escorting, they later said the bride and the groom would wear white African attire. All of the organizers would come in a special color selected by the group.

The Pastors and the family would also dress in African attire. As everyone was preparing Sister Hussy later said people the wedding is near and we have to move on. Two days later church was in order and the hall ready for the reception.

At the wedding, the party assembled themselves and the African dancers came dancing as people in the crowd commenced throwing flowers and money on the group. Everyone looked happy and there were jubilation all over the place. The dancers really danced and the people were happy. Across the hall sister hussy yelled that is what I am talking about man this is a grand wedding and I am ready for this today! The dancers dance gracefully and they were welcome as many plants and different leaves were placed in their path. The occasion was blessed with the presence of many persons who were ready for the occasion. The hall was dressed and ready to receive the bridal party.

At the ceremony the Rev. Spellman, give a liturgical speech just before the ceremony started. He said that life is what you make of it. The life that a person chooses now determines his out come later. Mr. Spellman said many of us could become channels for God to bless others. He later said that I am honored to have been in the right place at the right time to be used by God so that this wonderful man received his rightful place in life. He later said that you too can become a channel only you have to be in the right frame of mind to bless others when God chooses to bless them. Today God's will is been done; Rev. Crawford later said I am elated too that I am the vessel through which God has blessed my daughter. Look at Marylou, she knew what she wanted, she saw it when I didn't see it. She brought her husband to church and waited for God's time. Look at where God has allowed them to be now. Folks please let us enjoy this great day and make it a wonderful one. At the completion of his statement, the Deacon came and announce that the people are ready and the wedding is about to start. I am telling this story because of what influences it has on my personal life, and that is self-determination and the fortitude to be somebody despite the unfavorable circumstance.

The Deacon:

Listen everybody, and understand this one thing. This wedding is prepared for those who are properly attired. We are prepared to have all the readied guests to come up front and those in their western form to sit in the rear. We are the readied people read to see Brother Clearance and Sister Marylou ready and we are determined to see them through today. Men, Women, guest from Liberia, Senegal,

Sierra Leon, Nigeria and Ghana, come and let us enjoy this blessed day for this is the day that God has bless us With joy; rejoice! Prepare yourselves and see what God has done!

Later Timothy walked up and saw Clearance in the hall way and they embraced, and thank God together. They praised God and worshiped Him. Timothy later said my Brother I am sorry that I didn't understand what God was doing, but now I know that God is real and that no good thing does he hold from those who walk up right. Clearance said yes my brother I understand and forgave you for everything. I am glad that you have found the Lord. Come on let us get in there for I have a woman to marry.

The wedding moderator:

Instantly as the wedding begun, the moderator started describing the wedding garments of all of the participants. She was extremely correct when it came to addressing the beautiful Garments. The wedding people seemed overly joyous, and prepared for the occasion. No one seemed out of place everyone were ready and the bride and groom were excited that God has blessed them to be together. The moderator expressed the sentiment of the union and told the guests that God's hands had ushered the festival. She proclaimed that nothing could interfere with the day, because God had sanctioned the occasion. While the crowd was gathering, Sister Hussy quickly jumped in the middle of the floor and started her traditional dance. All of the organizers joined in, and while their dances went on the Pastor conducting the wedding yelled, "Come on Sister Hussy and others we have a wedding to perform here!" He later said to the moderator are we ready to bring in the bridal party? If so come on everybody, the party has begun!"

The moderator later walked up to Clearance, whispered in his ears, and said, "My man I hope you are ready? Please stop shaking, because people can see you" He later smiled and said yes madam I am ready! Sister Deanna later cried out by saying oh my God look at Hussy, look at the way she is acting, I mean that woman is crazy. Deanna later said the Pastor is ready and come on hussy let the people move on. The moderator later said I agreed with that and let the ball roll. The moderator later called in the traditional dancers and as they danced, the crowd started jumping and everybody were happy. The guests were seated in the formation, which was described by the moderator.

The families of both couple came in and were seated. Marylou's mother and father came in first. Clearance parents also came. They were traditional Africans and wore the real garments that displayed the appearance of the occasion. Pastor Spellman came in looking astonished and blown away. The beauty of the wedding party carried him away. Clearance mother commenced speaking her native dialect. She ran to Pastor Crawford and Pastor Spellman, spoke broken English, and said "Pastor made my son a great man" You have caused him come to this great country"; "God bless you oh! God bless you oh!" Clearance's father a bit eloquent came and, said Spellman and Crawford men of the most high God you all have made our lives blessed, and may the great Lord bless you all for the wonderful interference you have caused in our lives we are no longer sad; we are happy because God's blessings is with us. Mrs. Crawford later said to the parents of Clearance "My people I thank the almighty God for the great son that you all have given to my daughter for husband, and I oh! Did I say we are happy to have him as our son in-law?" We thank the almighty God for his wonderful blessings for today speaks for the kind of person you have as your son!

While this was on going the Moderator once again said my people my family, here come the bridal party, come and let us see what the Lord can do! The music started playing and the people were dancing, suddenly the party came in, and the Pastor went to the front of the hall. Two by two, the party walked up in formation. The beauty of their garments, were splendid, and the people looked well manner as they walked the hall. The moderator later started her descriptions. Calling everyone by names, and by formal escorts. Clearance was trembling as the moderator spoke Marylou comforted him. As the sweat ran down his face, Marylou wiped them away. Later Deanna yelled come on man!

Come on see what I told you God is about to bless the situation. The wedding party was anxious and pacing back and forth. The moderator as eloquent as she appeared walked down the hall.

Then came in the party and God was blessing everyone as the whole house were affixed on the beauty of the occasion. The traditional garments were stunning and the people loved the appearance.

My God yelled Sister Hussy what a show! What a show! Look at what is going on here! Then the little bride walked in with her garment on, the moderator later expressed the appearance of everyone! One by one, she described the look. She spoke of the exquisite designs of the garments and hailed the originations of the designers. As the party entered the hall, the people remained happy and helpful. The bride and the groom came walking in after all of the party had assembled within the halls.

Overwhelmed by the crowd and the jubilating experiences, Marylou and Clearance were over taken by the crowd's acceptance. The entire scene was encompassed by the splendor of the wedding, and the African attires. Gracefully the party came in the crowd waved and the wedding begun. The bridal party carried on the waving of branches. The Pastor later welcomes the group and blessed them After the ceremony the Deacon came in and announced that the wedding was over and that the traditional dance was about to start. He said everyone grab your partner, take a hold of the woman or the man, for this is a festival that we all must enjoyed. The bride and the groom shall lead as the family followed, this is a feast and come on everyone let us begin the function. This is the traditional dance and everyone must have a partner. Mr. DJ please let us have the sound that pleases this occasion. As the deacon spoke, the bridal party commenced their dancing and the folks stood up as the cord drill rolled on.

~Bobby tell his heart about the story~

This was the story my children and I also wished the same for us all, but there are some virtues, which we all can understand, and when we do well; all of us can be as Clearance. He showed us the real meaning of life and the purpose of struggles. In life every trial are not meant to be destructive; they are for developing and modeling quality character within individuals. Clearance knew this well and that through spiritual means and commitment to faith; one can realize his desires. Vows are meant to be kept and directly they are kept, yet there are circumstances in which they are broken for good reasons, such as my hope for reconnecting with Melinda, and this is my greatest prayer.

Vows, which are not considered when, made via emotional convictions; faces test and trials, which unearth the hidden realities. Things become glaring when the storm is over, and it is when reconsiderations of the obvious purport themselves as evidence that the decisions were not the real intentions but rather they were superficially orchestrated. The couple asked Brother Bobby if he thought it was possible to reconnect given the situation. He replied that with God all things are possible. Melinda may have been emotionally convicted to help, but it wasn't God's intended purpose for her! Oh by the way, guys, we need to understand these virtues, which I spoke of, and they are as follows:

~Love~

Love originates deep from within the core of God's purpose; it is spiritual it is one virtue which the creator carefully breathed into humankind. It is intended to promote greater emphasis of caring for another person other than oneself. Love is a quality in grind into man's heart. The opposites to love are hatred, distrusts, suspicions and grievous animosity. Love lends herself to acceptance, consideration, accommodations with good intentions. She is not puffed up but extremely sacrificial, and this is to say; one person dies so that the other lives. Most of the time individuals at this level make the hearty expression as "I have find my soul mate". Folks the world is changing today and this change is rapid. We have to identify what are the necessary tenets by which we spontaneously realized the fuel for rekindling a stayed relationship.

These things don't come along unintentionally. They do by commitment and unconditional support. Pretense cannot support the fundamental mandated criterion by which real expressions of the heart survive the tumultuous arrogance of individuals falsified connotations of fitted realities of love; rather a transparent relationship with selfless goals ushers an awesome sanity driven purpose by which everyone is securely actualized as a unit; properly fitted with unified objectives for growth and family development. It is this prospect by which the relationship is ideally centric for greater lasting acceptance just the way you are. I am my brother's keeper aspect of love.

Once you feel it and can support it, then trust it, respect it and invest in it. Love needs to be nurture, appreciated and reciprocated. Oh no I don't mean real death, but rather it is been patient to the point at which you are completely selfless and considerate. You see folks there are three types of love and they are explicitly in origins by way of the Greek language.

The first is called the **Eros,** the second is the **Philia,** and the third is the **Agape.** Each has its own denotative impacts. The Eros is not a word found within the scriptures but the actions are implicit, and applied to married couples. Eros is important within in married relationships. It is an emotion created by God. It was sanctioned by God and given to Adam and Eve as a process for participating in the procreation process.

> *(Genesis 1:28) Be fruitful and multiply, and fill the earth, and subdue it; and rule over the fish of the sea and over the birds of the sky and over every living thing that moves on the earth."*
>
> ***The same can be found within Genesis 9:7 "As for you, be fruitful and multiply; Populate the earth abundantly and multiply in it."*

Today extreme eroticisms has given rise to negative connotations of Eros, on account of extreme excessive sexual desires and excitements. This aspect of love has been misinterpreted, and the interpretation has become the foundation for extreme exploitations and belittlements. This is not love because it is temporary and entirely conditional with focus on appeasing oneself. It is only the satisfying of a desire of the flesh at the expense of a defrauded one party. Extreme Eros is about disguised intentions; which deny the real meaning of life. I am sorry but I have to submit to you some scriptural backgrounds; kindly permit me to digress just a little and forward sentiments which have grossly impacted descriptions of Eros in lieu of " Evil in the Last Days"

> *** 2nd Timothy 3:2-5 " 2For men will be lovers of self, lovers of money, boastful, arrogant, revilers, disobedient to parents, ungrateful, unholy, 3unloving, irreconcilable, malicious gossips, without self-control, brutal, haters of good, 4treacherous, reckless, conceited, lovers of pleasure rather than lovers of God,..."*
>
> *Marriages with meaningful Eros excitements between a husband and a wife; refreshes the relationship.*
>
> *** (Hebrews 13:4) " Marriage is honorable in all, and the bed undefiled: but whoremongers and adulterers God will judge".*

Today people use the phrase "make love to me!", "prove your love to me". Folks no man can make or manufacture love, no man can prove love to anyone or else you would end up within a critical delusional condition in which you become a victim of abuses and exploitations. Eros rules the realm of infatuations and misguided sensuality. Negative Eros (eroticism) is not of God it has a negative impact on humanity and it is enormously illusive in the end.

Some people think love is to be flirtatious with anyone; this is eroticism and the erratic spirit operates on this realm within such disguise with utterance of trickery and illusive kindness. They come as friendly as they can be with such statements "How was your weekend", "I hope you did not get yourself into any trouble". All of these are illusive and evasive statements to spark an erratic moments as an opening to the gate of sensuality with innuendos, which leads to appeasing an erratic appetite. Eroticism is not love; extreme Eros is the feel good results of exploitation and conditional merits for the advantaged at the expense of the disadvantaged. People who get involve at this level and get married soon end up into the divorce courts with broken vows. Extreme eroticism is not love!

Extreme Eros is not friendship based; it is conditional and merit based. Whenever you have to be remunerated for a display of a sensual emotion, you are not in love because your actions are based on satisfying an end. Eros can be extremely devastating, and it is also the root cause for many abortions. You use your imagination and understand sex out of marriage and the process of procreation. I rest my case! Think about it! The Bible is clear about sexual immorality (extreme Eros), and it is manipulative. (*1 Corinthians 6:18; 1 Thessalonians 4:3*).

~Real Love~

Real love is distinctive and it is the complete opposite to extreme Eros! Real love starts with friendship it is the second type of love; the Philia. Friendship based love is unconditional; it requests no refund nor is it merited. It is the foundation of life and on this threshold; individuals can trust, respect and support one another.

The Philia love makes you selfless, courageous and trusting. It has no animosity and seeks no merits; its criterion is wholesome friendship and spirituality. It seeks to promote the wellness of everyone caring on these bases.

Friendship is necessary for this kind of love. Caring for one-self is ideal in this dimension. Promoting everyone within which it connects; is paramount to this foundation of love. To understand philia love, we need to take a look at the other types of love. Storge (Greek word describing love) is an affectionate love, the type of love one might have for family or a spouse. It is naturally occurring, and it is an unforced type of love.

Some examples of storge love can be found in the stories of families promoting and supporting one another; it is with lovers who hearts are united. It is also an example seen with siblings ; such as brothers and sisters, mothers and fathers. Storge is actually a better degree of Philia. Unconditional love is not limited to anyone's definition, but rather it is rooted in the immaterial part of an individual. It is from the soul, it makes a person to become entirely sacrificial.

Adam could have walked away from Eve, but instead he succumbed to her on account of the knowledge he had gained from love for his help meet; flesh of his flesh and bones of his bone. Folks; people caring for one another in marriage or any relationship have to be considerate and supportive. Adam permitted himself to become as Eve so that both could face the consequence. True love would make you do some crazy things. Only friends would look out for another and sacrifice time and resources in support of the other. Real friends fall in love and see the unconditional good for the other. In St. John 15; Jesus calls us the believers his friends and said that He has chosen us we did not choose Him and as a Friend of our He is the source for the nutrients supplying all of our spiritual and physical needs for productiveness. Real friends sacrifice so much to perpetuate the harmony of a lasting relationship. Get to know God and get to know your friends and most of all support as much as you can and fall in love over and over again; as many times as you can.

The Bible says (1ˢᵗ. Timothy 2:14 "13For it was Adam who was first created, and then Eve. 14And it was not Adam who was deceived, but the woman being deceived, fell into transgression. 15But women will be preserved through the bearing of children if they continue in faith and love and sanctity with self-restraint").

Love would make you stay where you are no matter what. Love would make you understanding and approachable. It makes a person selfless and supportive. True love would make a man to stand up for what he believes. It has no conditions or merits. Its foundation is strictly based on trust and good reciprocity. It makes a man to reach out and takes a lady by the hand; draws her closer and securely protects her at all times. This love is what makes a person to regard another person a friend. It only keeps the hearts warm, united and helpful. The Philia love is not experience by a person who is not a friend. My Children all of these virtues are things which make the heart to grow fonder and stress free. In continuance of this discussion; you need to understand that life is better lived once these virtues are operational in your everyday living.

~Joy~

Joy is necessary for every one of you; seek the joy of the other and this is necessary for better family deportments. I would encourage you all to seek the joy of the other, and when you shall do; the happiness of the family shall be magnified. The human strength comes from God almighty, and if joy is brought into the family life the presence of God would be visible in the physical life of the family. The scripture implicated successfully that when God is happy; it becomes our point of strength **(Nehemiah 8.10)**. Joy is an intrinsic virtue actually deeply seated in the soul of every one, it is cautiously important that it is fostered and stigmatize in the life of all relationships by the triggers unconsciously placed. Binding with God helps this virtue in all dimensions; be it spiritual or physical. It transcends the core of the human sentiment of satisfaction. Spiritually we can permit the voice of the Most- high God to be heard in our relationships as this virtue is sealed by our supplications (*Psalm 28:7*). *When we operate in Joy and gladness of God's free spirit; we are approve by God and accepted by man.* Roman 14:14.

Let joy rule in your hearts; keep the life of joy for the unseen things. Helen Keller noted that "The best and most beautiful things in the world cannot be seen, nor touched, but are felt in the heart." I recommend that you all search deeply for this virtue and keep it above the shoulders of your relationships with God and yourselves.

~Peace~

Peace starts with the power of forgiveness:

I have heard people say "I can forgive, but I cannot forget". I have heard people also say I" hate the pains and this is repeated over and over the same thing over and over". I have also heard that it is best to" forgive but keep a distance"! Yes these are all true, and the fact is that no one enjoys pains of hatred, rejections, betrayal nor undermining; yet those who have experienced these elements of pains are accosted to make concessions by faith in accepting those who hate them, wrongfully despise them, and attempt to relegate them to mediocrity. It is a truthful saying that only your friend knows your secret and only he can hurt you with them, but when he does you have to forgive. I guess you would ask; why? And the answer is straight forward; it is your duty as a believer! Having the ability to forgive; would enable you to live peaceably with everyone including yourselves.

St. Luke 6:27-29 "But I say to you who hear, love your enemies, do good to those who hate you, 28 bless those who curse you, pray for those who mistreat you. 29 "Whoever hits you on the cheek, offer him the other also; and whoever takes away your coat, do not withhold your shirt from him either"

Listen the very acts of forgiving and been forgiven; take loads of people and bring about joyfulness in people lives. Jesus expects us to be mature at this practice. The very act speaks volume about the quality of characters. There is so much power in writing all of your hurts which people inflict upon you in sandy places, while spending much time remembering and carving in stones the amount of times you were delivered from personal trespasses by God almighty first and then by folks closer to you. Notice I said folks closer to you; it is said that way on account; that strangers don't hurt you, but it is the person you trust, respect and love; who inflicts the knockout incisions. I don't know about anyone's feelings but trust me; it does hurt! O well it is what it is; just learn the lessons, dust yourselves, move on with love in your heart. Therefore if you read this and if you are at odds with someone; make concession; agree with them, work with them in this process, get the stuff of your chest and live in peace with a clear conscience. Don't be afraid of words spoken by man; seek the love of God, live soberly and be above reproaches! Forgive your selves and others and then be forgiven by God almighty. Peace and love

~Longsuffering~

In relationships with the Creator and man; it is extremely important to exercise patience. I am encouraging you all to be sacrificial and accepting. Wait and understand the conditions or root causes of all upsets. Learn to know the other person more than yourself; this comes with endurance and heart felt circumstances controls. Therefore press forward; just shake it off! Stump it down! Keep your affections on things above. Make no friends with dismal yesterday or a call back to the day before dismay! Keep your focus on today's peace and let go of the weighted unnecessary. Take a good hold of your now and walk with God with an assuring view of tomorrow's bliss! Don't give up! Keep on trying for every round with God goes higher and higher! Peace and blessings God knows the details of my life; He is acquainted with all of my steps. My low moments and high ones are all seen and acknowledged by God. I am persuaded that He is able to create a balance in my life to keep me afloat of the unknown.

PSALM 139:1-10 He knows about my anxieties when I am relaxed and when I am troubled! I have no fear; for I am of more value to God than sparrows! Comment Amen if you know that God cares for you! Therefore be patience and hopeful in your caring one for the other; after all it is your happiness.

~Kindness/Goodness~

Do not become lost to a life of love! Demonstrate your maturity in kindness and goodly responding to the needs of the other. To be successful; become selfless and submit one to the other with a fundamental value which support the goals of your love life and commitment to your ideals. Be always sacrificial in love, because once it is gone; it is gone. Appreciate the time and serve one another with graceful acknowledgments. Love is happiness once it is carefully reciprocated. Show always kindness in support of the other person. Always seek to be good at serving one another in nurturing your love life.

~Self-Control~

Always subdue your passions and have respect for yourselves. Do not live by assumptions cure the jealous feelings. It would only complicate your good will in love. It would cause you to live a life of love in suspicions and this can be catastrophic if you do not have self-control. Keep the truth about your heart and execute a deliberate structure for good family living with a sense of appreciations. Always reach out to you inner passion in submission to integrity and interpersonal appreciations and compliments. The Day's session ended. He reminded all of the counselees to remain steadfast and committed to the given instructions, conjunctively. He noted; "I am thankful to God and all my Friends; he reiterated that during the morning while walking towards the bus stop; one of his neighbor called, and when he returned he realized how late he was, and that he had to stop and talk to his neighbor. "I did, and we started walking but she was a bit slower than I was, the bus came; I had to rush, but I realized that she was interested in talking to me about her experience, and so walking slow, we missed the first bus. Oh well I stopped and paid all the attention; finally another bus came and we boarded that one.

While sitting she said to me Bobby thanks; "for waiting for me I really needed someone to listen to me, and now I am feeling better" I responded; you are welcome! Then it dawn on me how grateful she was just for a moment of my time and the patience which I exerted at that moment. This led me into thinking about our Savior's encounter with the ten lepers; they were delivered and only one was grateful and returned to express his gratitude. Many people are blessed to have others in their lives, but somehow; shows no gratitude at all. If we can just take a little time to review constructively people conditions around us, then we would realize that they cannot be taken for granted but rather, respected, honored and appreciated. In so doing; we just might entertained a child of God as I did on the bus. We have to take time out to show love to others in demonstration of the Savior's acts of kindness. Today we can all become demonstratively positive about our attitudes in representing the Lord's love and care in preserving us; His children. We must all be appreciative in all aspects of our lives; more so in all the ones which are considered trivia.

Every sustaining moment; which we encounter is the Lord's. He watches over us; assuring us of his cares in leading us every step of the way towards His good will pleasure and purpose in time. You could be lonely today, forgotten by friends, neglected by family members, opposed by church members, but just take a look at you! You are better off than what you were 10 years ago. There were others who tried to be in your position today, but failed at it. Just look at who you are today, and where you have come. Isn't it a reason to be grateful!

Just understand that God cares to listen to you and He wants to hear your conversations with Him. Only be thankful and grateful for all of your friends and family who have been there for you along the way. Take the time to call someone show some as for me I am thankful to God and all my Friends who have; over the years never given up on me! More so to those who never ceased my trying moments as opportunity for laughter; but rather supported me when I was down until the grace of God lifted me 30 plus years ago! I am thankful! In getting his points across, he instructed the counselees to hold and never lose hope about any situation in their lives. He stated that no one should count himself out of any victory until it is really over. He told this story the at the next day session: I am not counting myself out until I see the end.

Chapter 10

~A Sealed Victory must be tested~

Psalm 31:15-16 "15 My times are in Your hand; Deliver me from the hand of my enemies and from those who persecute me. 16 Make Your face to shine upon Your servant; Save me in Your loving kindness"

I watched the New York Knicks and the Indiana Pacers game on Wednesday night; it was a wonderful game and the defensive coordinators works of excellence were demonstratively evident from the orchestrated plays at both ends of the floor. The game was at a height; with the New York Knicks leading the Pacers at 00:05 left in regulations; and the scores were 89 Knicks and 86 Pacers. There were great adulations in chants towards the Knicks and people were celebrating for once a change and a real victory. I saw the reasons for such a moment, and I thought to myself at last; these guys would redeem themselves; instead it was the other way around.

The Pacers had the ball in the last seconds and from a three pointer's range, the young man from the Pacers went up, I guess in desperation to redeem his team from falling, he missed the shot. However, it was not over because Iman Shumpert went up to contest the shot, which Paul George shot, oh well there it went. Paul George while coming down got touched by the tip of Iman Shumpert's fingers. The rest is history.

You see this had me thinking; I pondered deeply about pre-matured victories I pondered deeply about pre-matured victories in our lives, meaning before we go out in wide spread celebration; we have to assured ourselves that the victory is sealed. Nothing is over until the final whistle is blown. Your chances in life are not over until the expected end promised to you by God is experienced. Until then we can be certain that God's grace is not over towards us until He says it is. Make sure that your victory is actually sealed before celebrating because in every game; under-dogs have opportunities to re-bounce; once time is on their side.

Therefore, be like King David who relegated to trust in God and not the temporary prosperity of those who believed to themselves that they have victories over him. There is something about the present appearances; they are shadows and shadows don't have the same impacts as the actuals. Only God sees the end and knows all about the ends of our times and every situation in time. Therefore; remember that everything about you; have been made; also be knowledgeable that everything about you have been made beautiful, God made it so.

Fret not yourselves when you see others moving ahead of you; it means nothing; just be the under-dog because once the final call is in the hands of God; the time Keeper; you still have an opportunity of making just that last buzzer beater's shot. I also believe in this; once your steps are order by God then; your Times are in His hands as well. Watch how you celebrate; assure yourselves that God is actually in control of the situation, don't fret because of what you see now; hold unto God for He sees tomorrow. Promotion comes from Him. Tomorrow one is lifted and tomorrow another is humbled. Therefore those who are in great admirations or exaltations of a victory; please let God almighty sealed your victory; before it is taken away at the last buzzer beating shot! Ps. take an advice from the playbook of the New York Knicks; trust in God, and not on your own merits.

When Adversity comes, God intercedes! He won't leave you; no not alone! Salvation belongs to the Lord God almighty. He knows your down sitting and He understands your uprising. He is the greatest of all! I am so confident that I shall come out of this situation. I am going to get married, I know that time, and destiny is on my side. I shall see Melinda again and trust me when I say again that I mean just that. I am determined and selfishly I am praying that love; real love would induce her to reconsider the real will of God for her life. I honestly believe that she was put on earth to be the object of pure love and serenity. I know that I shall be a part of that serene.

~In the interim Bobby was nearing the end of his two years stay in Africa~.

He had worked successfully with Jacqueline, Jimmy, Mr. and Mrs. Larry Moses, and the adopted son of his Amos. Jacqueline and Jimmy followed keenly the instructions given and were successful at supporting one and the other in love. They got together and the Priest, Father John performed their wedding and they were happy. They became a model couple at the parish and successfully aided Brother Ross in meeting and counseling others. Jacqueline often worked with the women and children and supported the nursery. She was committed to the services and became regular in support of single mothers. Jimmy started a youth program and enlisted Amos help in reaching the younger men of the parish. Amos was kind; determined to become a priest as his grandmother had wished, but he later decided to discuss the plans of his life with Brother Ross. Amos started serving weekly mass with Fathers John and Peter. He loved the priesthood; he made promises to one day become a better priest as Father John and Peter.

~Brother Ross Meets Amos~

Brother Bobby was to meet hurriedly with the young man and thus questioning him about his real feelings about not having a family of his own and denying a young woman the privilege of motherhood. Amos eyes lighted up astonished at the line of questioning, he shy away from the discussion. Brother Bobby Ross would insist, for some reason Brother Ross equated Amos becoming a priest to the situation with that of He and Melinda. Bobby thought the young man was making a mistake. Bobby was a good believer, a good catholic who believed and advocated for priest and nuns to have families of their own. Bobby focus was obeying the commandments of God. His view of been fruitful and multiplying was to be upheld and respected as every other commandment of the Holy Scriptures. God's command *Genesis 1:28 "God blessed them; and God said to them, "Be fruitful and multiply, and fill the earth, and subdue it; and rule over the fish of the sea and over the birds of the sky and over every living thing that moves on the earth."*

Amos, this is the word of God and His command given as a responsibility and authority to act as God. Why should this aspect of the scripture be missed aligned and disobeyed? This was a beginning command, and all believers must adhere to it. No matter how committed and sincere a person is about celibacy, it is only a choice completely volitional and not divine. God created the act and actions for pleasure and procreation; therefore any creature of His; perverting this act for proliferating humanity and God's command; that person or creature is in complete disobedience and committing the act of omission; and this is an affront to God. It seemed as if Bobby Ross was embarking on his personal journey to reverse the mandate of the Catholic Church.

Bobby told the young man about a former priest at the St. Francis in Liberia. He said the man was a good priest who understood the words of the Holy Scriptures, but had eyes for women. While he was a priest; he was a disciplinarian and brought up the young men on the campus with an iron hand. He travelled from one end of the country to the next. Consistently nuns and priests came from the city to visit the parish, at night there were laughter coming out of the parish house, the noises came from the nuns and priests eating and drinking at night. They were happy but at times discussed the opportunities of being real parents. One afternoon Father Power made one of his trips; while returning to the campus; he ran off the road; broke his collar and chest bones, been severely injured; he had to return to the States after years of service in the mission field. Father Power later disavowed and became a regular man of faith living in the United States.

He later sent for one of the African sister, married her and today they are parents of four sons and a daughter. So Amos you see; you can still be a man of faith and live the human part of you; this is your responsibility to humanity. We have to be fruitful and multiply. We are to continue the process of procreation. This is a human responsibility and we shall commit to this because generations before us were committed to this and this is why we are spontaneously here today! Why must this process halt because of a desire, which at times made out of frustrations, distrust and brainwashed. Everyone woman or man has a right to obligate himself to God and man. There are no special benefits or accolades in preventing children from having parents because of a religious permanent celibacy. Denying your sexuality and interpersonal relationships with others, thus preventing from the earth. the next lawyer, doctor, nurse, scientist, presidents or any great leader from the passage through your blood line is also a spiritual and supernatural genocide.

This is wrong and not promoting nor supporting the purpose of God's creation. I refuse to accept this for you Amos. Not if I can help it; son I am right now frustrated and flabbergasted. I shall mentor you and by the way; upon my return to the States you are coming along with me. Your grandmother out of support for you might have been seeking assistance for helping you. She thought becoming a priest was a means to this end and son; act the real you! I shall get your documents together and I am taking you along with me. On the other hand the former priest is happily married and enjoying the company of his wife and children. This is also intended for you Amos. This is God's will. By the way, I must tell you a little about God's possibilities in your life.

~God's Possibilities for you St. Matthew 14:22-33~

God wants us to be able to walk on impossible foundations and surfaces. Conditions may seem not possible and things may not appear as they should, but if Jesus is in our focus; we can talk like the Apostle Peter "Lord if it is you bid me to come". Trusting God is all what really matters, and in this some of the most impossible challenges can become doable only if and when we focus by keeping our eyes on the destiny ahead;

towards Christ Jesus! Everyone may not get the opportunity to walk on water as Peter did, but certainly everyone can take a chance with God and reaching forward upon the command of the Lord "come unto ME all ye that labor and are heavy laden; I will give you rest".

When Jesus bids us "come!" then we have to listen and move forward. No matter the challenges, we have to move in the name of the Lord in taking hold of our destiny. We cannot mind the waves and the intensity of its boisterous, tenacious movement; we have to take a hold on the fact that Jesus is in our view and He is the ankle for the souls. God's possibilities have carried many individuals to levels they didn't imagined. People down through the years have looked at the impossible things in their lives and have come out with greater achievements on the bases of God's enabling possibilities.

Peter had no means of connecting to a railing or climbing back into the boat; he had no inclination that he shall return to the boat, but rather he saw that; if Jesus was doing it; he could get out there and do the same. Jesus knew Peter's limitation and He very well anticipated doubts, which would set in because of fear. Folks it is your fear and mine doubts, which might prohibit walking on water as Jesus, did, but He is always there when we are falling; to lift us up from sinking water, sinking sand, and sinking life styles. God has greater possibilities for you, therefore affixed your eyes upon Him and out from impossibilities; He shall lift you up to possibilities. Therefore, walk by faith; do more faith walking and get the blessings Jesus' has in store for you.

~Looking at Possibilities- Walking by Faith~

Practicalities are the normal facets, which bring about various rationales as to why faith walking should be abandoned. It tells you that what you see is only what is possible. Therefore you must base your evaluation on the foreseeable tangible not on the abstract, because the abstract is unknown and cannot be evaluated **(Matthew 13:13-16)**.The down side to practicality is that it is short sighted; and cannot elevate the faith walking process. Walking by faith is to believe in that which is not possible to be possible. Walking by faith causes one to take the **Davidic steps** and approach to every project or process in life. Let us look at what were not possible that became possible as a result of the leap of faith:

~Faith has foresight (I Samuel 17:34-37) ~

Faith can see, and it is productive; faith can take a timid individual and makes him into a Giant killer. Just imagine in your lives when you always see those high hills and unreachable peaks, which you have to climb in other to become what you are, or will become what you want. Faith tells you that it is possible, while the practical you say wait a minute; this is just not possible, because you are not up to the task, but faith says yes you can, and so you pressed on. I have to press on; and I am pressing on! In total disregard to what the world may say; I am pressing on with my inner drive towards a greater perspective for achieving my life focused goals; which are living happily, with my wife and children. Pressing on, yes I am with foresight in achieving the impossible. Like King David; I am trusting on the Lord and I know that as I bring my desires full focused into His presence; I am obtaining my impossibilities. In my position I stand as the King to face my challenges without pretense; rather I am determined to gain the impossible; for with the true and the living God; resides justice and greater sensible realities. With Him, I can take greater chances; and I know that from the depth of my heart; He sees the sense to my realities. Trust me He knows that Melinda and I; are His realities. I am persuaded this much, I have no doubt as Thomas; who almost missed his blessings of being with the LORD ALMIGHTY.

~The Apostle Thomas Almost Missed his Place with Christ~

Thomas almost missed his place with God because of practicalities. He wanted proof for everything; he wanted insurance that the awkward (ill at ease, out of depth, uncomfortable and embarrassing) things were not hindrance to his position of satisfaction or reasons to go along. (John 20:24-26). As a result Jesus said to him "Do not be unbelieving but believing" in Verse 29 Jesus also said "Blessed are those who have not seen and yet believed". Thomas problem was sight. Amos! We have to have sights; we have to see the unseen as seeable.

We have to extend our focus extensively, thus reaching the ideals of the most High God! In other words we all have to connect deeply with the spiritual side of us or else the inner other would suggest to our faculties that we are not the possibilities of God. Amos Jehovah has embedded in us greater will and tenacities for reaching for those things which seem unreachable. We can go after them if we dared to, and justifiably position ourselves for receptions of the impossible which are made possible; by greater desires of us in full connection with the spiritual dimension within which we are a part of us, and we are placed.

People are committing suicides today on account of ignorance. I say ignorance in an extent of the Christian reality and presuppositions. Many people are totally oblivious to their spirituality. Once a person realizes this aspect of his make up; he would seek to purposely align his spirit with the Supernatural for invigorating his soul and body, so that the uncontrollable realities can become controlled. First thing is to understand the realities of the spirit domain. From this domain comes inner strength for establishing the physical realities of one's life;

Isaiah 26:9 "At night my soul longs for You, Indeed, my spirit within me seeks You diligently; For when the earth experiences Your judgments The inhabitants of the world learn righteousness.."

No one who connects with such spiritual side succumbs to negative realities in life. They are always able to repel the opposite and leverage the inner authority, which resides on the inside. This is while the Apostle Paul carefully said:

"For what man knoweth the things of a man, save the spirit of man which is in him? even so the things of God knoweth no man, but the Spirit of God"(I Corinthians 2:11).

Every man who intends to be control from the inside, and successfully deals with life issues; he must first know himself and the spirit dimension. Thomas the disciple; almost missed this when he spoke with Jesus. We are blessed whenever we do not see, but believe what is not seen.

Logic and other empirical systems of thoughts limit the individual's trust on his inner strengthen and spiritual realities. The absent of empiricisms actually produce an opportunity for soul searching, and thus promotes a lasting trust on his spiritual will. God wants us to deal with him blindly so that He holds our hands and lead us with foresight.

(I Cor.2:9) "Eye has not seen, nor ear heard, nor have entered into the heart of man the things which God has prepared for those who love Him".

Faith finds the things of God, which are in the abstract for us! If you behave naturally and practically, you shall not see the things of God for your lives. Faith walking is ignorant of what is seen "Walk by Faith and not by Sight" Sight means "appearance" Jesus Christ is not physically present, therefore we are to live by faith. The Bible also tells us that we have God's guarantee. Jesus said to Peter come; and those words were good enough for Peter. Amos in life we have to walk the walk and talk the talk therefore; you take the walk.

△ △ △

~Taking the Walk Amos calls for you to begin a process like the Apostle Peter; the reasons why are as follows: ~

Peter had great faith – develop faith in God without a doubt trust Him

He did not say bid us come; Bid me come- Walk alone, seek God and stand on your faith

He allowed his own faith in God to control his steps- Walk by your convictions and not others

He did not wait for James and Andrews and the rest- Motivate you; flow with God alone

His rationale was not a factor to his first steps- just walk and stand on the promises

Jesus word "Come" was good enough- follow the command of God and listen for Him

Fear was not a factor when he was focused- Never mind the waves of problems

Faith was the factor when he was focused – Walk the first step in Jesus' name Shalom

He did not wait for others to support him- move by what is in your heart only you know you

He was fueled by his curiosity- Taste and see that God is good. He is able to support your steps

When you never think you can complete something walk with God!

When you think all is lost;- walk with God

When your burdens get you down walk; with God take the leap of faith and walk.

When you let your mind get the best of you, you start to look at all kinds of waves which can do you no harm band instead; you make them a factor for fear. Godly Information liberates you, you know who to call when you are sinking! Listen to this son and I mean list to this very well: ~Not to stay focus on Jesus is to be expose you to the following~

• *More impossibility to situations*

• *To many unnecessary waves*

• *Timidity*

• *Out of principle*

• *Poor reasoning*

• *The reality is that what is seen cannot hold you and support you or balance you.*

~Therefore these Conclusions must be adhered to my son~

- *Waves will come into your lives, but it does not mean you shall go under*
- *Just walk by faith no matter what comes your way*
- *Wait on no one; not even if they stay within their zone of safety*
- *Call on God when you can no longer hold on*
- *Know that the devil will make you see things his way to distract you*
- *Don't mind the waves they cannot sink you when Christ is near you.*
- *Don't let go; keep your eyes on Jesus, he cares for you.*

Understand the value of love and loving someone as thou self. Love does not fail, love does not cease. The permanence of love is found within this phrase, "love never fails." In the Bible; Apostle Paul used a Greek verb for "fails". The Greek word is *ekpipto*, it really means, "to fall apart." It was used of a flower or leaf that falls to the ground, withers, and decays. In this it saying that love never "falls apart" It is meant in the sense that love never falls away and disappears; it never quits; it is never used up nor does it frustrates. Love will never collapse, love will never fail; positively love is everlastingly flowing. Love not supposed to hurt nor is it supposed to frustrate!

~Amos Spoke Back to Bobby Ross~

Amos then spoke to Brother Bobby Ross about his relationship with women. He told the Brother exactly as he felt. Speaking to Bobby in a subdued manner, he was curious to know why Brother Bobby has not been speaking with any single women. Why didn't Bobby have a lady in his life and why was Bobby pushing him as he did when he has never been seen with a woman before. Long story! Long story young man! I am glad first that you brought this up! Second and foremost, I am able to become a part of your life. Yes I was in love; my young man, but my woman decided to become a nun; depraving me of my God given desires.

She was or by the way; she is not was but is the best woman I would ever have wanted. I know we are to happen in the sight of God almighty. The young man spoke to Brother Bobby and said you are confusing me with this "she was or is not"; I am sorry to say confusing! Kindly be clear! Okay Amos; I love her; I respected and I craved and am craving her. She is Sister Melinda Yates. Moreover, she is my heart desire. Brother Bobby come on get real! She is already a nun! Brother Ross please get your act together Sir.

$$\triangle \ \triangle \ \triangle$$

A BROKEN VOW

~Brother Ross Talks~

I am here in Africa because she left for the convent. I know that she made a mistake and she knows that as well. I hate to say this but as Jacob worked for his wives; I have also labored for my prized and choice wife. I have kept myself all these years and it's time; I am going to find my bride. I told many stories in resemblance of my situation to keep the memory fresh in mind, and it worked well. By the way, I am predicting that you shall be in my wedding son and I am going to marry Melinda Yates. Her father knows it; her mother knows it, you would see it as well, and I am telling you son I have never been more direct in my life than right now.

You see I fixed things with the help of God almighty for many people around here. Jimmy is happy; Jacqueline is happy, Mr. and Mrs. Larry Moses are happy as well. I know that God is working behind the scene somewhere to grant me the desire of my heart. Amos astonishingly glanced at Bobby and pondered in his heart "WOW!" what sort of fellow is this? Bobby Ross said to Amos young man don't be surprise, on account of these expressions, but once a man lays his heart on real love; every fiber of his being is focused and determined as I am, and son come and let begin the process.

~Bobby and Mrs. Moses~

Bobby met Mrs. Moses and disclosed his desire for mentoring Amos not in Liberia instead in the United States; predicated upon her approval. Instantly Mrs. Moses responded praise God! I approved this is God's will. Bobby said just so you know this; he is not becoming a priest, God wants him to be faithful at loving him and fulfilling his will. While speaking to Mrs. Moses; Bobby's telephone rang and it was Melinda on the phone.

~Melinda on the Phone~

Hello Brother Bobby! Hello Bobby this is Sister Yates! Oh Sister Yates; how are you, and the church? Melinda responded wonderful. Melinda quickly said Bobby can you believe this? He responded, "What? She instantly spoke freely; with vigor and joy by saying, it is Starr and Fillmore! He quickly asked what about them, is there some kind of trouble?

79

She responded, "No Bobby no! I have never seen such a thing in all of my life Bobby! Melinda come Sister tell me; she said I have not seen the display of love as seen with Starr and your friend Fillmore!

He responded, "What? If this is the case; then all things are possible with God and that includes you breaking that vow. I thought that Starr and Fillmore would have never been not in this life!

Starr had a 360 turn. She is like an angel just out of heaven's door. I mean respectful, polite, loving and extremely courteous. Truly when love finds its path, like water, it flows and creates good pools and streams. My God! I was carried away by such display of honesty and genuine quality of individuals feeling securely belonging to each other. I spoke with Starr and questioned her actions; she said it was the working of love and its spiritual guidance through the voice of Molly.

Bobby I strangely felt jealous, and hoped it was I. Melinda you are only experiencing your true emotions of love, and to be love by me, Bobby Ross! What are you saying? You mean to tell me Sister Yates you are feeling jealous about Starr? Wow! Oh my God; I thought these things don't happen to someone as you! She replied Bobby I am not a dead piece of wood; I am alive and more so acquainted with human emotions as well. I made a decision by given myself to ministry and that was it, nevertheless; I am also a person first. Brother Bobby quickly interrupted her by saying Melinda I have to tell you.

I woke up this morning with you on my mind! Had so much in me knowing that you would be there once I am awoke. Imaginations upon imaginations flooded my heart! Questions after questions rained down as snow covering mountain ranges. At the sound of every beat of my heart I felt a better peace deeply within and the thoughts arose that this is real!

Oh how would I have missed the opportunity in finding such a precious ornament such as you; I was thinking that this might be unreal but across the floor at got a glimpse of your person and quickly and then I knew that it was only a figment of my imagination. I got an image of you in that scarlet dress at the theater and there you were in the flesh I imagined reaching for your hands, then I realized that I was hallucinating on account of overwhelming thoughts of you. I reached out for your hand and touched it; oh dear I was dreaming then the phone rang and I knew that you are special but my thoughts were getting the best of me! Melinda responded oh Bobby I think I am falling in love with you, but my faith! Bobby responded Melinda your faith is my faith.

You need to consult God all over again, because His intended purpose for you is that you become my wife because it is my honest prayers to Him daily and I am persuaded that He would answer my prayers; I have labored extremely hard for you and my hope and faith that you would be my wife; Sister Yates.

A BROKEN VOW

~Melinda Silence on the Phone~

Melinda went completely silent on the phone and it seemed like Bobby knew what he was talking about because Melinda was developing strangely; thoughts of actually renouncing the Sisterhood and becoming a wife, mother, Wonderful and committed Christian to God and humanity. She struggled with these thoughts as to what would happen to the Kingdom of Heaven if she would disavowed and become a normal Christian, enjoying all the best of relationships with God first and Bobby Ross. She knew that the decision would not kill nor destroy any one other than becoming a better mother with beautiful children and living with one of the most dedicated man in the world; a man who has sacrificed everything because of her.

In the main time Bobby was screaming at the height of his lungs; Melinda! Melinda hello! Melinda Hello! She softly spoke yes Bobby I am here. Bobby wanted to know why the silence and why it took her so long to return to the phone. Melinda in contemplating a response; could not tell a lie but rather hesitated a little and just when she was about to express her thoughts; Amos walked into Bobby's office choked up with tears.

~Death in the Family~

Amos' grandmother has just passed away. Amos thought about his current difficulties and struggles and the good deeds of his grandmother, which with Divine intervention brought him into contact with Brother Ross. Amos pondered hardship and problems after problems.

Bobby's Response to Amos Hardship trials struggles worship joy redemption

God is in the hardship of life see these scriptures read them

> Romans 6:1-6-7, psalm 30:1 Jeremiah 10:1-17, I Corinthians 4:1-9 Nehemiah 8:10 God is in the hardship.

After this convincing teaching, Amos decided to follow the dream of his grandmother to become a priest. He asked Brother John what was necessary for realizing his conviction. He felt compelled to take a vow of fellowship. Brother John encouraged Amos to become an Alter-boy as a start. Amos gladly accepted and commenced his weekly mass duties. He prepared the alter for weekly mass and father

Peter, an Irish priest, became his mentor. For three years, father Peter mentored Amos to the point that he believed within his heart that he would enter priesthood. After this tragic —death of a matriarch the grandmother- which was a blow to Amos, Eric and Obed, the three could not handle it. Eric and Obed asked not to return to campus; Amos returned but endured serious depression didn't know how to deal with death and dying - brother Bobby stepped in.

Chapter 11

~Brother Ross intervention Steps with death and dying~

The debating blow Amos; I couldn't have understood why? When all seemed to be getting along just fine; Bobby worked with him; informed him that this was a reality in life and it comes early and sometimes; it comes later, but the impact is always the same no matter at what time it comes. Amos continued with the weekly mass but was filled with blame and this almost caused him his faith. He complained about how the only person who ever give him a chance growing up was his grandmother. After all, everyone left him alone to fend for himself, but his grandmother believed in him and struggled with him. Death didn't seem appropriate at this time.

Brother Bobby spoke of this with greater understanding! One of the most difficult experience in life; is to take a young person through the reality of death! Death may seem evil, wicked, unkind and not understood, but it is without prejudices. It doesn't matter whether those left behind are strong or stronger. It only acts the assigned time. There is a time to grow and gear up for growth. Only one thing matters, and it is a problem with painting our peace in the sky.

Chemistry with God matters in relationship; within which we find ourselves when death comes. Brother Bobby said find a project that heals; Amos suggested helping others he called his project "no shirt! No shoes! No problem; loving and living life.

Most people don't realize how relevant they are to others until a shifting occurs within their personal lives.

Bobby Ross in Africa discovered living life; while making a difference in someone's life. He mentored and counseled most people; who couldn't find the solutions to their situations at all, but Bobby's impacts upon them; were impeccable. He utilized the skills of biblical counseling realizing that many individuals had many unresolved problems and encounters, and by this he recommended coaching along with people inner strengthen; for resolves. Bobby said Amos a conscience resolves lies within people's connections with the spiritual domain; he allowed himself to be approachable while the usefulness of empathy, integrity brought together with honor and respect for restoring the dignity, which the people desired! Amos stood astonished and motionless; Bobby retold his own experience with disappointment; yet he was not bitter but instead he channeled bitterness into strength with which; others received healing.

Bobby later told Amos that his life was just beginning and that the plan to take him over to the United States was still happening. Amos kept on with his project in helping to collect used clothing and shoes for those less fortunate than he was. He knew all about been without and he therefore participated in helping those in need as he once was. He prayed this prayer; my honest pray this is my honest. T

~The Prayer~

My heart to you I give. I surrendered all my will. In union unpretentious, Oh Lord this is my honest prayer. I pray to humble to your will; as I glory in your presence I bow before your throne filled with your goodness. I pray this my honest prayer. I seek your promises sure and new. I reached forward for your hands in humble adoration so that I may know you Lord in my heart. This is my honest prayer, to seek your will and to become renew every day, as you are always faithful to me in Jesus' name, Amen! Bobby heard Amos prayed and said Amen as well! Amos to Bobby; Sir you know God is a real friend; I mean A real Friend. Jesus you are a friend to me whenever I need you; you are there for me; I am never without love from you! I can call you in the morning even in loneliness and the loss of my grandmother; noon, night and day! I can always count on you; for you are a real friend. I can always count on you for you my friend; their friend; for you are a real friend; we can always count on you for you are a real friend; Jesus you are a real friend! Lord, I am asking that you hold my hands; I am asking that you take control of me! Lead me and direct my every way; I trust you with all my heart; for you are a friend who always there and cares; never complaining for you are my real; my one and only special friend I always count on you my real friend! Lord, I thank you for Brother Bobby.

~Bobby's Advice to Amos~

Bobby advised the younger man Amos the following: To die to self; is ridding you of independence to become totally dependent on God for everything in your life; cultivate a heart so that it sees reality for what it is relinquishing you of self-wisdom; rely upon God for directive for understanding your perspective with Godly presupposition. Forget the futile thinking, but subject your cognitive views in service to God; guarding your heart and mind. Amos functionally we are noetic (thinking related to effect of the fall). With all your heart fully depends on God; He is able to move you higher with your own children and a wife at your side.

Amos said, "What?"

Bobby said, "Yes children and wife don't fool yourselves in becoming frustrated people. God wants you to participate in the continuity of procreation and this is what you were called to be a man thus participating in the human process; filled with emotions, which God Himself created and said it was good. Today this still stand and it is still good for all the family of Jehovah God.

Things might seem impossible now but God shall see you through! It seems impossible now and they say you wouldn't make it! Say you went to court they put you down say there's no hope for you. You are not qualify and you are guilty of your past and now you feeling like you can't go through and no one to help; stand still my God shall see you through! Stand still my God shall see you through don't you give up; hold on. Don't let go my God shall see you through. In spite of the impossible situations which seem unbearable. You've got to hold on and wait! Wait on the Lord hold on to His promises He shall see you through. Stand still my God; He shall see you through. Say you have a problem that you don't understand; you don't know what is wrong; you turn left trouble; so many troubles on the right side. Stand there in the midst of your tears hold up your hands; my God shall see you through; He shall see you through. In broken circumstances of situations untold. He shall see you through! Young man your best is yet to come. My best is yet to come; I know I shall see Melinda.

~Bobby Ross call Melinda to Read a Poem he wrote for her~

Time and time again I live in solitude
Thinking what it would be to be satisfy with you
Had no thought or hope that there be a moment in
Time that you would come along
Alone I couldn't imagine the possibilities
But there you were and one look; it took my breath away

My days shall never be the same just for this moment!
And for this moment I am living
And for this moment I am living
Taking back my time; turning it over to you
Just in time for this moment
You favor me with your tenderness
Your loving care cover me; you did not compromised, but have chosen me to partner with you, And just for a moment as this I am turning back
Seeking your love from this moment; Melinda my wife to be soon; from this moment.

~Melinda Reacts to the Poem~

The Nun (Melinda Yates) was over taken with great flabbergast, and was appalled at the sounding of his voice. Romantically it rhymed in a sensual mood and she was carried back in time of their first encountered; she quickly refocused and stood a pretentious ground; responding not coheres; she reaffirmed her position with tears running down her face; she said Bobby I am a nun and I am devoted to my calling. Bobby would not relent, and he uncannily stated my Dearest I have no fear other than to fear God himself. Yes you took or made a vow but to whom did you commit to God or the Pope. I am a catholic myself and a very good one as such, but I disagree with your position. Your life belongs to God, you and I! I know this for a fact! I can tell also from the cadences in your voice that you also believe that I am right. Melinda or Sister Yates; I believe that like Jacob I have labored for my bride and God is responsible to grant me the desires of my heart. Sister you are the desire of my heart and without you there is no me. In am making preparations to return. I am going to speak with your parents; I know that this is awkward, but I have a conviction and it is supported by the word of God

> (Mark 11:24King James Version (KJV) 24 Therefore I say unto you, What things so ever ye desire, when ye pray, believe that ye receive them, and ye shall have them).

I believe the word of God is true and says what it means and means what it says. Melinda you are the good which I desired. You are my desire; God is who I worship and you are whom He has blessed me with. I love you Sister Melinda Yates. You are the earthly source of my completion. As Bobby spoke; there was an interrupting noise at the door; Bobby told Melinda that they would complete this discussion and that someone needed his attention. She hung up and promised to return the call later during the day. It was Amos at the door and he had a story to tell Brother Ross.

~Amos' Story~

Brother Ross you see I understand your position, and I mean I really do! I have been struggling with the question of feelings and convictions. I have discovered that feelings are not necessarily emotions, which drive focuses rather; they are impulses which misguide a person with great anxieties for confusions and other sorts of fantasies. I have seen folks with great illusive attitudes, but yes; illusive it was all what it was. I have seen folks who have been convinced of something, which is not obligatory. Sir you are so focused and determined to marry Sister Yates; how sure are you this is what God wants? How sure are you that Sister Yates is your soul mate as you have vehemently proclaimed?

Bobby I love you as a brother and really admire your work, but I am struggling with the idealistic focus of yours. You are entirely focused on getting married to a nun, a woman who has made a vow to Jehovah God; aren't you afraid; trying to persuade this woman to become your wife. Have not you thought you might be interfering with God's plan? Bobby intensely interrupted Amos. He said wait a minute young man! What is this all about? Why are you coming across as such? I know what I feel and I understand as per your opening that feelings are mere emotional impulses without permanent benefits!

Yes, I may come across as a man desperate to have a nun disavowed her commitment to the Sisterhood, however my young man I know and knowing is not mere feelings; it is a knowledge derived from the foundation of humanity. God made man, and God made a woman to walk with the man and that the two together can become one flesh. My son my philosophy is not with cunning words of man's wisdom but they are relegated within the annals of the Holy Scriptures. If God wanted a celibate individual on earth, He would have sat the example within the origin of humanity. God instead made a man and a woman and told them be fruitful and multiply; now how do you understand that? Not listening to the words of God by formulating a form of righteousness is actually an affront to God. Monks and others who have given themselves to celibacies are doing it on their own, and trust me avoiding contacts with another person of the opposite gender because of one's belief; is not the will of God! People call it sacrifices but it is not God's will. God's will is that we worship Him, praise Him, procreate and live in harmony with the God's creations.

I am not appalled at your assertions at all; this tells that you are focused and a good thinker. I appreciate your concerns and to be truthful; I needed someone to push me to the point so that I can ascertained my position and conviction.

Yes, young man Brother Amos; I met Sister Melinda Yates prior to her entering the convent and yes we experience these realities which confront us today. I know for fact that she is reconsidering her position as well. Son, everyone who loves God can love Him faithfully and by desire afflict themselves with the avoidance of certain humanly pleasures, but to deny one-self of what God has created as a continuance of His creative process for humanity; I honestly find this absurd, I mean it is totally incongruous to God's plan for the continuity humanity. There is nothing illogical about this and I mean it. It might seem ludicrous, outrageous or foolish on my part, but a conviction based on the tenets of the Holy Scriptures is valid and upon information and beliefs convincing to the heart of a real Christian man as myself. Amos these are my philosophies, and the word of God have fathomed me into this character of which I am; son I am persuade that neither height, distance, time and place would interfere with this knowledge.

~Amos Response~

Brother Ross; kindly pardon my assertions! I had to come across as I did, I needed to validate my thoughts so that in supporting you; I would share the same views as you do and Sir, to be honest with you I am to follow your footsteps; you are my mentor and role model. Thanks for taking up the time to explain yourself as you did; honestly I concord. Sir when I was a boy my grandmother called me to tag along with her to church; I totally ignored her request. I sat around, playing the fool, share some rum with friends, and proceeded to the second level of our home. I sat on the balcony of the house on the left wind. A friend brought over a pair of slippers as a gift since I was to return to the all boys' campus, a catholic school for young men and those who would later become priests. I was elated that I did not go with granny to church and I thought it was a time to act up since she wasn't around. Sir a strange thing happened. I bend my head over to try on the slippers, and with the rum in my body which I totally forgot; I lost my balance and from the second level of the building I hit the ground head first, beneath me were steel rocks, broken glass bottles, I mean everything which could have killed me.

When I hit the ground everything went black, I saw myself going further from everyone, I left my body for a while, could hear from a distance people saying he is dead, some insinuating that he would be paralyzed. No body falls head first and survive. I saw a great blackness and from that distance I faintly heard the voice of my sister screaming Amos! Amos wake up; oh my God wake up! All of a sudden I saw myself returning to my body and then I started to move my hands and when I finally gained consciousness; there was this great crowd standing over me. My sister later held my hand and took me up the stairs into the living room where she administered first aid as granny has taught her. I slept and then my grandmother returned from church, they told her what has happened, she laughed and said I was praying for him while in Church.

I didn't know why but something told me to pray for him. By the way Amos come here and go to the store for me. I thought this was real mean; granny saw my pains and yet she is sending me to the store. Later did I remember she was applying faith that what so ever you desired in God just believe and you shall have it. My grandmother was applying her faith. She wanted to see it in actions. I woke up; pulled myself together and this time around consented quickly to do what this woman of God requested.

Oh how do I missed; her dearly? Oh how she believed in me; when no one did! I am what I am today because of her faith in God. She was not moved by my conditions she trusted God for healing me. I went to the store in pains got what she needed, and came back. The neighbors could not believe that it was I walking the streets after such a fall. Upon my return from the store; grandma called me over to her, she sent for the holy oil, put her hands under my rib cage and said I think you have a fractured here, but please God complete this healing process in Jesus' name. She rubbed me down with the oil and told me to go to sleep for God has done it. She told me that God wants you to become a priest and I am presenting you to the Church. I accepted it, because who wouldn't after what God has completed on my body, God healed me I never went to any hospital, God healed me the fractured ribs were never touched by any medical doctor, other than the Doctor of all doctors; Jesus himself!

Therefore brother Ross this is my story and reasons to why I spoke as I did. Nevertheless, I would give myself to fasting and I would definitely welcome the opportunity to follow you. As a matter of fact, I had a dream the other night and in my dream spirit of the LORD told me to get up and read **Proverbs 25:25**, and this is what it says "As cold waters to a thirsty soul, so is good news from a far country" Brother Bobby I knew then that God has made a way for me to become someone special. Your love for Melinda is genuine and I am with you Sir. God wants us to have the perfect union in His name. He has provided all of these possibilities; idealistically for the development of humanity, and by this we grow in his favor or grace. The older Brother Ross, stood motionless, and with his eyes filled with tears staunchly steered at the young man Amos. He said Amos I am glad that I have gotten to know you and that you have become a partner with me in this work of God. We are from now on family; you got that. Yes Sir Amos replied.

~Bobby talks to Amos about Clerical Celibacy and the Catholic Church~

St. Peter who was an Apostle walked with Jesus; he was married and the Catholic Church also claims him their first Pope. Scripture shows that St. Peter wife followed him everywhere he traveled on his evangelistic journeys, and being a husband never stopped his faithfulness. He remain faithful and with full anointing authority; until his death.

In the early years of the church the clergy were married men, I Corinthians 9:5. The Apostle Paul taught that those who would guide the office of a Bishop, Pastor and Deacon must be the husband of one wife. This is the teaching and traditionally the scripture has emphasized this to be the way; and it is factual. It wasn't until the time of Pope Siricius that he declared celibacy the "Directa and Cum in unum" meaning the rule; and this became the mantra that clerical sexual abstinence was an apostolic rule which must be kept; since February AD 385. Pope Siricius succeeded Pope Damasus I; Prior to Pope Siricius the priest cohabited with their wives and children. It was stopped in February AD 385 because of the "Directa". Clerical Celibacy is only a spiritual discipline and not a rule from God. Man came into being over Six billion Years ago and far from AD 385. Prophets we marring and given into marriages thus proliferating procreation prior to the papacy. This Pope after his perusal with life and other glaring unholy realities constructed the "Directa". This was man's doing and it was not the work of God. God's command was to be "fruitful and multiply" we cannot ignore the words of God. By convictions and other measures; people are given into this practice. It is manmade and not scriptural. From AD 385 until now men and women who could aid in the procreative mandate of God, "Be fruitful and multiply" are denying themselves as a consequence to self-denial. Celibacy retains its original meaning for the unmarried to observe for continence abstinence until maturity for marriage. The married may observe, abstaining from sexual intercourse for a season of cleansing and commitment to fasting for a period of time (I Corinthians 7:3). This obligation to be celibate may seem significance; in that a person obligates himself to observe perfect continence for the sake of the Kingdom of heaven for a period; after such a time they may return to one another.

Others who support clerical celibacy may see it as "a special gift of God by which sacred ministers can more easily remain close to Christ with an undivided heart, and can dedicate themselves more freely to the service of God and their communities. Yes, this may hold some validity, but this is not a gift from God. It is a practice initiated by man; and it has been successful for some; who through constant conditioning; accept the life style. This was not meant to be and for this cause, many priests and some nun who love the faith are severely struggling with their sexualities. Many have also left the faith because of this stringent condition and submission to personal denial of an emotion, which Jehovah God created for pleasure and procreation. Today many priests continue to struggle and many nuns as well. The Church is been defamed because of this stringent thought out means of piety by Pope Siricius; a man who never saw Our Lord Jesus Christ as the Apostle Peter did. Many priests and nuns are forced to forge their truth passion for human development such as having children and becoming parents themselves.

Law suits upon law suits are the problem of the church today; on account of priestly improprieties. Clerical Marriage was ruled out by the Catholic, Eastern and Oriental Orthodox churches, and there was no exception to this rule. Consequently, no one could become a priest or nun while married. This is crazy but we can see the impacts, which this condition for ordination has on the church today. The law of clerical celibacy is considered to be not a doctrine of the Christian faith, but a discipline of a religious organization. I am an advocate for clerical marriages, and Amos the church would be even more grandeur if this manmade rule would dissipate and people are given the opportunity to love God, their faith and become productive parents. I believe Clerical celibacy should be a thing of choice and not a mandate for enforcing a perfect continence for the kingdom of heaven.

Priests and Nuns must be given the choice for clerical marriages and that of celibacy. Sister Melinda Yates love the catholic faith and would love to serve her faith as a nun, she might not of account of her recent expressions of love and concern for me. She also envied Starr and Fillmore's relationship and indicated to me that she which this was happening for her. Amos this is where I am coming from. I have prayed and I have declared the obvious for me and my family life and that includes you as well. My son Amos there is nothing in this world, psychological, social or religious for which God don't understand. He knows all about us and how we shall interact one with another. He has planted in us a way to seek Him. Therefore no matter what may come our way God shall see us through. He shall see you through It seems impossible now and they say you would not make it! Say you went to court they put you down say there's no hope for you are not qualify and you are guilty of your past and now you feeling like you can't go through and no one to help; stand still my God shall see you through! Stand still my God shall see you through; don't you give hold on don't let go my God shall see you through. Regardless of the impossibilities and situations which seem unbearable you've got to hold on and wait! Wait on the Lord hold in to His promises He shall see you through; stand still my God He shall see you through; say you have a problem that you don't understand; you don't know what is wrong; you turn left trouble so many troubles on the right side Stand there in the midst of your tears hold up your hands my God shall see you through. He shall see you through. In broken circumstances of situations untold; He shall see you through! Be strong my son joy is coming after this storm.

~Amos spoke back~

Once in my life there is no turning back going forward with Jesus; I v got a made up mind can't lose hope now I have come too far; got to go on; this is my time and God is in control with Jesus leading me on my way. Once in my life I am taking control I am going to let this little light of my shine. Brother Bobby I am taking back my joy; no turning back got a made mind with heaven in view I am taking this train ride in full control got no intention of losing hope. I have seen the light and out of darkness; I come with God in control I am moving forward with eyes on the prize; I am pressing forward. Oh once in my life I am moving on In Jesus' name. Brother Ross there is also something about God's truth which I have discovered from listening to you. You see God wants us to know, hear, acknowledge, and understand the tenets of His truth; hear and your soul shall live; acknowledge Him; He shall direct thy paths-Jesus is God's truth. "Ye shall know Jesus and he shall set you free" The Truth comes by the Holy Ghost (John 14:6) the way, the truth and the light are grace which came through Jesus Christ. Jesus mission was to reveal the truth for knowing and understanding of the mind of God. Having a living knowledge of the living truth brings a person into accepting God's timing for one's life. I am a witness; look I have lost my best friend my grandmother and on the other hand gained a father, brother and a friend; Brother Bobby I find these qualities within you. I also realized that a person can acquire God's truth by Scripture reading, learning the application of the scripture and the realities of our daily lives.

I also discovered that the word of God is settled in Heaven; consequently whatever we desire within God's will; becomes ours' so long as we believe them to be in Jesus's name and by the Holy Ghost (psalm 119:89, Matthew 11:24)- God's truth is comprehensive and absolute-(psalm 119:104) Psalm 119:105 light to path ways. Today my eyes make me to understand your precepts. Knowing Jesus brings to light the secrets of the kingdom of God (Matt.13:11) Let us look at psalm 119:142 "Your law is truth" now compare with (I Corinthians 2: 9-10) God's truth through the written word and the living word (John 1:14). Bobby was astonished and he related how amazed he was given Amos' perusal of the scriptures.

He said "Amos these are signs of great awareness, keep the faith"; but Amos there is only one thing which you must understand today and that is Marriage is a sign of union and it represents togetherness between a man and a woman. With marriage comes blessing and trials. However as with every relationship there are blisses and regrets, but once a marriage is based on godliness then the foundations are assured. Seemingly no two marriages are the same in terms of personality, and physical make up yet the values are the same once its' foundations are based on Christian values with Christ Jesus the focus.

△ △ △

~A Spiritual attempt at Stopping God's plan for your life~

Amos! Something just came to my mind, and it reminded me of the many trials in life. These trials are not without a purpose. The Bible alerted us to count it joyful when trials come, and the reasons are for creating a quality character within. The fall which you had in March of 1975; it was an attempt on your life. The devil knew at the time God had placed His hands upon your life, and for this cause he the devil intended that you never make it. He wanted to stop God's purpose for you. Satan tries to kill every birth in which God plants a seed. If you are call to service by God; Satan tries to stop that process. Revelation Chapter 12 speaks of the attack Satan leveled at the woman who was about to give birth to the CHILD; however the angel of the Lord stopped Satan's destructive and disruptive plans. Amos before any good plan of God can be birth within His children there would always be a plan by the devil to abort it, God had His hands upon you son. You see, once we travel to the States there would be opportunities for you to become a Minister of the gospel and married with children as well.

Remember this is prophetic, and this is what God wants for your life. The devil knows this; therefore he works in the spirit realm; he planned every attack meant to destroy you. It failed and that is why you can talk about it today. Amos God calls many people for worship and praise and there are others who are called to leadership for directing people who are in relationship with God almighty. Son you have been called for this purpose and Satan knows it, but God would not let you go. There are Churches in America seeking quality Ministers such as you. Trust me I am the channel for your trip to your blessings and position in time. I said in time because everything about every man, woman, boy or girl is positioned in time by God almighty **(Ecclesiastes 3:11).** Sadness and many sorrows would come your way, but they can no defeat the purpose of God on the inside of you. Many great men God has called to ministry have faced attempts on their lives by Satan and his cohorts. Some, Satan attacked with all sort of sickness, some with unfortunate deaths, but God made them resilient and faithful to the end.

God does not make a plan for you and renege on them. God is a not a man to promise and do not come through, it is not is His personality or His makeup to tell lies, what He promised; it shall come to fruition. I know this for a fact young man God is with you. The anointing of God is upon your life and His purpose for you is like a mountain of favor. God's special grace is increasing every day in your behalf. God has hedged in your life. Your walk to leadership and approval is in your view. Son, all you have to do is to keep the faith which has brought you save thus far. In my career I have seen many young men in ministry or trying to come into leadership but I have not seen one as you. It is apparent that you grandmother and others did do a wonderful work on you for the kingdom of God. You would see young man what God has in store for you.

Chapter 12

A s Bobby spoke; his cell phone rang; he picked up the phone and commenced speaking; hello! Oh excuse me Amos, we shall talk later! On the other side of the line was Mr. Yates; Melinda's father. Hello Brother Bobby! How are you today? I am fine Sir! Have you talked to Melinda lately? Yes Sir; I did about three weeks ago. Well son, I think you need to give her a call for there is a development around here and you have something to do with it. What development Sir? What development; is everything okay? Yes all is well, but kindly call Melinda! She has been trying to call you and has not gotten a response from you! I therefore took the time to find out for myself what is the matter? Nothing is wrong Sir! I thought she was busy with the convent and other matters around the church, but I intended calling her today. Bobby my boy just moved ahead and placed the call to Sister Melinda Yates! Call Melinda and talk to her about her emotional upset about you! What about me Mr. Yates? Bobby laughed and said what did I do?

~ Mr. Franklin Yates on the sentiment of Real Love~

Mr. Yates spoke and said; son love is something that no man can halt, it is a miracle from God and He God fashioned it in such a way that once it meets the level of mutuality; it is vastly unstoppable; call Melinda please! Thanks Sir I shall do that right away. In my understanding, this primary fruit of the spirit is what humanity and faith is based upon. The devil is busy attacking the sharing of love. He has created a distorted version of love. His version has to do with conditional exploitation. I said conditional exploitation because of the misguided sentiment, which people use in taking advantages of the lazy and the have-nots. Ungodly men with little resources utilize those resources for taking advantage of those who are without and are barely making it. On account that you perform for assistances you get these benefits; this is exploitative and not love. People are cruel, mean and unthankful.

"The heart is deceitful above all things, and desperately wicked: who can know it? (Jeremiah 17:9) "

Bobby God has positioned you in time and space to be a good man and out of a good man's heart comes love for his fellow man. The Kingdom of God is within the heart of every believer and love is the key to the treasury of the soul. My son the love for God and the love for man is magnified; when it is share with others. It is your responsibility to call Melinda if you want to a troubled soul overtaken by loneliness! Thank you my son; we shall talk later.

~Bobby Calls Melinda~

Hello Melinda! Hello Bobby or rather Brother Bobby Ross! Melinda I sensed some cadences in your voice; what is the matter? What is the matter? For three whole weeks, you did not take my calls and I tell you what; I was upset and worried Mister! After all you are in Africa, a single man and very handsome. Sister Yates you know that you are not supposed to speak in such a tone right? I know but Africa has so many beautiful young women attracted to a man of your caliber. Melinda did you say worried? Are you still trouble or jealous? Oh, by the way Sister I am sorry that you have to demonstrate so much concern for a friend. I understand you care for me, but my feelings are deeper than just a concern for another person. Sister Melinda Yates I have to tell you that I have strong desires for you and they are not delusional either, rather they are real and purposeful.

I have asked God to make you my wife and I am sure that you shall be. What is your view to my desires since you are so worried? Well Bobby! I am in prayers myself and I know that this is difficult, but the more we talk, and the more I don't see you the more my heart tightened within. I have asked God to make this possible if this is His will, and gradually I am coming around to this point of my life. It is a very difficult task to undo; how this is going to take place; I just don't know. I am encouraging to continue to pray for this and if this is God's real purpose in my life; then by all means I submit to His divine and perfect will for my life. I am not against God's purpose in my life Bobby. If I am to be what He wants me to be I shall by all means submit to His call as I did in becoming a Nun; and if it is His will that I become a wife and a loving mother then, I am praying for the success of His purpose. The Lord prayer states that we shall pray so that the will of the Lord is done in heaven; even as it is on earth. Bobby I am in agreement. However let Him cause this to happen. I must admit I love you but I have committed and I am waiting to see how God would resolve this matter and make me your wife. Melinda I do respect the sentiment of your faith; I also share the same and am also committed to the same I am seeking also His perfect will and I know that it shall come to pass in Jesus precious name. His words declared:

(Psalm 84:11 "For the LORD God is a sun and shield; The LORD gives grace and glory; No good thing does He withhold from those who walk uprightly"). I am therefore trusting on Him because you are; Melinda Yates the good in my life. I have sacrificed everything to His perfect will so that you are mine, and I have the faith that even as we speak; He is working in my behalf. I thank Him and I magnify His most Holy name and like Gideon declared in Judges Chapter 6; Jehovah Shalom! Yes, God is my Peace in this matter and He shall permit this good situation in our lives to come through in His name. Okay Bobby I heard you and I shall start the process in prayers. I shall also check on Starr and Molly to see how things are turning up on that side; Bobby love between two people can be so wonderful when it is God's approved! I envy these folks and am learning from them. I am going out with Starr, Filmore and Molly tonight; I shall let you know how things turned out. Melinda that is wonderful; I am so happy to hear that. You see over in Africa there is a song, which is sang "Jesus is working for me! I shall not worry about such complexities! I know God is working something for me and you, for God's words declared that (II Chronicles 16:9 "For the eyes of the LORD move to and fro throughout the earth that He may strongly support those whose heart is completely Him"). I am so certain that God loves us; those who trust His will and He divinely set them up to gracefully please Him in all their ways. Melinda hold on to your faith and I am holding unto mine don't be pressured; God is in control of our situation.

Man creates circumstances in our lives but God has His own timing and purpose for the life of everyone. When the "Letter of Pope Siricius to Bishop Himerius of Tarragona, 385. Ed. Pierre Coustant" came about no one knew his mind set nor his mental state at the time, but his instructions for the abolition of matrimony for priests and nuns were in my view not ordered by God and therefore not essential for a perfect life style for Christian commitment to faith and divine purpose. This I have already discussed with Amos and I am reiterating it just for your reference; just think about it and pray for God's perfect will. I have begun some research on the subject and once I am through with it; I shall inform you. I am researching prior popes, children and prior popes who were actual children of other popes. I know that the Eastern Catholic priest and bishops are some married and active. I am wondering why these folks placed many burdens on the Clerical leaders. It wasn't always this way. I am seeking answers to these questions for my benefits and support of my decision. While Bobby spoke, he was interrupted by the visit of some of the other clients.

~Clients visit Bobby Ross~

Mrs. Moses walked into Bobby's office and sat down, a few minutes later Amos walked in; saw his Sister sitting and asked to be excused. His sister later called him back in as he turned to leave. She asked Bobby if it was okay that Amos sat in the meeting. He replied okay it is just fine with me if you don't mind Mrs. Moses. It is fine with me Brother Bobby. As the matter for fact I came to discuss Amos with you and I am hoping that you have the time. She later said Bobby you asked my permission to mentor Amos and have agreed to the request. I am however here on a request as well. To the point I am requesting kindly that you sent Amos ahead of you to the States so that he completes his education. I know that the both of you have discussed and argued about the priesthood, and that is strictly up to him. I am in agreement with you as to Amos becoming an educated man and a child of God, most of all a father to some child, children and a husband to a beautiful and blessed woman. He possessed such quality and good character to fit those roles in life. I don't think anyone should be denied that. Amos bowed his head towards the floor as if to say why now; this discussion has already been put to rest, but if this is how it is going to be then; I am yielding to my sister. In the main time Amos commenced a poignant ponderous moment in thought as to the teachable moments of God. He asked the question!

What is God trying to teach me now? He continued with these words!

Have you walk into a room or a meeting feeling isolated? Feeling all alone and that everyone is sensitive to you? And you try to understand what's wrong; when you have done nothing wrong to anyone? And you have also seen that the many infractions of the day are overwhelmingly frustrating, and you've tried to understand what's wrong? Oh well just be patient; ask yourself in a sincere manner "What is God trying to teach me now?" At times, we are just too busy running about totally inundated with other issues; I mean totally besieged by conditions with family, friends, children, and most of all folks on the job. Seemingly, there is no ending to the saga of the day. God at these points in time is patiently awaiting a call from us, and because we are swamped with circumstances, we placed Him on the back burners. We isolate from Him and yet He reaches out to us with these words "The Lord hath appeared of old unto me, saying, "Yea, I have loved thee with an everlasting love; therefore with loving kindness have I drawn thee (Jeremiah 31:3). When God is drawing you closer to Him; He permits circumstances to come about in your life so that you take time off, I mean a total solitude and solitary moments in which you come closer and closer to Him. In this you have to become unsocial and self-contained. I guess you would say why? It is because in silence and complete quietness God teaches greater lessons. You may be misunderstood as friendless, but it worth the time for projecting, refocusing and careful foresights.

This action means that you have entered the classroom of God! Consequently; when you see and hear the noises in your time of trial; listen out for the silence moment don't fright because of the estrangements; the Master Teacher is before you. The Prophet Elijah experienced this moment; (1 Kings 19:12) "And after the earthquake a fire; but the LORD was not in the fire: and after the fire a still small voice". There would be ramblings, inner conflicts, and external conflicts. They would appear with greater misunderstandings. At times, you would get abused and used by others who need you as a bridge for getting closer to others. They rendered you a culprit of bad luck. You also get labeled as the evil one, the jealous one, but no matter what, you must not feel alone! You have to listen for the silence moment when God would reveal to you directives for your victory. (Zechariah 4:6) So he said to me, "This is the word of the LORD to Zerubbabel: 'Not by might nor by power, but by my Spirit,' says the LORD Almighty". Amos continued in agreement with Bobby and his sister to travel abroad for studies. Amos called himself the little light and explained the meaning behind his name to Brother Bobby Ross and Mrs. Moses Amos' sister. Bobby discovered that Amos and Mrs. Moses were related.

This Little Light which I am

Sometimes people would say there is something about you, I just cannot put my hands on it, but there is something about you! You are left speechless, in a way, you become flattered, but then you realize that it is because of the love of God; which has transformed you into that special light with greater brilliance. God has made us lights; he has made us torch bearers, which illuminate the surroundings within which we find ourselves. We have a responsibility to others who are away from the light and in darkness, sadness and lonely places; it is our responsibilities to channel hope of brilliance into their dismal conditions. Jesus said "You are the light of the world. A city set on a hill cannot be hidden. Nor do people light a lamp and put it under a basket, but on a stand, and it gives light to all in the house. In the same way, let your light shine before others, so that they may see your good works and give glory to your Father who is heaven (Matthew 5:14-16)". We have to be the little lights bringing hope to those who are lost, bringing directions to those without. Whenever situation arises in which your light may seem dimmed; quickly reach out to God for refueling; remember we have to feast on the word of God so that the spiritual you is functional in proportion with the natural persona. We are to show forth the praises of God almighty freely and without fluidity.

The next time you walk into a room, a church or a social hall no matter where; you have to walk in with dexterity, great strength and be focus with a commanding presence; that you are different and unique by the quality which Jesus has made you into "The Little Light which you are". Whenever you are looked upon; permit them to see the glowing you; the you which express a quality of the Savior's Love; wear it on your face that you are a light whose presence embodied something further from the reach of man; yet approachable and comforting.

"This Little Light Which I am" is only possible because of the precious blood of Jesus Christ. "For all have sinned and fall short of the glory of God", being justified freely by His grace through the redemption that is in Christ Jesus, whom God set forth as a propitiation by His blood, through faith, to demonstrate His righteousness. Because in His forbearance, God had passed over the sins that were previously committed (Romans 3:23-25)." In essence, it is benefiting to know that the Love of God always restraint His absolute doom actions and usher His long suffering, tender mercies and loving kindness to keep us in His presence, so that we are constantly illuminated to be that little light so bright. So if you are thinking that you may be less significant than you are; just think again: you are that Light sitting on the hill whose presence radiates on account of the forbearance of God; He doesn't see your past negative activities and transgressions; previously committed. Once you call on His name; He accepts you and transforms you into His righteousness because of the acceptable price; paid by his son Jesus Christ.

For me today no matter what people say about me; I see me as God sees me "This Little Light which I am". For the Bible says: "But God commendeth his love toward us, in that, while we were yet sinners, Christ died for us (Romans 5:8)." I am therefore somebody because I did the following: "That if thou shalt confess with thy mouth the Lord Jesus, and shalt believe in thine heart that God hath raised him from the dead, thou shalt be saved (Romans 10:9). Bobby Ross was astonished at the brilliance of Amos and said to him; young man I am fully persuaded that you are called by God to be a witness of His promises to humankind. I shall become the mentor, which God shall utilize in bringing out the best in you. Wow, I am greatly impressed. Wait until Melinda hears this about you she would be swept off her feet. Wow, I am greatly impressed. Truly, God does use the stones, which are rejected by the builders.

Chapter 13

Starr and Fillmore in the United States

One afternoon Starr sat motionless and poignantly in awe; thinking to herself how wonderful it is to know that someone genuinely is attracted to her; cares about her without prejudice about her antics and other behavioral blockades. She knew that Fillmore was an attractive lawyer; an outstanding gentlemen. She knew that Molly words of encouragements were forceful and imbued with life directives for a careful selective husband, but what bothers her that most was how come at this juncture ; she had to do the opposite of her plan. Things were automatic and gracefully felled into place as if to say her words were nothing and that fate had her born and readied for life with Fillmore. She was deeply in love; she could not go a moment without think about Franklyn Fillmore as God sent just for her benefits on this universe. She called Melinda to tell about her greater expressions of her inner combustible exuberance, and soon the women were engulfed with the flow of peace and love from their hearts. Starr told Melinda that she Starr would have never thought about caring for a man and understanding the reasons why God created mankind if Molly had not been forceful about the dignity and quality life style which she Molly now enjoys. Starr said "Melinda I just opened up my heart and all of a sudden I had a rush; I was at peace with myself as if a heavy load was lifted off my shoulders.

I permitted a peaceful moment into my life while sitting in my apartment all alone and thought about the fulfillment of my purpose on earth. As a professional woman and a mother to be. Melinda once I did, I felt like it was my call in this life to love and be love by my children, my husband, friends and family. You know Melinda I have since taken back my vows, and I have given my heart to Franklyn. Cousin I am in love and wow; I never thought how different life is once you find the proper fit. I know this is alarming but we have to be sensible and permit Godly chances into our lives. Melinda halted for a moment and said Starr what did you just say? Starr replied Melinda I have said many things; which one actually alerted you and that you have become awakened all of a sudden. Starr you spoke about God's chances into our lives? I was moved by that expression!

Normally Starr would not have spoken about God! Molly had a greater impact on Starr she was able to tell Starr about Jesus Christ, and got Starr started attending Church and finally accepted the Lord Jesus Christ as her personal Savior. Franklyn Fillmore also accepted the Lord Jesus Christ as his personal Savior and they were both attending a Full gospel Christian Church. Melinda was moved by this development and she thanked God for His benefits. She later pondered her personal situational dilemma. She envied the new Starr and envisioned herself in similar position. She wondered what if she broke her vow; leave the sisterhood and just become a devoted Christian would she go to hell? Would she be held responsible to God because she broke a rule. After all, she had undergone in becoming a nun. She questioned herself to the point of hysterias. She knew that this wasn't a distraction and that it had many real roots in the nature of a mankind to love and be love by someone other than oneself.

First, it is a good to be love by God. Secondly, it is a good to share God's love with others so that justice, mercy and acceptance are equitable within the heart of man. She knew that it was the duty of man to fulfill the command to replenish the earth and that every living creature under God's heaven; male as well as female had a part in this great command. She realized that her decision in denying true intimacy with Bobby was not a fulfillment of her God giving duty. Melinda sadly hung up the phone with Starr. She walked towards the convent sat on the bench and whispered softly to God "lead please me; guide me along this path; I need you to help me now"!

Your Choice is not necessarily divine but permissible

You see, too often we run our lives on euphoria; instead of a true Christian call to ministry. We confused a momentary epiphany with that of a spiritual lead for a call to do something outstanding in the guise of commitment of faith. People offer themselves as sacrifices, which are not acceptable to God; because the decision feels good, seems acceptable by a decided norm, they hastily rush into vows without considering the real choice, which God has for their lives. This I find quite alarming; when individuals give up godly directives for man rules and regulations.

A true call of God would have no second guesses; it would have no alternatives to His purpose. God knows what he wants and calls us to what He expects. If you feel strongly about a call to do something or become what you think is your divine directives, then look again and question yourself if your feelings or decisions would cause you to look back and wonder what if? If your focus becomes diffused by something, which you might want to give up; then it is not the call of God for you. Instead, it is necessary to always seek God for the real answers to the things, which we feel strongly about. Feelings are mere emotions and not a conviction.

Convictions

Convictions do not come along with second thoughts; they are properly defined and control by God. If what you feel seemingly is God's call for your life, then walk towards that purpose; just be sure that it does not conflicts with God's thoughts and purpose in your life. Trust me God shall lead you always into that direction, and not without temptations from the external to pervade God's purpose for your life. A child needs a mother, a mother needs a child, a father needs his family and they all need a union within the will of God. Jehovah God intended man to love and share love one with the other so that the family here represents the family of heaven. The nature of man comes from God the Father, and He has placed within us His quality; therefore with this quality resident in us; God expects us to continue this example by perpetuating love, respect with procreative prospects. Walking in God's will; is doing exactly what He expects; as per His word.

Godly Emotions come from God Himself

Melinda was struggling with her real emotions. She struggled and confused emotions with convictions. Emotionally she became religiously convinced that it was God's will for her to deny her sexuality for the choice of celibacy. She envisioned herself as been more committed and completely set aside. Within in her belief she successfully fathomed the idea of one's dedication to faith they had to give something up, and given the idea that she wanted to become a dedicated Christian; she decided to give up her God given emotions for adherence to the catholic belief of celibacy. As the scripture implied, "Be ye fruitful and multiply" is a direct sanctioned of the deepest human emotion of real love and procreation. This is a command of God "be ye fruitful and multiply" anyone who disallow this aspect of God's command is also in disobedience to the word of God. No man must on his own account, prohibit another person from falling in love and becoming parents of the children God promised to be given. God created man and so did He; in his OWN Image and Likeness created He man. God instructed man to build up and multiply and this command or instruction from God cannot be ignored. Many people would love to become priests, and nuns in the catholic denomination today, but the prohibitive requirement of engaging in love and marriage has driven away devote individuals. People cannot suppress this created emotion; it was created and sanctioned by God to be good. It is a human factor which cannot be turn on and off. The Apostle Paul was forceful on this subject once it came to celibacy, love and marriage.

He clearly stated that married people cannot deprive one another of their expected benevolence, and that celibacy can be practice for a moment only account for fasting and after such period they must united as soon as possible to avoid temptations (I Corinthians 7:3-4). Throughout the scriptures; it is evidence that 99% of all the prophets had wives, almost all of the Apostles who walked with Jesus; they too had wives. The Prophet Moses; he had a wife, Father Abraham, he had a wife. Before this century Priests, Nuns and Pope married and had children; why is it so wrong today for the aspiring persons as Nuns and Priests to be married. The question here is why disobeyed the commandment of God; why silence a God created emotion, cannot you see the danger it has caused?

There are many lawsuits against the Catholic Church, because of self-denial, and sacrificial commitment to ones' faith. This leaves many of the nuns and priest burning with passion, and not been totally committed at keeping to the vow which they have vowed; they walked in total secrecy and stealthily engaged their passions. Some priests and nuns have been misguided in controlling the intensity of their passions that they burn deep within the attention of another person and when this is not fulfilled; some of them turn on the people; they are called to shepherd.

This same saga is played in other Christian Organization as well. Folks denying the will of God and been misguided they assumed they are doing God's will. Denying fatherhood and not becoming a mother of children; is not the will of God. God's will in this aspect of our humanity is to become parents, husbands and wives to develop our community and extensively participate in the security of humanity , with love, respect and dignity. God intended man to demonstrate love, honor and respect one for another in great communities upholding His mandates in the process of development and spontaneity as seen within the Garden of Eden prior to the fall.

This blissfulness is God's desire for humanity, and in this we can show forth His greater praises. No one can keep God's intended purpose down; no man's rule can stop the process and the progressiveness of God's will for mankind; through selfishness others would attempt to distract the order of nature, but they cannot stop the power of the soul and its connection with the things of God. Bobby Ross realize this greater aspect of faith and hope; he knew that once God is in a plan no matter what the world may say or do; God would bring forth that which He has promised.

Whatever a desire is; if it is praise worthy, hope building with in the construct of faith; the unseen realm becomes subjected to reality. Bobby gave his life to Christ and completed the social requirement as seen within the 58 Chapter of the book Isaiah. This chapter calls for fasting and making sacrifices for developing the less fortunate. In this chapter God promised a blessing of protection and deliverance; once an individual socially promote the wellbeing of the poor. Bobby understood this and he therefore went into Africa to bless many families who were socially deprived. He knew that God would turn things around, but he had to wait on God's time.

The Eden Experience

Anyone seeking a favor from God; would have to follow many Scriptural based principles, and once these are adhered to; the presence of God is invoked and He thus seeks to award the requested favor. Commitment to something worth the while in God's will, and it brings God to attention. Look at Molly in the story, she was hurt, abused, and despondent; yet she was not discourage nor faithless. She took her time explaining to Starr the significance of forgivingness and the joy, which comes with it. Starr was educated but was spiritually dead. She was overcome by her eloquence and financial status, and yet she was empty and lonely. Molly shared the importance of spirituality and loving another person, Starr decided to give it chance and she later found out that it was great being in relationship with God, which counts the most. The human experience is very important; knowing the importance of needing another person to share one's experience and lifetime with is an ultimate need for security, belonging to and actualization.

Once these factors of the human experience are satisfied; then there can come the bliss of Eden. The Eden experience is paramount within everyone's life. Everyone has to search for it, seek it, and make all necessary preparation to protect it, enjoy, and nurtured it. This is the God given emotion, which a man must feel for his wife and the wife for the husband, it is call pure, and protected love of God shared within His creatures. There is nothing more appealing to man when he falls in love, and in the process realizes that God is invited into the matter for blessings and protection. Unconditional love invokes the presence of God; it breaks down the suspicions of the ordinary and catapults a heartfelt yearns of truthfulness and greater desires, which are reciprocated.

The scope of the Eden experience is within the scope of Adam's experience and his acceptance of his wife after the fall. Forgivingness is key to this experience; people wanting to be happy; learn to accept others for who they are, and by seeing them as God would regard your person. The Eden experience is what bubbles in the heart of a man, a woman when he fines true love. IF and when love hits you unconditionally; you would know! It comes with a flavor of favor unpretending but rather deeply rooted in the heart which says "I shall never leave you; I shall be at your side; no matter where you are from; I am yours'" that is real love, unconditional love. The Eden experience would cause a person to cover up for the one he/she is in love with. It would make you want to develop everyone and everything around you. It is a special kind of love that would not let a person down; it always makes the experience worth the while.

Chapter 14

Melinda Heartfelt conditions

M elinda started to feel like a woman of God aligned with her emotions created by nature. She felt deeper inner peace every time a thought of Bobby Ross came across her thoughts; she wanted to be embrace as a woman and loved by the special man who understood her so well; bobby Ross! However, she had to struggled with the thought that she was still a dedicated nun.

Wow what a dilemma; which she faced with inner desire for a man; she found herself in a dilemma. She had a heart of gold and seeing children; she yarned for some of her own, but she insisted in another lifetime. One day during her morning's meditation; her telephone rang, and it was Starr. Hello Melinda! Hello Starr! How are you doing today Melinda; I am just great and doing well with my work. Melinda said Starr; have you heard from Bobby Ross; yes of course she responded! How is he doing Starr said; I don't know because he was in one of his counseling sessions and I told him that I would call back, but I did not. Melinda that is just not cool; Starr insisted. I understand Starr but he was busy and I had to deal with my heart situations. What heart situation Sister Melinda; Starr said. My heart situations are the inner struggles I am encountering; that Bobby Ross has caused a problem for me.

Honestly, I am confused and am falling in love and I mean deeply in love; Starr I am starting to feel as a regular woman. Starr replied, "Oh I know what you are talking about Sister Melinda; believe you me I know all that so well. You see Melinda when love for another person hits your heart you really do have a heart situation. I vowed once and you can remember; not to give my body to man, but I found Jesus Christ, I found true love and I got the cure; Jesus took away my toughness and gave me a heart of flesh where I could greatly love myself and love Franklin Fillmore. You see Melinda that is the condition, which I have come to understand and trust me; Sister when it is real and control by God Almighty; you, can accept the situation. I am sorry Sister Melinda, but like what Molly said and I say the same to you give yourself a chance and follow your real heart not what man said you should become in religion.

I have got a great deal of problem with religion and religion is not faith. Faith is belief in God and the principles of His son Jesus Christ. Religion is what man put together and formed denominations for controlling other people. You can have faith Sister, know God and be control by the Holy Scriptures of God and not some denomination. Melinda you can definitely become a beautiful wife and an outstanding mother! You must follow what really your convictions are. There are no reasons to go through life pretending to be something that you are not. You cannot accept what others decide for you; you have to desire what makes you who you are, and trust me; you with your dedication can become an outstanding Christian, married and doing and fulfilling God's will as a beautiful woman of God and at the same time have your beautiful children. As Starr hung up the phone, Melinda sat motionless.

Melinda sat motionless

Melinda was amazed at the change of heart, which Starr presented and it had her speechless, she could not handle the facts and it kept her motionless for a while. She could not believe that it was Starr; the convicted Starr instructing her about realities. She had a mouth full and she had an awe moment. What was that all about just now; Melinda asked? What was that? Was it a message from above? Was it a message to my heart? I know what it is; it is a confirmation for me to make that big move, but how? In the main time, she reverted to her chores around the convent. As she got up to continue her walk, Molly called hello Melinda! Hello Molly! How are you today? How is your son and how is life over there? Life is great and I am doing just wonderful at Church. Molly did you see Starr today? Have you talked to her today?. No Melinda; I have not seen Starr and more so she has fallen deeply in love with Franklyn Fillmore. Melinda the woman is a different woman; she found Christ and has since been saved. Starr is a devoted born again Christian; Molly said.

Well Molly no matter what she is or who she is; she has really had me on my heels; my God she is really converted and convicted by her faith. She spoke soundly to me about my desires and my choice and also encouraged me to leave the nunnery. Mine oh mine she was forceful and committed to her quest to diffused my belief. Molly please for God sake how can I renounce my vowed? Melinda the real answers to that question is within you; I think you understand the situation, which is going on here, and it is about obedience to your heart. What is your heart actually telling you? Is it saying falling in love with a Christian man a bad thing to do? Is in violation of any moral law? Now tell me Melinda why live a life which has not been given to you by God? Why refuse the call of God to become a wife, another Christian woman who would love her family; nurture them in the admonition and control of the Spirit of our Lord God Almighty. Melinda; there are children within realm of the Spirit; who are waiting on you accepting the call of motherhood to be birth. You have been chosen to be fruitful and multiply.

Your life in the convent is not what has been planned for your end. My assertion to this point does not; in anyway allures your position, in my opinion you are the perfect woman for Bobby and the both of you did not crossed paths by mistake. It happened because God the creator of all mankind desires that for you. Bobby has been praying to God asking for a long time for a wife and he believed that god would one day sent her his way; and guess what it was you and, unfortunately for him; you had a decision made on account of your past experience. You know all men are not animals and all men are not monstrous creatures. There are men out there who have given their hearts to Jesus Christ and they sometime get stuck with the wrong women who do not know how to appreciate them nor be thankful to God for creating such wonderful men. Some women are actually abusive to these guys who respect their mothers and sisters, and do the same them for these unappreciated woman. At the end of the day these mean seek alternatives to their maladies. Melinda; Bobby being a professional marriage therapist understands the situation and he lives to help others find their way back to God through successful marriage counseling. He has refused to become a victim of his own experience. He believes that any man or woman must understand the severity of marriage and that despite of all the turmoil; life can be lived with gratitude and with grater appreciations. He knows that you are the answer to his prayers, but I am sorry that he has to succumb to the convictions of his heart that now and sacrificially; he is living in Western Africa helping families with this aspect of his life which he hearted desires.

The flipped side to his saga; is that the woman he loves so dearly is a Catholic Nun. I really don't understand this complexity, nevertheless with god all thing are possible. Saying this I kind of question myself would Almighty God answer the prayers of Bobby? Would He cause Melinda to give up the nunnery; would this be fair; Melinda thinking about this stuff I am becoming even more confused. It is like the funeral Director praying for a better business; while on the other hand people are praying to get well and not die. Would this relegate itself to a level of selfishness or are they not selfless in just giving up and let the course of nature takes it course. I know somewhere in the will of God Almighty there is the scale of justice which lends itself righteously to the mind of God. I know that in this event, there are significant adorations toward the things of God and I know that whatever our desires are; God grants the good the opportunity for stepping out from the light. Melinda some of our actions and choices are not necessarily God's choice for us, no matter how good they may seem. God's will for us come to past.

Bobby's Message

I was at a meeting one day and Bobby was speaking; I said to myself this God is send by God. Just listen to what he spoke: God is bringing Judgment into Victory Hear and your soul shall live, hear only the words of God and Know the truth; God's truth and they shall set you free. Jesus came not to condemn you; but to save you, deliver you garnish you, into a sweet flavor person who is able o let his light shine; so that God is glorified. Have an excellent spirit so that the Holy Ghost can use you, Pray; Because you can see, hear and understand spiritual things you shall be Converted; you shall be protected from the strongman no matter how well he multiplies. Your soul shall live it shall be covered! Therefore take back your control, deny access to the enemy. Keep Jesus in your heart, He shall sup with you. Today I pray that you hear the call of God on your life, I pray that you answer the call of God don't hold nothing back; God understands where you are! Peace and blessings in Jesus' name. Below are the Scripture references. I was shocked to see such well spoken word. Matt 13:16, Matt 5:16, James 4:7, Rev 3:20, Isa 55:3, Matt 12:44, St. John 8:32, John 3:17Just listen to this Melinda he later spoke about many things over time and I recorded them; I am hoping that these words would speak to you hear about the nature of the kind of man who awaits you upon your return. Here are some of the topics, which I have heard him speak.

My true brother is my friend!

Bobby Ross; in one of his many messages to his client spoke on brotherhood and what the scripture, in this he noted that the best brothers and sisters most of us have had; have been the friends which continue to be near and closer to hear us when we call! Jesus calls us His friends and it meant so much to Him, because He laid down His life for us;

His friends. I am a friend of God, and I have many anointed and saved friends are you one of them? (John 15:13-15) The counsel of a friend in Christ is sweet to his friend in Jesus Name Amen! Solomon said, "9 Oil and perfume make the heart glad, so a man's counsel is sweet to his friend. 10Do not forsake your own friend or your father's friend, and do not go to your brother's house in the day of your calamity; Better is a neighbor who is near than a brother far away. 11Be wise, my son, and make my heart glad.

That I may reply to him who reproaches me...." (Proverb 27:9-11) In the same process, he alleged that the love of God is unconditional but Salvation is conditional; by belief and confession, based on personal faith. In this case, to know God one must make the relationship personal by heart belief and mouth confession and these are the conditions based upon personal faith as the scripture declares "That if you confess with your mouth, "Jesus is Lord," and believe in your heart God raised him from the dead, you will be saved. For it is with the heart, that you believe and are justified, and it is with your mouth that you believe and are saved. For "everyone who calls on the name of the Lord will be saved." (Romans 10:9-13)

Maybe you had some storms in your life. Maybe you were overwhelmed or inundated with matters beyond your control. Maybe you suffered the loss of a family member or maybe your hardships were more severe than usual. Maybe you had a tough time getting a job. Maybe you were a little disappointed, you got all kinds of mishaps; Maybe your pains were greater, you almost give up but you didn't; you held on, you changed your hope for faith, you trusted in God to bring you through; you stood your grounds and turned; your hope into faith. You are still standing, you did not lose your faith, Christmas has come and gone, you are still standing. You didn't think you would have made it, you are still standing. I love Melinda so much she left me but I am still standing; I know that I shall see her soon. I never lost my hope. MY trip back home is right around the corner; I am still standing. Praise God I am going through now but at the end; I shall finished in Jesus's name Amen! I have changed a new hope for New Faith.

I told myself that I would take down pride; that I would no longer worry about things I cannot change; but instead put more energy on things I can achieve as I leave the impossible ones to God Almighty; and then I started talking about other things; after all there are things better to be done with my time! As I contemplated a takedown of my pride; the telephone rang and it was Sister Melinda Yates; just as I begin talking to her; the telephone line went dead due to circuit problems. I became overwhelmed by this and then all of a sudden the priest standing behind me said " you just don't know how your writing helps me during the day and thank you so much" and then he said " I may not comment but truthfully it helps" In my mind I said praise God from whom all blessings flow. Friends I am going to talk about God and express my thoughts about my Savior's love and His gift towards me.

My experience the other day

Two Christians I assumed were engaged in a fight the; one to the other "I am not competing with your righteousness" the other responded, "my righteousness doesn't depend on your perfection" I saw this as extremely interesting and became an interloper to the fight. It baffles me that Christians would engage in fights about righteousness and perfections. However the fight continued. The other said, "this is why I isolate myself from you because I don't want the world to see me with you, and think I am like you, a hypocrite." The one called a hypocrite responded, "I understand you, but I know that Jesus died for me as well. My life and my righteousness have nothing to do with you, and I cannot live by what you consider righteousness. I don't want to mortify myself, but instead what I think of you would be kept to myself." This was amazing, seeing how the hypocrite person responded. I was wondering what in the world was going on and then I said WOW! It blew my mind and it brought me to a simple resolved as I stood in the midst of them; I realize how judgmental many of us are and the things, which we do to one another and consider them God's will. I thought about Jesus love and His special considerations for those who are humble on account of His death on the cross; and relating it to the lives of believers. I said OMG; some of us have really closed the doors to heaven on others in an attempt to demonstrate how holy and righteous we are; when we should get in the habit of saving souls and not bringing sinners to condemnations. The Word declared in St. John 3:16-18 "For God so loved the world, that He gave His only begotten Son, that whoever believes in Him shall not perish, but have eternal life. 17"For God did not send the Son into the world to judge the world, but that the world might be saved through Him. 18"He who believes in Him is not judged; he who does not believe has been judged already, because he has not believed in the name of the only begotten Son of God...."

~Bobby Spoke to Amos~

Bobby later said to Amos; we can put away the struggles and relax for a moment and say okay God please take care of my day. I am just so appreciative of being me. Thank God for me in Jesus's name; I thank Him for my late mother and father who took chances with God in my Behalf, and I am grateful! Amos, as I speak; I am going over my life, and I feel something good is coming my way. You see Amos, no man must go too far from whence he came. One day, my testimony shall be expressed on this. I slept on the floor at one time in my life and I asked the Lord for a mat. He gave me a mattress, I was evicted from an apartment I asked the Lord for another apartment, He give me a Home, thought I would not have made it this far, but the

Lord kept me through many dangers, toils and snares; and by grace I am still standing. Could not have made it thus far had it not been for the blood of Jesus Christ; I would have been stuck in my old paths with not a trace of my spiritual identity. Today from the hill where God has placed me; I am constantly reminded from whence I came. I am so thankful, truly thankful for all the wonderful things God can do within a person' life. It is good to know Jesus even when it does not look all clearer for you; He makes the lasting change only if you let Him. Tonight somebody can trust Jesus He is able to see you through. Amen! Son I woke up this morning thanking the Lord; I turned on the TV on CNN; first news I heard " Bill Cosby is been investigated by the police" for all those allegations! Given his status and act of Kindness, but you see Amos I really don't know the truth, but money and power can make good people bad; you would think all would be well, but what is our world coming to son? WOW people we need prayers the devil is busy these are the last days. Everyone who thinks he is standing must take heed lest he falls! Please stay under the blood of Jesus Christ. Please keep your hands in God's hands please love your neighbor as yourselves. Please make a change before time runs out on you. A Pastor suggested finishing 2014 strong, you must draw closer to God and He shall be right where you are. Listen son; a real battlefield is not in Iraq, not in Yemen nor Syria but it is your mind and environment; where the battles are fought daily against hatred, jealousy, fake friends, self-righteousness, sin and haters who are going to hate no matter what! I thank God for my haters. Psalm 2:7 the Lord has decreed and declared that I am His son. If they fight you or me they are fighting God. So let them hate!

Chapter 15

~Every Event of your life is important~

The word of God declared that every event of my life is significant and purposed. For God has made them beautiful in His time. I am therefore letting go of all of my anxieties and I am succumbing to the will of God because I am a product of His; in time. Amos we are WORK IN PROGRESS; as per the word of God. We must feel very grateful and I am gratefully thankful; that we have come this far by faith. Not letting up now we must keep on moving while favor is in our view. Mr. Ross questioned about his origin and testimonies he said; I was sitting the other day and a friend asked; are you an African from Liberia; I replied yes I am and I am glad that I don't have the opportunity to change who I am. Or else I would become as others avoiding the stigma and denying their origin. I am a mixed breed, and yes off course I am a Liberian and I am not a plague either; I am an educated man who love God so much. This pride I wear in my heart, on my mind and within every fiber of my person. Kindly pardoned me; if you are limited, and cannot idealize the construct of my person; on the other hand I pardon the extensive ignorance, which is plaguing others. Just so you know yesterday prior to the massive awareness of this Ebola virus; I was a Liberian and today I am the same individual fully capacitated by nature; a Liberian; I am not a virus rather I am compos mentis with greater ideals out of the heart of West Africa-Liberia; my mother's home. I stand by this and live by this fact. This is why I have chosen to give back by volunteering over here.

In Jesus's name and by His Grace from every valley, hillside or mountain top fear we declared in Jesus's name we decree finishing strong with greater impacts without the assigning distracted forces or even within their presence. For it is written that, "He shall prepare a table before me; even in the presence of my visible enemies possessed by satanic forces and also the invisible enemies. For He shall give His Angel charge over me to watch out for my victories over the snares of the fowler; in Jesus's name Amen! God has not spoken in secret; listen! God is the Holy ONE of Israel who teaches you to profit, He leads you in the way you should go; pay attention to His commandments so that your well-being can become like a rive, and your righteousness like the weaves of the sea OMG today is a good day and wow! God is so good I thank Him for His Grace; for His mercy and all that He has placed and shall place in my path. Thank Him for Jesus and the opportunity for embracing quality God is with you; shout it on the mountain top! Make it echo in the valley and most of all feel it freely in your heart! I love Him for He has heard my cries. Today I sing glory!

Glory to His name! I know my wife shall me Malinda Yates in Jesus' Name, Amos; Amen! There is a past to every beginning no matter whether good or bad God's grace keeps us going. When I think of His shared blood and the price paid for grace God's love becomes more magnified in our weaknesses today we all live in Him and we all have our being perfect or imperfect God's grace sees our weaknesses and it is His will that none should perished but that all should have everlasting life. This is "An ideal I am willing to die for" whither fake or perfect, sick or confused no one takes the joy God has granted to us all! Hell belongs to God; so does heaven and I am so glad; I mean so glad that the blood of Jesus lifted us all! Praise God from whom all blessings flow; praise Him all creatures here below, praise for the father, the son and the Holy Ghost- The Lord Jesus Christ! Strict apostolic!!!

Effective Communication

Effective communication is possible when people who have something in common and I mean something positive; which is worth the time for promoting progressive growth is possible; and they are able to impact the progressiveness of their commonality; when the understanding of people is directed by the Spirit of the Lord. The ambiance of commonality lies in trust, respect and speaking the truth of what is prevalent in the heart. Therefore, if you do not have something in common with God; please don't expect anything from God! He only seeks those whose hearts are towards Him so that He may bless them effectively! So folks if you were further away from

Him; please don't expect Him to come closer to you. God wants you to make the first move; draw closer and He shall come closer to you. Amos if you don't call Him, He will not answer you. Just do this; seek Him first, His kingdom and righteousness, and when this is done; He promised to sit with you, dine with you, communicate with you along with the all-time great in faith; Abraham, Isaac, Moses and Jacob, and most of all, shall bring you to His banqueting table were love overflows! People improve your relationship with Him; become an effective communicator in good relationship God.

Sometimes you might feel out of touch with God and be at a low point; or maybe you are troubled with unresolved situations or problems; they can have a negative bearing on you as well. Even if your problem overweighs you; disregard the weight of the situation and tell it to God. God is moved when the broken hearted; the contrite heart, the poor in spirit, the needy and the outcasts seek His assistance. When we are full of our selves; God cannot filled us, but when we are emptied of ourselves God can use His ever fountain to fill us to an over flowing point.

Today, there are great men full of themselves. They have come to positions in time where they compare themselves with enticing words full of man's wisdom thus hypothesizing the Divine Providence of God to fit their presuppositions. Whereas, the simple and the down trodden consistently seeks the Divine mercies of almighty God with complete devotion while invocating. They lament so that the compassion Spirit of God is touched by the feelings of your infirmities. There is an adage "empty barrel makes the most noise" and that is true within the natural sense as they do, however within the spiritual sense; God seeks the empty barrel making the most noise in godly lamentation! When a heart is broken, it must cry to God! When in need of help from an emotional drained; cry to God! When confused and cannot figure out why? Cry to God; make the most noise in the spirit and invite the presence of God into your situation. At your low points seek God first; rid yourselves of the reasons why you are where you are and be filled by the invited presences of the most High God. He would not despise the broken hearted; nor would He reject the one contrite in spirit; if we call on God; when we are in lowly situations or at the upper heights in Him; He abundantly pardons. No matter what your circumstances are God wants to fill you with His presence and flow within you joy so that you are strengthen from within and out.

Once our moments meet the conditions of God; without the self-righteous attitude; He raises us from the low to the upper and He fills up the emptiness. Friends and Family Remember you have to call on God in the time of trouble; seek His mercy in the time of need, Christ came to this earth on account of our lowly moments and for this very reason to rescue us from those who would pressed us down. Once we are emptied of all those issues of life tying us down and present them to God, He is certainly able to mount us up on wings of eagles. Today let the peace of God rule the day; and I declare for you in the name of Jesus of Nazareth that there would be no bad feeling of rejection or guile of bad spirit of emotional drain; keeping you down. I nullify the enemy plans and declare by fire that they are defeated in Jesus' Name! AMEN!

Molly to Melinda

I have to be going now; we shall take up this matter once again. Those words, which you heard, were messages from Bobby's counseling sessions and previous works, which were recorded. Melinda I am certain that for now you have come to an understanding of the kind of man who is seeking to have you break your vows as a nun; just to be become his wife; the woman of his hear and the answer to his prayers. I don't know Melinda sometimes I think Bobby should move on but then; I am persuaded by his deep faith in God and his commitment to loving you. I am sometimes convinced that by your actions and interest in discussing Bobby; that you are struggling with this feeling of falling in love and breaking your vows; if not why do you always call. Melinda said Molly please; do not put me on the spot; you know where this situation has led to; you know the circumstances of the matter, but I am in prayers. I shall speak with mother superior this afternoon; by the way you may go and leave me to myself; I need to pray and meditate more on this. Bye!

Melinda at Bible studies; she speaks on the power of forgiveness

I have heard people say "I can forgive, but I cannot forget". I have heard people also say I" hate the pains and this is repeated over and over the same thing over and over". I have also heard that it is best to" forgive but keep a distance." Yes, these are all true, and the fact is that no one enjoys pains of hatred, rejections, betrayal nor undermining; yet those who have experienced these elements of pains are accosted to make concessions by faith in accepting those who hate them, wrongfully despise them, and attempt to relegate them to mediocrity. It is a truthful saying that only your friend knows your secret and only he can hurt you with them, but when he does you have to forgive. I guess you would ask; why? And the answer is straight forward; it is your duty as a believer! St. Luke 6:27-29 "But I say to you who hear, love your enemies, do good to those who hate you, 28 bless those who curse you, pray for those who mistreat you. 29 "Whoever hits you on the cheek, offer him the other also; and whoever takes away your coat, do not withhold your shirt from him either...." One person responded, "Forgivingness can be cold at times, cruel as well". Listen the very acts of forgiving and been forgiven; take loads off people and bring about joyfulness in people lives. Jesus expects us to be mature at this practice. The very act speaks volume about the quality of characters.

There is so much power in writing all of your hurts which people inflict upon you in sandy places, while spending much time remembering and carving in stones the amount of times you were delivered from personal trespasses by God almighty first and then by folks closer to you. Notice I said folks closer to you; it is said that way on account; that strangers don't hurt you, but it is the person you trust, respect and love; who inflicts the knockout incisions. I don't know about anyone's feelings but trust me; it does hurt! O well it is what it is; just learn the lessons, dust yourselves, move on with love in your heart. Therefore, if you read this and if you are at odds with someone; make concession; agree with them, work with them in this process, get the stuff of your chest and live in peace with a clear conscience. Don't be afraid of words spoken by man; seek the love of God, live soberly and be above reproaches! Forgive your selves and others and then be forgiven by God almighty

Molly Speaks "I am thankful to God and all my Friends"

This morning while walking towards the bus stop; one of my neighbor called me, and when I returned I realized how late I was, and now I had to stop and talk to my neighbor. I did, and we started walking but she was a bit slower than I was, the bus came; I had to rush, but I realized that she was interested in talking to me about her experience, and so walking slow we missed the first bus. Oh well I stopped and paid all the attention; finally another bus came and we boarded that one. While sitting she said to me Molly thanks; "for waiting for me I really needed someone to listen to me, and now I am feeling better" I responded you are welcome! Then it dawn on me how grateful she was just for a moment of my time and the patience, which I exerted at that moment. This led me into thinking about our Savior encounter with the ten lepers; they were delivered and only one was grateful and returned to express his gratitude. Many people are blessed to have others in their lives but show no gratitude at all. If we can just take a little time to review constructively people conditions around us, then we would realize that they cannot be taken for granted but rather, respected, honored and appreciated. In so doing; we just might entertained a child of God or a stranger; as I did on the bus.

We have to take time out to show love to others in demonstration of the Savior's acts of kindness. Today we can all become demonstratively; positive about our attitude sin representing the Lord's love and care in preserving us; His children. We must all be appreciative in all aspects of our lives; more so in all the ones which are consider trivia. Every sustaining moment; which we encounter is the Lord's. He watches over us; assuring us of his cares in leading us every step of the way towards His good will pleasure and purpose in time. You could be lonely today, forgotten by friends, neglected by family members, opposed by church members, but just take a look at you! You are better off than what you were ten years ago. There were others who have tried to be in your position today, but failed at it. Just look at who you are today, and where you have come. Isn't it a reason to be grateful! Just understand that God cares to listen to you and He wants to hear your conversations with Him. Only just be thankful and grateful for all of your friends and family who have been there for you along the way. Take the time to call someone show some love and be appreciative for the life God has given to you. As for me, I am thankful to God and all my Friends who have; over the years never given up on me! More so to those who never ceased to pray for me; during my trying moments; I am rather glad for those who supported me when I was down until the grace of God lifted me 15plus years ago! I am thankful! Thank You Jesus for greater love; my family and friends! When Adversity comes, God intercedes! He won't leave you; no not alone! Salvation belongs to the Lord God almighty. He knows your down sitting and He understands your uprising. He is the greatest of all! As the class ended, the members were elated and they thanked Sister Melinda Yates for such profound message.

Melinda encounters an older Lady

The Mrs. Crawford steered at Melinda all through the Bible class; she was not a member of the church and wanted to address a matter with Melinda. She politely requested the time and Melinda been obliged responded positively. Mrs. Crawford; said listen my child you are blessed on account of God' remembrance of you. The preacher said, "God remembers! God has an agreement with you and He is about to fulfill it in Jesus's Name. If you had or are having a praying mother, grandparents, father and every time they blessed their generation they included you therefore they are in covenant with God and on you shall the blessings pour as well, magnify God today for a new thing is coming your way in His name you must trust. Tell Him who you are and that every good word or words spoken in your behalf; you are claiming them today in Jesus's name Amen! God remembers (Psalm 105). Today I rest the Name of Jesus Christ upon your life for blessing Amen! The preacher also said, "Freely give freely received". As the Lord blesses me with His words, I shall share it with you as I am instructed. Some preachers maybe bless by these expositions of inspiration while others may reject them but those of you who are commenting on them; telling of your faith; you are the reasons why I rise up early in the morning to pray and to speak blessings into your lives. Please be blessed and use these scriptures, as the steadfast love of God is new every morning.

Great is His faithfulness. I love you all in Jesus's name Amen! You know Melinda I also heard the Preacher talked about the "Victory in every battle waged against you today; you shall be ransom unharmed, every sickness and other attacks are powerless against you in the name of Jesus Christ of Nazareth! Your calls and cries to God at morning, noon and evening are heard by God; today is your day for rejoicing in Jesus's name Amen! Psalm 55. Don't be surprised at the how and whys? After all you are an over-comer in Jesus's name Amen! Keep the faith and hold fast to your calling in Jesus's name Amen! My child the message is made so simple that I look forward to it. I heard that you are struggling with your feelings about your vow to the Catholic Church; I do not know; how this might help; I heard another line from that preacher and he said "Train your heart ". What occupies your mind determines what you speak in relationship to God, to man and to yourself.

Therefore; if your heart is filled with honesty it shall be faithful to God and to man. Truthfulness sets you free and guides your heart; when you speak from your heart peace, love and kindness; then your soul is in fruitful action mode (**John 15:2**). What is in your heart now? A good person produces good fruits, a bad person produces bad fruits all from the treasury of the heart (Matt 12:34-35). Train your heart to know humility, honesty and good quality and then you shall be a repository of goodness from the heart, what is in your heart? Say it! Good or Evil. MAY THE LIFE of JESUS CHRIST GUIDE YOUR HEART IN SERVICE AMEN! " My daughter these are the days for you young people to get up and stand up for Jesus; my God that preacher is something else; another one of his messages was "Arise my friends and shine, give God the glory, for today your peace is upon you. Your favor is sure and God's graces have spotted you. So press forward and take a hold of your position your victory is now in Jesus's name Amen! Arise, shine for your light has come. The deep shadows can no longer hide you, walk in the light of God. For the Son of God has caused you to shine. So shine today in Jesus's name Amen! Praise the Lord for He has made Peace your governor and righteousness your ruler; therefore shine in Jesus name" We all have to shine for Jesus and it does not matter where you are or whence you came; believing in Jesus actually makes you to shine.

People would see you and know that you are the child of the most high God. My child, train your mind and follow the lead of your heart. Do you hear me? If you out here today reading this; God wants to speak to your situation, and declare that your season has come and your prayers are at your feet with results to make you live in Jesus's name Amen! This is your time to live in Jesus's name Amen! Speak life now into what seems fable and break out this morning with peace and joy in the Holy Ghost after all you must shine; for in Jesus's name this is your time to shine! Melinda in all that you do my daughter you must "Understand the laws of life, sin and death, be controlled by the Spirit and not your nature, in this way Goodness and Mercy shall be your front and back protectors. Be controlled by the Spirit so that you can please God by obeying the Spiritual laws of life! If you want more blessings in your life, be controlled by the Spirit of God, seek peace and follow it. Live by faith and not by sight. If you please God, you shall be satisfied with long life. Romans 8, Psalm 91. In Jesus's name Amen!

Sister Yates, reach out more to Friends and Families things around us may seem prolonged and some might even get tired of trying, I want to admonish you today not to give up. Your help is nearing right where you are, don't be weary. the Word of God declared "but those who hope in the LORD will Renew their strength" Isaiah 40:31 Your flight to victory is now press forward and take control in Jesus's name Amen! Melinda I want you to know that I Corinthians 8:3 declares "But the man who loves God is known by God". I want you to know that God knows you and He is working it out for you. Hold on all of your good are about to step out of darkness into your view of light for harvest time and with more reaping in Jesus's name Amen. For this is your day; God has given you; the former has gone and today God is about to do a new thing for you, but He has said that before the New thing is done He God shall show it to you; Isaiah; chapter 42. Therefore whatever new you want done in your life; trust God it shall and it shall be done in Jesus's name Amen! My Dear Daughter God is real; God is real, His angels are real; the Spirit realm is also real! God speaks from Heaven to the heavens and the Earth hears His voice. Can anyone tell where did the voice come from, when the mother die, the baby strapped in the car seat for 14 hours in frigid waters, after an accident! On CNN the Police Officers and the other rescue team said they heard the voice. Right now I am saying Great Jehovah; Thou are ALPHA and Thou Are OMEGA; Heaven is filled with your glory, while You controls the heavens; deep calls unto deep as Your everlasting glory constantly and consistently delivers as YOU o LORD Shines from the hills of Mount Zion. In you do I put my trust, and I am not a shame to lift up praises of thanksgiving unto your Holy Name. From Everlasting to Everlasting YOU are LORD; God the Lord; God is sending you a breakthrough, get ready to receive your reward, there is an open door set for you, and no man can shut it. Believe it is yours and press forward in Jesus's name Amen! Sister Yates these words I am giving to you just see them and use the for your devotion this week my daughter they shall encouraged you dearly

Isaiah 38:18 Don not be silenced Now

Hezekiah's Song of Thanksgiving

17"Lo, for my own welfare I had great bitterness; It is You who has kept my soul from the pit of nothingness, For You have cast all my sins behind Your back. 18"For Sheol cannot thank You, Death praise You; Those who go down to the pit cannot hope for Your faithfulness. 19"It is the living who give thanks to You, as I do today; A father tells his sons about Your faithfulness....

Psalm 30:9 What is gained if I am silenced, if I go down to the pit? Will the dust praise you? Will it proclaim your faithfulness?

No, I cannot stop praising Him. I am still alive my voice shall boast of His grace and mercies. Psalm 67. Melinda the preacher said also "This one is for you and if you are reading this with an open heart. Stop pleasing man; start serving God, AND MOST OF ALL start pleasing GOD! He gets upset when you please man. Focus more on your godly relationship, after all God needs your attention Jeremiah 17:5. God needs you to stay focus for the blessings of your life. A big difference is that God knows your heart, and man doesn't and cannot reward you as God can. So whose blessings do you desired; man or God? If God; He has an approved plan for you. Therefore draw closer to Him and you would see how great He is. " OH TASTE AND SEE that the LORD IS GOOD and HIS mercy lasts forever" It is all well to be antagonized for the things of God; for antagonism is going to bring you closer to your destiny; just persevere the Man of God said Is it okay to talk about God or preach on Facebook without an offense. Only the spirit of a man knows what is in the heart of the man likewise only the Spirit of God knows the things of God therefore God is a Spirit and those who worship Him must worship Him in spirit and truth. Satan does not cast out Satan; only God can cast out satanic activities. Jealousy can cause people to become judgmental, self- righteous, isolating on the guise of doing God's business. Listen know the fruit by the tree.

Bad tree don't bring good fruits so be careful how you act to others who are serving God after all your determination of righteousness cannot be imposed. Let us walk by faith, live by faith renounce jealousy it is a tool of the enemy to distract and cause isolation, which is not godly. Prejudging with prejudice and not after a Godly manner; is demonic, be careful least you become a resting place for a deceitful imagination. Truthfully, are you in the faith; have you examine yourself. Let God be true and everyman a liar; what is really eating you up; is it my attitude; my love for God? I have a desire and that is never to fine myself in a second heaven attitude, come and walk with me, then you would know what is speaking, love, peace, hope or greater walk towards my destiny. In extension, ask God what is leading him. Is it man or is it the grace of God? Please for God's sake; hold on to your faith. After all I have to express what God places in my heart. This is the walk I walk in Jesus's name Amen! No comment is just right also; no likes is just right also at the end of the day; God is real and I can feel Him in my soul. The life that I live shall one day speak for me until then

I have works to do. I am a sojourner just as you are. Am I talking to you? I hope not, but walk the walk I am taking the faith walk. This is how I was lead after my meditation! **(Job 36)** Just know that Authenticity is of a concern when the foolishness of the gospel is committed to you and your dedicated spirit increases above the natural realm.

We are committed to doing the things of God and by faith, we are moving on Melinda. Therefore, my child, do not let your strength fail you, do not let situations get you down. Stand up for your heart felt conviction and let the Lord rule your heart for Proverbs 24:10 says " If thou faint in the day of adversity, thou strength is small." Therefore, don't let your strength fail you in trials hold unto God's hands. Melinda God wants you to be strong and encouraged, because that stronghold formed against you is coming down today; in the Name of Jesus Christ of Nazareth! For I declared the word of God found in Isaiah 54:17 "No weapon formed against you shall prosper". Sickness is coming down; any other conditions are also coming down in Jesus's name Amen!

Melinda later asked Mrs. Crawford, "Why are you telling me all of this?"

The silver hair lady responded, "Just consider me the voice of God in this situation and you shall see my child. God knows who we are and what is conducive for everyone. At the appropriate times, He sends His angels in the form of man to speak prophetic words to the minds of His people. Thanks is to God for a big heart as David the King of Israel. Don't run from anything which might seem enormous; face the challenge with God on your side your Goliath shall fall. I Samuel 17:26-36 Amen in Jesus's name! Give God the praise tell Him from your lips "You alone are worthy Lord to receive praises and honors. You have been faithful from generations to generations; even this morning you are protecting me from the evil humans who should be praying for a healthy relationship with you as I do so bless them Father. Lord today because of your faithfulness I see a new mercy and grace this morning.

So Father retracts the curtains so we all may see from whence we have come and that we are appreciative of Your Kindness in Jesus's name Amen! Now "Pray a little more, connect with God a little more; don't you know God wants you to call upon Him so that He can show you the way through your struggles? Just stop for a moment and think again try Jesus; after all He wants you to call upon Him so He can reveal the unsearchable things which you seek. He has the answer to what you are going through right now. If it is healing; he paid the price; Money seek Him more; He has the answer; joy He would make you glad. For in sorrows; your Comfort shall God always become. He told Jeremiah in Chapter 33:3 these words call to me, and I will answer you, and show you great and mighty things, which you know not. Jeremiah 33:3; call unto me, and I will answer thee — "An expression manifesting God's favor and loving kindness; that he was ready to comply with the first intimations of his servant's desires." Sister

Yates; God wants to answer you and to reward you for calling upon Him. Give Him the praise and make a praise call! "Almighty Father; Maker of heaven and earth; the Keeper of my soul, in You oh Lord my soul takes delight; I call upon you for a right now favor; I call upon you Omnipotent Father that what are unseen to me would become visible as they concerns the benefits of my life and that of my friends and family. I thank You so much as your word declares that nothing can separate me from you, not even my struggles as a person nor any man or thing can separate me from you. I take delight in you and the care you have shown towards me in Jesus' Name. Sister Yates kindly understand that these words found in Gal 5:22-23 (The products of your faith tried: Joy, Peace, Patience, Kindness, Faithfulness, Gentleness and Self-control) Trust in God and stayed humble; produce much more fruits; after all Jesus wants us to be productive:

Matthew 7:18-20
A Tree and its Fruit
...18"A good tree cannot produce bad fruit, nor can a bad tree produce good fruit. 19"Every tree that does not bear good fruit is cut down and thrown into the fire. 20"So then, you will know them by their fruits.

Always make the fruit in your life worthy to be seen and blessed by. Put away the struggles and relax for a moment and say okay; God please take care of my day. I am just so appreciative of being me. Thank God for me in Jesus's name; I thank Him for my late mother and father who took chances with God in my behalf and I am grateful! Melinda we must be grateful to God at all times for all of His blessed opportunities which he has afforded us as His children, because nothing is permanent; I Woke up to this morning thank the Lord; turned on the TV; first news I heard " Bill Cosby is been investigated by the police" for all those allegations! WOW people we need prayers the devil is busy these are the last days. Everyone who thinks he is standing must take heed lest he falls! Please stay under the blood of Jesus Christ. Please keep your hands in God's hands please love your neighbor as yourselves. Please make a change before 2015. A Pastor suggested finishing 2014 strong, you have a fee weeks; left draw closer to God and He shall be right where you are. Peace and blessings in Jesus's name. You see my daughter, as I am speaking to you for; there are many wars which would have to fought, and the A real battlefield is not in Iraq, not in Yemen nor Syria but it is your mind and environment. where the battles are fought daily against hatred, jealousy, fake friends, self -righteousness, sin and haters who are going hate no matter what. Like the preacher said "I thank God for my haters. Psalm 2:7 the Lord has decreed and declared that I am His child. If they fight you or me they are fighting God. So let them hate!"

~Daughter we are a work in progress! ~

The word of God declared that every event of my life is significant and purposed. For God has made them beautiful in His time. I am therefore letting go of all of my anxieties and I am succumbing to the will of God because I am a product of His; in time. ECC. 3:11 I AM (WIP) WORK IN PROGRESS as per the word of God. I am feeling very grateful and I am gratefully thankful; that I have come this far by faith. Not letting up now got to keep on moving while favor is in my view. Isaiah 48; says favor is my boundary. Therefore In Jesus's name and by His Grace from every valley, hillside or mountain top fear we declared in Jesus's name conquered; with greater impacts in the faces of the assigning distracted forces; within their presence; God shall established a standard of forwardness in Jesus Name.

It is written that "He shall prepare a table before me; even in the presence of mine enemies: There are visible enemies; meaning people possessed by satanic forces to do you harm. No matter how difficult things shall appear; God would grant you victories over the invisible ones as well; for He has given His angel charge over you; to watch out for your victories over the snares of the fowler. In Jesus's name run your life with diligence and follow the leading of your heart if Bobby Ross is your happiness and if you shall believe that; God shall bless you with children; only if it your desire my child. Melinda by all means you must always be led by the convictions of your heart. Isaiah 48:16-18 (Paraphrased) God has not spoken in secret; listen! God is the Holy ONE of Israel who teaches you to profit, He leads you in the way you should go; pay attention to His commandments so that your well-being can become like a river, and your righteousness like the weaves of the sea.

OMG today is a good day and wow! God is so good I thank Him for His Grace; for His mercy and all that He has placed and shall place in my path. Thank Him for Jesus and the opportunity for embracing quality education. I love Him for He has heard my cries. Today I sing glory to His wonderful Name. If God is with you; shout it on the mountain top! Make it echo in the valley and most of all feel it freely in your heart! After all "greater is He that is in you than the he that is in the world". True life is with God and to tell you the truth I never thought life with God would have been this good; until I learned to endured tribulations, trials, disappointments rejections and masquerade conditions from acquaintances; then I realized it is when joy comes; once you go through holding on to the Name of Jesus the SAVIOR and COMFORTER! Know this " count it all joy when you f all into various trials" James 1: 2 in my life at my age my child; I can Shut up! Stop complaining! Praise the Lord; you are better than what you were ten years ago! So give Him all of the Praise .God is good all the time and all of the time; God is! I am so grateful to God for life. I know that you know Molly very well, she is my granddaughter and that girl is on fire for the Lord. She is also the story of my life she knows much about the devices of the enemy and as she spoke to me, I realized that I am bless not baffled, truly bless; woke up this morning anticipated the devices of the enemy, quickly fed on the word and armed myself.

Ready for today's challenges; resolved to the point that with Jesus on my side; this day is going be a great day in Jesus's name and also I am resting in God, and it starts with justification, sanctification with greater access through hope in our Lord Jesus Christ. Romans chapters 5 and 8 and Today I blessed the Lord; my soul remembered God to "place all of my time in the hands of the eternal father" Hebrews 12:5-6 Psalm 31:1-13 I say the truth I lie not " God is good; and all the time God is good and good all of the times. I am blessed and grateful that at one point in my life; I was a nobody but Jesus, with His special love; dispatched Bishop William Lee Bonner to Liberia, West Africa December 12, 1979 to host a national Crusade. I was one of the hundreds that got saved. I am so grateful that God saved me from sin and saved my life. I am not a slave to the past; God changed my status to a friend of HIS and a leader who has become somebody because of our Savior's love! My family is blessed I am looking forward and like my predecessor "Bishop William Lee Bonner" I am taking chances with God and people. People must be developed, given opportunities to become somebody not only for heaven but for living meaningful lives on earth as well. Thanks to God for greater moments in my life. So grateful and thankful!

~Molly and I are sadden by the sudden death of Pastor Bonner~

That is why I am taking chances with God, I am grateful for the life of that great man, and I have realized that I can Praise God for the day. Survival is key to making the best of every opportunity in my life, A preacher, An IT professional, an adjunct college professor, Certified New York State' paralegal; all of these were junks; seeking the mind of Christ is the best profession with eternal rewards! Amen. You see Sister Yates; Molly understood so well that There is a past to every beginning no matter whether good or bad God's grace keeps us going. When I think of His shared blood and the price paid for grace; God's love becomes more magnified in mine weaknesses; we all live in Him and we all have our being perfect or imperfect God's grace sees our weaknesses and it is His will that none should perished but that all should have everlasting life. This is " an ideal I am willing to die for" whither fake or perfect, sick or confused no one takes the joy God has granted to us all! Hell belongs to God so does heaven and I am so glad I mean so glad that the blood of Jesus lifted us all! Praise God from whom all blessings flow; praise Him all creatures here below, praise for the father, the son and the Holy Ghost- The Lord Jesus Christ! Strict apostolic! Melinda one thing you must know and that is the:

Chapter 16

~The power of forgiveness ~

have heard people say "I can forgive, but I cannot forget". I have heard people also say I" hate the pains and this is repeated over and over the same thing over and over". I have also heard that it is best to" forgive but keep a distance"! Yes these are all true, and the fact is that no one enjoys pains of hatred, rejections, betrayal nor undermining; yet those who have experienced these elements of pains are accosted to make by faith in accepting those who hate them, wrongfully despise them, and attempt to relegate them to mediocrity. It is a truthful saying that only your friend knows your secret and only he can hurt you with them, but when he does, you have to forgive. I guess you would ask, "Why? The answer is strict forward. It is your duty as a believer!

St. Luke 6:27-29 "But I say to you who hear, love your enemies, do good to those who hate you, 28 bless those who curse you, pray for those who mistreat you. 29 "Whoever hits you on the cheek, offer him the other also; and whoever takes away your coat, do not withhold your shirt from him either...."

Listen the very acts of forgiving and been forgiven; take loads of people and bring about joyfulness in people lives. Jesus expects us to be mature at this practice. The very act speaks volume about the quality of characters. There is so much power in writing all of your hurts which people inflict upon you in sandy places, while spending much time remembering and carving in stones the amount of times you were delivered from personal trespasses by God almighty first and then by folks closer to you who truthfully care about the well for you. Notice I said folks closer to you; on account that only your friends can have this sort of access, and that strangers don't hurt you, but it is the one you trusted the most, respected and loved; who inflicts the knockout incisions. I don't know about anyone's feelings but trust me; it does hurt! O well it is what it is; just learn the lessons, dust yourselves, move on with love in your heart. Therefore, if you read this and if you are at odds with someone; make concession; agree with them, work with them in this process, get the stuff of your chest and live in peace with a clear conscience. Don't be afraid of words spoken by man; seek the love of God, live soberly and be above reproaches! Forgive yourselves and others and then be forgiven by God almighty. I encourage you to pressing forward; just shake it off! Stump it down! Keep your affections on things above; make no friends with dismal yesterday, nor a call back to the day before dismay! Keep your focus on today's peace and let go of the weighted unnecessary.

Take a good hold of your now and walk with God with an assuring view of tomorrow's bliss! Don't give up! Keep on trying for every round with God goes higher and higher! Peace and blessings. Child listen I have done much preaching to you and as soon as you get an opportunity; call brother Bobby Ross; open your heart and tell him about your peace. God knows the details of my life; He is acquainted with all of my steps. My low moments and high ones are all seen and acknowledged by God. I am persuaded that He is able to create a balance in my life to keep me afloat of the unknown. PSALM 139:1-10 He knows about my anxieties when I am relaxed and when I am troubled! I have no fear; for I am of more value to God than sparrows! Comment Amen if you know that God cares for you!

~Mrs. Crawford ended her conversation with Melinda; Molly had called for her~

As the older lady left she promised Melinda that that they shall revisit the conversation and continue their discussion. She had to respond to Molly in the main time Mrs. Crawford said Melinda pardon me just permit me to leave these words with you as the preacher said "A great man once said, [it is not what you say but it is what you are not saying is what matters." Assumptions can consume you and it just might affect the people around you. So have good quality judgement, have peace with yourself be sincere in what you are doing never mind what is going on the outside of you; only control your Spirit, your inner man and then your soul man shall aligned with you. The real you need spiritual satisfactions which relinquish you from that inner conflict, not knowing what to do, what to say you find yourself assuming, prejudging and extremely self-deceived, and most of all; at war with yourself. That is the real warfare and you don't need Facebook for this; my good Bishop Bonner in his book the "Uncontrollable emotions" said a situation as such; is when you need prayers.

The weapons of our warfare are not carnal but mighty through God to the pulling down of Strongholds. Please Read Matthew 12. We got to fight strongholds, and stop assumptions of who likes you, dislikes you just live now in Jesus's name Amen! Truthfully, tomorrow is really not promised if you permit mere man to drive you into hell. Melinda it is not worth it at all for 32 years of my life I have seen and fought many battles but none was special until I applied Psalm 94.

Therefore down with Satan and up with Jesus!" As Mrs. Crawford was about leave for attending to Molly's crisis; Melinda ceased the moment and said waiting a minute I feel that I should testify that I really love the Lord, He woke me up this morning, and I have send up my petition and I am awaiting my expectation. At night my soul desires my Lord and at morning my spirit search for Him. God is good to me so good to me. I may not be where I want to be but I am far very far from what I used to be. I have renounced those easily be setting things and have find a better way with Jesus, never mind if I am offensive; I am only enjoying my own space in the Lord and it is my right to do. So down with Satan and up with Jesus. Mrs. Crawford Read Isaiah 26 and get inspired preachers and people of God!

~The Next Day over in Africa~

Amos held devotion at the parish, and everyone was seated along with Bobby
Ross. The Young Amos, like the Prophet Amos, walked across the floor cleared his throat greeted everyone. He said, "My fellow Christians, keep calling on name of the Lord. Keep trusting in His Name, for the Bible declares that, this shall happened to you as you lift up the Name of the Lord. Your heart shall understand knowledge, your tongue shall speak clearly, the wind shall serve as your deliveryman, your words shall reach the heart of God, and for you it has been declared that the Spirit of God shall pour upon you more blessings from on high. Stay with God, trust in God be not dismayed, your wilderness shall be fertile, your seed shall grow, and the devour of your plenty shall be stop and quieted in Jesus's name

Amen! I have prayed for you and applied Isaiah 32 to seal these words in Jesus's name Amen! The folks responded Amen. Before he could be seated, a lady said, "Brother Amos isn't the passage of scripture which you just spoke from is about the kingdom of God and righteousness and also about the women of Israel?"

He responded that is true, and to be correct; you are actually on point; however the acts of the bad women represented sin, the very nature of sin ascribed to our generation, and it is deeply seated in disobedience and rebellion. The good women represented the Church the very essence of repentance and righteous oblations to God the father and if you take into totality my dear sister you would find yourself closer to a kingdom of righteousness as you sitting right here right now begin by magnifying God for greater graces and mercies. I say this and I lie not God is in control of every situation and it is only the matter of time when from the heart men would praise the Awesome God for all that He is! Brother Ross was not only astonished but flabbergasted at Amos and the level of profound spiritual growth which he had attained. Brother Ross later said "Breakthrough – every weapon formed against you are scattered and are useless in Jesus's name Amen!

My Friends and family I declare victory for you and your family in Jesus's name, my prayers this morning is that you see your way and not only that but that your breakthrough comes by the word of God from your heart. GOD is waiting for you to speak your desires into the atmosphere and His angels are ready to deliver them into your cares. Your ideals and within the position of thoughtful realities; your prayers therefore on this foundation is to speak your breakthrough, and support it by the word of God; Jeremiah 1: 12 assures us that God watches over His words to perform it. Therefore pour out you heart to God; He awaits your request. I sealed these words with (Jeremiah 23:29) God's word is like a hammer that breaks the rocks in pieces. Today is breakthrough day in the name of Jesus

Christ of Nazareth; use the hammer and stand on Christ the solid ROCK. AMEN! I am entirely grateful to the God for seeing the way in which this young man has developed. A young man neglected from childhood now finds himself mastering the words of righteousness; all praises be to God Almighty. Family expressions must made sincerely at any-time; anywhere in God's way, excuse me for a moment; thanks to God for a time of peace and blessings must always be near our hearts and lips.

~Bother Ross later instructed the group that we are Temples of the living God ~

He said Temples! Yes, we are temples of the living God, containers for the Holy Ghost. Paul said "don't you know that you yourselves are God's temple and that God's Spirit dwells in you (I Corinthians 3:16)" therefore my friends God is returning His anointing to His temple but it has to be tested for quality. God knows you; who you are, but you have to be shaken, stripped of excess weight in other to be filled with God's glory; lift up your heads; for today as Jesus said "salvation is returning to your house" in Jesus's name Amen!

I don't know what trials shall come your way, but I know that you shall come forth as a vessel thoroughly tried and ready for the Master's use. (I Corinthians 3:12-15).Wherever you are right now, find a moment and praise God for two minutes, lift Him up for today joy shall fill your hearts, and you shall overcome in Jesus's name Amen! Everyone know that you are temples of the living Lord; for His Spirit resides in you in Jesus's name Amen! Peace and blessings! In this, we have to take care of what God has given us. I am thankful that everyone here understands this implication. I am certain that as we come to grips with this little concept we would feel responsible to our spouses, friends and neighbor. In my conclusion May the peace of God rule your day, may His loving kindness brings you comfort and security. All your good plans in Jesus's name Amen; shall follow you and evil shall not overcome you. May your day be delightful. To help you along the way I have prayed (Psalm 64:2) that God shall "hide you from the secret counsel of the wicked" and I have bind and rebuked every spirit of Sanballat and Tobia (Nehemiah 6:1-6) in the name of Jesus Christ of Nazareth. Every evil plan against you is scatter in Jesus's name Amen! Peace blessings; have a good God Monday in Jesus's name Amen! I am pondering right now and I Couldn't feel any less better than when Jesus warns that a man's worst enemy would be that of his household. I thought about this and the word came to me again. Glorify God and He shall lift you up, acknowledge Him and He shall acknowledge you, draw near to Him and He shall lift you up. Jesus can set us on fire and we have to keep the flame ignited. Don't turn the flame out in your lives. Amen in Jesus's name Amen! Matthew 10. LEV. 6. It is good being in the Lord's presence.

By understanding, that God's words are His will for us. We must use them as tools for salvation, as power and authority for healing and deliverance as protection from the unseen evil (Matthew 10:1), and as light to your path out of darkness. Use God's words wisely and it shall shake your spirit and set your soul on fire. Use it to defeat spiritual stagnation and release in you a glorious joyful, sweet presence into your day. I sealed this with (Jeremiah 29:11). God wants to prosper you; He has good thoughts and peace designed just for you in Jesus's name Amen! In this I pray that Goodness and Mercy follow you on the left and right side of you and before and behind you; Love and Peace to protect you in Jesus's name Amen! Oh magnify the Lord with me come and let us exalt His name together, let us make mention of His excellent greatness. Oh praise Him for grace given unto us in Jesus's name Amen! Christians let the praises of God be on your lips and from your hearts let the mention of Jesus be increased in the precious Name of Jesus Christ of Nazareth. Today use the weapons of praise to defeat the nay Sayers and unwanted presence.

The Clients concern about Melinda

One of the clients later inquired about Melinda. She needed to understand if the Counselor was gaining strength from his work. He replied "Let us today glorify the Lord together, let us also lift up His name together. Today whatever you are doing stop for a moment and give praises to God for He woke you up this morning and He has placed blessings into your day. The word of God declares that "those who look to Him (God) are radiant: their faces are never covered with shame"(Psalm 34).

You are covered and protected; for an angel of the LORD has been assigned to you to bear you in their hands in the time of trouble. Have a blessed day and have peace with your fellow man and then with God and in this; your day shall be filled with joy in Jesus's name Amen! I am certain that God Melinda is my wife and that God has fixed this for me. Mother Crawford is God sent and she is on the case.

Out of now where Mother Crawford called me and inquired about my where about; I explained the situation to her, she promised to talk to Melinda, and since then I am believing in God for my victory; not caring what man might say. I am bound to Melinda and she is special and God has declared her for me that no good thing would He God keep from me. He also promised that If I neglect myself for others; he shall give me the desires of my heart, and trust me I do desire Melinda and she is a very good armament for joy and blissful heavenly life.

Therefore, I want you all to praise God in the sanctuary, praise Him for the little things He has done, praise Him for His greatness, and praise Him for His kindness. Today speak God's graces sing about them and how they delivered you. Tell about His mercy, and how it has helped you. Speak into your situation your desires and declare your victories because the authority to use the power of God is in your heart therefore speak as God has directed you. Tell every obstacle to step aside because you are the child of God. I sealed this with (Romans 10:8) The word of faith is in your heart to declare it so in Jesus's name Amen!

All praises be to Jehovah God; Amen! The Client responded Brother Ross you are actually a man of faith. "Yes I am he!" said Yes I am" and I am praising Him for His goodness towards you in Jesus's name Amen! As you face this new week; face it knowing that God has given into your spirit strength to go through, and for your safety and protection; I have applied (Psalm 119:114) God shall be your shield and your hiding place, speak into your day your good desires and God shall see you through in Jesus's name Amen! You shall hold on and endure every test of the day in Jesus's name Amen! (2 Timothy 2:3).May the peace of God keep you strong and steadfast in Jesus's name Amen! I am as certain as I can be that mother Crawford knows right from wrong and she understands that this is a matter for God. he later said "Followers of Christ Jesus be reminded that there is a precious gift of God on the inside of you, but you have to fan or stir it into flame. Let it come forth today with joy and gladness in the name of Jesus, for the word of God declares " For God has not given us a Spirit of timidity, but of power, of love and of self-discipline (II Timothy 1:7).

At any location today, you must release your joy, release your faith into actions and give praises to God; for He awaits your worship. Therefore, in serving Him today release it from the love from within. Have a blessed day in Jesus's name Amen! In closing today, I have a question and you don't need to answer it he said "Who are you attracting? What are you putting into the atmosphere? What are you declaring? Are your hands ready and fingers aligned? Scot moto "be ready, and be prepared" Choose your battles; know what to take on before it takes you out. God is in control! Take on the winnable battles and leave the stronger ones for God. After all "the battle is not yours' ; it is the LORD'S" As for me I have placed this hope in Christ and I am very certain that victory lies ahead for me for I have attracted Jesus and His angels to fight my battles. Satan wants to stop the family of God and so he tries to stop my life with Melinda, but this is a battle already won in heaven! My prayer this morning is that we lift up the LORD our GOD more and more in fear, respect and honor; so that His bidding angels can see us in the process and with recognition act in our behalf, for they are about to transport our words of declarations along with our morning requests before the presence of the LORD for actions.

Today the love of God is moving in our directions as from everlasting to everlasting and securing us greatly in Jesus's name Amen! Be blessed for God favors you in Jesus's name Amen! Read Psalm103 and I release into your day peace in the name of Jesus, love and understanding. I bless your hands for greater breakthrough, I declared by the word of God (Jeremiah 29:11) your success; your peace your prosperity and your good end in Jesus's name Amen! I pray that as you go about your business the countenance of Jehovah God shines in your pathway so that favor goes before you. Today is your day of blessings; receive it in Jesus's name. My friends and family blessings upon you all in the name of Jesus Christ of Nazareth: The word of God wants you to know that " the boundary lines have fallen for you in pleasant places and surely God has a delightful inheritance for you" God has positioned your blessings for delivery stand still and see the power of God in your circumstances for in Jesus's name you shall prevail. Keep pushing and pressing for your line of blessings have been drawn by Jehovah God. Be glad and rejoice in Jesus's name.

Blessings for you (Numbers 6:34-24) May the Lord bless you and may He make His face to shine upon you and your family, I also pray the words of the scriptures that God be gracious unto you and lift up His countenance upon you and give you peace. Confess today that you are favored by God on account of His name upon your life. More so that the Holy Ghost shall be upon you in Jesus's name Amen! I speak peace into your day and declare healing and good health for you in Jesus's name. Friends and family some are thinking that I frequent this world of social media too often, but I am glad that God blessed this innovative apparatus for multiplicities of Groups with divers views and beliefs. For me I take it as an opportunity to preach every day and I know someone out there is blessed by this; and it has become my obligation in spreading the word of God via this media. Every now and then I achieved my photo via posting them on my wall, just in case friends and family out there seeking to connect with my person can view them, and more so when I am gone to be no more someone who seeks to connect with me in memory; would have a repository and a genre of details; as I now do with my late Brother Wellington O. Deline (my twin).

Sorry if you find me offensive! I am only doing what I am convicted to do and I enjoy it; only pray for my health and strength so that I am able to bless someone with the steadfast love of God which is new every morning. I want to share this scripture with you, 2 Samuel Chapter 2; you must sing the praises of those who offend you, love and rejoice for them and hold no malice. Always have a clear heart so that your inner man is gracefully calmed and then it shall surface upon the outer-man. God wants genuine services from everyone, and therefore rejoice with them that hate, pray for them that use you and always remain humble and attentive to the things of God. In this your blessings, your protections, your healing and your victories shall be sure. If this is you then you are walking with God, and as we Understand this; you are love so much by God and that daily.

He carries your burdens therefore no matter how heavy the load is; God is your Savior praise Him always for caring your load. GOD shall arise for you and He shall make your enemies scattered, they shall become foot stools. Know that Jehovah is your God who saves you even from the strong enemies. Shine where you are; be positioned and see your victories for God is your Salvation now; Stop! Look! Listen what the word of God says for you today in Jesus's name Amen! God shall be a shield around you and a Greater WALL OF PROTECTION. Cry aloud today, sound your trumpets God shall answer you from His Holy Hill, I don't know where you are located but where you are positioned; I am speaking into the atmosphere your deliverance from your strong enemies and blessings upon your life in Jesus's name Amen! I am speaking into the East Wind commanding your victory in the name of Jesus. O LORD by the POWERFUL MIGHT OF YOUR HOLY SPIRIT; let Your blessings be upon Your people in Jesus's name Amen! Be courageous, go forth God shall teach your hands to war and your fingers to fight, stand today in the name of Jesus, for the restored joy. The night is over and your day is now, come out of obscurity for before the eyes of the enemy Jesus is LORD TO THE GLORY OF GOD Almighty.

~Amos Spoke with Brother Ross~

Amos later asked Brother Ross what was getting into him; he replied the joy of the Lord and signs of my love, my live and peace with Melinda. I want you to pay close attention son. There are people who are watching your life for opportunities to out shine you, and every moment they get they would cease it to do justice for themselves, but THE APOSTLE PAUL said you have to keep doing what God has called you to do, and boast the most in your disappointing moments. Most about God delivering you from pains, boast about God's salvation for your life, and boast how you have overcome sicknesses, hatred and isolations. Remember God gives more graces to the humble, the fainted. Most of all God makes His strength perfect in your weakness. So if you are weak boast that God is bringing you through (II Corinthians 11:12).

Chapter 17

~Molly's Sister Joyceline crisis~

Mother Crawford ran as fast as she could, but was disappointed Joyceline testimony "May 12th will be a date forever engrained in my memory but in that same day the Lord put a song in my heart that gave me the strength I needed. She said, "There were dangers awaiting me destruction was sure to be, but thank God for Angels that were shielding and protecting and looking out for me "Thank You Lord". The devil had a plan to kill me, I know But God intercepted his plan and told the devil, no God blocked it He wouldn't let it be so "(Kurt Carr). Thank you and special blessings to ALL that reached out in their own way. It is truly appreciated and not unnoticed. God first, my husband my parents, siblings, family & friends made my ability to cope so much easier. There are blessings written in the stars for you. Joyceline's mother included these words, "In times like these we have as savior, His name is Jesus, the son of God; "King of kings, and Lord of lords". My child, God bless you and your husband for the strength and steadfast love you two have exhibited throughout this entire ordeal. You have proven that your Faith in God; is unshakable. After the rain, your sun will shine again. Love you!

Mother Crawford later said the preacher told her that if "Circumstances have caused you to feel abandoned; don't feel rejected". God has deep compassion for you, what you are going through; it is only for a moment for in God's will for you; is an everlasting kindness beyond your pains, increasingly the favor of God for you is with deep compassion. For the LORD your REDEEMER; He Jehovah has an unfailing love for you which cannot be shaken no matter what the circumstances are; therefore who ever attacks you shall surrender to you; no weapon formed against you shall prosper." I am weak today, and this event has taken the breath out of me, but I know that I am coming through, and this is my prayer "Lord lift me up to where I belong; on mountain tops way up out of the deep dark valley; for the Bible says Jesus loves us and has shielded me with favor! What a joy so divine; in knowing that around me there is an angel assigned to bear me in their hands when lest I dashed my feet against a stone. There were many tears of sorrows and yet there were; many hope for tomorrow and in the midst of them all; O LORD YOU kept me and I won't complain.

Joyceline Mother – Molly Sister Prays

This Day Lord I pray order my steps and deal with all that are around me visible and invisible for my good; let blessings fall upon me; for my hurt; protect me. Open my eyes Lord that I may see; I know that there is a star over the head of my child Joyceline. It is not a common thing when the wicked one distresses God's children. Joyceline experienced a terrible moment in her life; she had a missed carriage; lost her first born child and yet hangs unto her faith. It is devastating; an experience which no family should have to go through; it is an ordeal filled with frustrations and bewilderment. Joyceline father cried, his wife cried, it was a great anticipated time in their lives, but that enemy of progress; intruded and stole their joy. Joyceline mother blesses her daughter "Lord I cover my child in your name and I protect her in your Name; the weapons of the enemy shall no longer come near her dwelling and I pray that your peace shall always rule her heart; in Jesus name"

Mother Crawford Response

It is always the case while you are out; work to mold and shape lives; something is always lurking behind closed doors, to impede progress. In as much as I would love to see the world at peace; I still cannot carry the whole world on my shoulders.

I struggled with the acceptance of my granddaughter's ordeal, but my faith kept me as it did for Joyceline. My greatest desire now; is to see Fillmore and Starr get married, Bobby Ross and Melinda Yates meet and follow their hearts and get marry. I was wondering about Melinda and Bobby; expressing thoughts to Melinda and then all of a sudden; my granddaughter was going through pains and suffering miscarriage. I visited her after the ordeal and assured her that God is able. I also thought about Melinda; more in regards to her vow which she made to God Almighty. I visited Mr. Franklin Yates, and the purpose of my visit was to ascertain his approval in the affairs of his daughter's choice for nunnery. As I approached the home of Franklin Yates; a feeling came upon me that I should search the scriptures in regards to a father's approval of his daughter's vows while she lives under with him. I was amazed to find out that Franklin always supported his daughter in everything, which she desired, but would then argue with his wife about her position of the events or incidence. Franklin wanted grandchildren as he told his wife but had no inclination on the bases of confronting Melinda.

Mrs. Yates opened the door for Mother Crawford and welcomed her into the house. She quickly offered to Mother Crawford tea and some homemade biscuits. Mother Crawford accepted the jester and enjoyed that down home cooking. As they sat poignantly; Mother Crawford asked if it was okay to pray before telling the purpose of her visit. They agreed and the mother prayed the prayer of faith and everyone said Amen!

You know at times we don't understand how things work, but they just work themselves out to the glory of God Almighty. Mrs. Yates showing concerns for the gentle Missionary; asked about the loss, Molly's sister had a miscarriage; it broke the heart of Mother Crawford, she had so many plans for that baby, but it wasn't the time the little man went back to be with God Almighty. You know when a young woman struggles dearly and finally gets an answer, but suffers loss before the actual time.

It can be heart breaking, with great hurts and disappointment. I have seen too many young women; struggling to experience this heavenly bliss and when it does the enemy comes and steals away this joy. No one ever forgets this. Mrs. Crawford trusted in God and His providence, but she was overwhelmed with the hurt. All she could do was cried for her child, and hoped that things work themselves out again. There is nothing like having a child of your child and there is no experience like seeing the bliss on the face of a daughter who successfully give birth; after all of the pains now she is with the fruit of her labor and the pride of her husband. This experience was a motivating factor for Mother Crawford; it encouraged her to speak with the parents of Melinda, and this brought her directly to the point.

Mother Crawford meeting at the Yates:

Franklyn I have a question to ask you, and I want you to be keen with me! Mr. frankly Yates responded; Mother Crawford what is the matter; I mean I heard about the loss of your grandchild, but what has that to do with me? Frankly! Frankly; the loss of the child is not in question here, Sir it hurt me, it broke my heart, it made me bitter not at God but at the spiritual enemy. I boasted about the coming of the child too early. I was sure that everything was sealed and that my victory was sure and so I went public and expressed my joy. I spoke of my future joy and it was heard by the enemy. To make me doubt my faith; my family was spiritually attacked. I from that experience have relegated to praising God in secret and keeping my joys to myself.

I need to have this bliss in my life and so I am claiming this peace and joy for my family and myself. Frankly back to the reason why I am here; and the purpose of my visit, is about Melinda and Bobby Ross. These children are meant to be together. I understand the will of the heart and the decisions made from the heart. I know that from early on Melinda decided to become a Nun, and you knew that you and your wife were not happy with the situation, but you went along because you thought it was a means to an end. Immediately Mr. Yates responded; Mother Crawford who sent you here and what is your mission? Did Bobby request that you speak with me? Melinda is a Nun and an ordained woman of God. There is nothing anyone can do about that she has made a vow. Hold it right there Mr. Yates I understand your point and very well she is an ordained Minister, but have you ask her about her desire to be a mother or about her love for bobby Ross. Listen we cannot no longer live in pretense of our inner heart desires. God Almighty has placed in every man and woman the reasons to become parents and in love and support of the family unit.

Only people have chosen not to on account of their preferences; however it was not intended to be this way. A man must love a woman and a woman must love a man without constraints. Do you have a desire of becoming a grandparent, and seeing the extension of your life through your grandchildren? Melinda thought she wanted the life which she is now living, but never thought God had a different plan for her.

Look at you and your family; you are wonderfully placed in society and blessed with many blessings in living as good Christians. Why cannot Melinda live the life as you do; happy parents and loving one another and still committed to your faith. Now here is my point; honestly did you with your whole heart approved of your daughters' decision; or did you just went along because it made her happy?

Franklyn quickly said; Mother Crawford I am inclined to believe that God have sent you here; my spirit has been troubled a great deal. My daughter is a beautiful young woman and I would love to see her offspring. I have thought about this over and over again. This situation plays in my head like a mantra. What would have been the real choice of Melinda; had I suggested other means? I know she loved Bobby Ross, but I thought she should follow her own heart. Missionary Crawford; I have thought about my life and that of my wife in continuance through our blessed daughter.

Certainly I was not in support of her becoming a Nun but I supported only her choice. Well said Frankly Yates. Your daughter is struggling with her inner feelings, and they are out of control. She is in love with a man and she calls him every day of the week. I was praying and Molly requested that I get involve and I did. You see Franklyn vows are broken every day. If a young woman decides to fall in love and become a mother; she is still in the will of God. if Melinda leaves the convent; she would still be a devoted Christian. She has to fulfilled he desire and become complete as it has been intended for her. Mother Crawford how can this be? How can she become a wife when she has already dedicated her life to Nunnery? Brother Yates I remember conducting a research on spiritual vows and the vows made by a young woman living in the home of her father.

> Numbers Chapter 30:1-2 did say "Moses said to the heads of the tribes of Israel: "This is what the Lord commands: 2 When a man makes a vow to the Lord or takes an oath to obligate himself by a pledge, he must not break his word but must do everything he said."

Yes brother; Yates these were the words of God given to Moses for the children of Israel, and they also apply today as it was then; however as according to same scripture it also stated

> 3 When a young woman still living in her father's household makes a vow to the Lord or obligates herself by a pledge 4 and her father hears about her vow or pledge but says nothing to her, then all her vows and every pledge by which she obligated herself will stand. 5 But if her father forbids her when he hears about it, none of her vows or the pledges by which she obligated herself will stand; the Lord will release her because her father has forbidden her (Numbers 30:3-5).

~Mother Crawford's insights~

If we underscored the wellness of nunnery; it would be easy to conclude that the sacrifice is beautiful, and that good godly men and women can come to such a decision of life time celibacy. People are wired this way for such a life. Others who are not wired this way cannot be cornered into acceptance of this life style when they would later look back and wonder "What things would be like if I get married?" Could I still love God and fellowship sincerely in relationship with Him as when I am celibate? Mr. Yates it is obvious that as a catholic believer, such tradition would come easy, and followed with intense psychological backlash at the choice to remaining super spiritual in pretense of the God given emotion in having the ability to love another human person. Most man made rules have caused religious people to control the independence of individuals seeking to be wholesome in approach to godliness and faith. Mr. Yates many of these rules are actually affronts to God's designed for humanity.

Now tell me Yates I want to know if over times; did you in your heart; objected to Melinda becoming a Catholic Nun? Yes mother Crawford; Melinda is a very wonderful child and she is so sweet, didn't want to put her down and oppose her desires, and I therefore went along. Her mother from day one of Melinda's journey towards the convent was saddened by this. I struggled with the idea and kept quiet. I forbid her behind closed doors; her mother and I were one on the idea but I said nothing, only one time which I can recollect that I asked her Melinda as to her conviction. I even spoke to her about Bobby Ross, I commented on their closeness but she quickly changed the topic and moved into a different direction. On another occasion; she and Bobby went out to the movie and I was glad that she was beginning to find attraction, but she ignored me. All this is to say I love my daughter and would someday want to be a grandfather. Well said Mr. Yates and as according to scriptures; Melinda has nothing to worry about if she wants to recant her vow, and do the right thing provided it is her soul desire. Thanks Franklyn this has positioned us right where we all should be, and that is see Melinda becomes the wife of Bobby Ross.

You see Yates my mission here is not over until we established this matter on the findings of scriptures. I heard you say all of the right things and what you intended, but are you feelings still the same? Yes they are now more than ever; I want my daughter to get marry and I need to see my grandchildren as well. This religion and religious mantra are just too controlling for me. Why cannot Melinda become a good mother and a good and committed Catholic Missionary? All of these qualities are within her and God Almighty has sanctioned her this way; why some man must control and enforce celibacy on the guise of adherence and true holiness to the faith. Moses was a committed believer who believed in God so much that God placed him in the cleft of the rock and he Moses was the only living Prophet who saw the back of God as He passed by. Now tell me why didn't Moses' relationship with his wife hinder his intense and holy relationship with God? Abraham was another great forerunner of the faith; he loved God to the point that God called him (Abraham) His friend. Abraham had his relationships and God blessed him with sons; why didn't God exclude him Abraham from the annals of faith. Today Abraham name is archived in the hall of faith (Hebrews Chapter 11)! Come on folks I think this is a travesty, and it is a darn dirty shame that one man who isn't our Lord and Savior Jesus Christ would change the course of history in disguise for material gained. Clerical Celibacy does make a man or a woman any more Holier; than neither Moses nor Abraham. If it is a life time commitment to fulfilling an end as orchestrated by man's ideology; it is then only disruptive to the plan of God. Marriage is the plan of God; God caused this institution into being and also He sanctioned the purpose of this plan; for He God sat the stage for this natural heritage of human genesis.

Chapter 18

Starr and Fillmore interrupted

Aunty Crawford good to see you, I am so happy that you are here. Hello Mr. Yates and mother Yates. What a surprise! Aunty Crawford I just want to inform you that I am in love. I am a Christian woman, saved and engaged to be married to this young and handsome lawyer. My life has changed and I have given up the old and sophisticated me to find God and fall in love. Oh Aunty just a little gossip; what is about what Starr; I guess the same reason why you are over here with the Yates. Mrs. Crawford laughed and said to Starr come over here child! You know prayers really change things. I heard about your transformation and the love for God. Molly told me about this joy of yours. I am elated. I just spoke with the Yates and we are all in agreement that Melinda's answered the call to the convent was a rushed situation. She is however a committed Nun, but she is not satisfied. She is in love and I mean deeply in love with Bobby Ross. We however got the understanding that the scripture allows Melinda the opportunity to recant her vow to the Nunnery. Starr responded; really and how? You see Starr I got the revelation through the scriptures that if the father of Melinda opposed his daughters vow while living under his roof; that vow can be broken. Melinda shall be made aware soon. Any way I am on my way to Church.

At Church Mrs. Crawford's Pastor Spoke

Chosen by God

When God chooses you for service, He makes you ready by the anointing of His Holy Ghost. He makes you a changed person. He places you in position of authority and power thus equipping you for the task ahead. He instructs your heart to understand with great compassion. Troublemakers might not approve of you; in their hearts they are the better ones, but God choose you to show forth His praises. Read 1 Samuel 10. God's servants are not perfect but God has changed them, He calls them His anointed ones. People only understand that you have been chosen by God to serve, only understand your place in the service of God. One Lord! On Faith! One Baptism! One Kingdom in every man! Christians the kingdom of God is within you. You have been chosen as habitations for the Kingdom of God (Luke 17:21). For the Kingdom of God is within you. What is in your heart? God knows and the more compassionate you are the more of the glory of God you shall see.

The Glory of Jesus shines brighter and brighter. For you are a chosen vessel; and everyone God chooses to service; he God makes them ready. You all know Bobby Ross who attended services here sometimes ago. He is really a chosen vessel of Go showing forth the praises of God in a foreign land. I have heard that lives are been changed and reunited with full commitment to the faith and life. Anyone when fully convicted by the Holy Spirit; relies on God for the life's fulfillment and completeness. Bobby' faith has taken him to Africa, and not only that but love, you all know the kind of love which makes a man's heart rate to move a little faster once he finds the right soul mate. I mean the real help meet. Bobby found that in Melinda Yates who is now a Nun at the Convent.

This man really believes that God is able to do the impossible. You know I am inclined to believe the same for him as well. I know that nothing is impossible with God; however, as selfish as it might be; our own Mother Crawford is working to see that Bobby's dream comes true. Therefore as selfish as it might sound; I need you all to pray with me for the will of God to be met for His chosen vessel in that of Bobby Ross our missionary to Liberia west Arica. Amen! We cannot be taken by circumstances, but instead we must have a day of Increase.

Increase is the word for the day!

Genesis 13:15 God told Abraham to lift up His eyes and see as far he could northward, Southward, eastward and westward that he would be blessed. My friends we have to be honorable and committed to God and He shall reward us. Sometimes life, people and situations try to limit you to a situation of seclusion and marginalization, but pray for increase. Don't let past experiences limit you they are done, don't let people coin you into their vision, it is theirs'. Don't let your current conditions limit you. Pray for increase. Jabez in I Chronicles 4:9-10 saw his condition even his own name called him painful and he should have been subjected to it, but he prayed so that God could change him and enlarge his territory. God can change your positions my friends. He can make a difference for you. Pray so that your conditions are changed within your positions.

In the name of Jesus Christ of Nazareth; we can demand the most difficult things and go after them, because God specializes in transforming the impossible to greater possibilities. Seek the difficult things and trust in God always. Abraham trusted in God and he was blessed. Jabez looked beyond his position and place in life and asked for increase and God enlarged his territory. God is able pray for increase everyone. King of Israel; King David said "The LORD has heard my cry for mercy; The LORD accepts my prayer. All my enemies will be ashamed and dismayed; they will turn back in sudden disgrace" Maybe something strange is happening to you and you don't understand why? Things are not as usual as they used to have been, and you are anxious about the situation.

God wants you to know that whatever is the bad; it and the intended purpose shall fail. You have the power (Mark 16:17) use it. Bind, break and cast down those forces of darkness. Look unto Jesus Christ of Nazareth. You are under attack; call on the Name of the Lord and He shall rescue today, now in Jesus's name Amen! (Numbers 10:9) Blast your trumpets; God wants to hear you calling Him. Yes today; there shall be sudden shamed persons or invisible agents; for you shall shine in Jesus's name Amen! This is the day to pray for those who give you the most trouble in the natural; bless them and don't curse them lift them up in the name of Jesus Christ of Nazareth. Pray for them that God shall forgive them, love them in Jesus name (Matthew 5:44) Jesus's reason for this is "that you may be sons of your father in heaven (Matthew 5:45)". FB Christians don't let no man stop you from going to heaven. Be Christ like. Paul said for in so doing; ye shall heap coals of fire upon their heads. It is a great thing to be free in the spirit. Therefore let everything go and treat everyone with respect, don't judge for God is in control. Love you and stay with God in Jesus's name Amen!

△ △ △

Back in Africa Amos thoughts to Bobby;

Confess your faith −deliverance~

Say I am I delivered from the power of darkness and adopted into the kingdom of God; my assigned Portion. Everything about you and everything about me have been assigned. Blessings have been assigned; struggles and difficult times have been assigned. God's map for you; are in God's time. Brother Ross I am getting you ready for a time of your life. David said "Lord you have assigned me my portion and my cup; You have made my lot secured". Christians our portions are assigned and aligned in God's timing. Solomon understood this and said, "There is a time for everything, and a season for every activity under the heaven". The steps of the righteous are ordered by God; our times are ordered by God. You might think it strange to wait on God, but wait and trust in God for your appointed time and assigned Portion. You see our waiting moments are also geared towards maturations and fulfillments of God's purposes within time. As spiritual beings residing in the flesh; there are pitfalls along the way, and waiting on God brings us; into a position allotted towards destiny.

Therefore, no matter the wait; socially we gained the socializing garth towards God's perfect plan for us. God's Son; Jesus Christ has given you power therefore say; (Col.1:13) I tread upon serpents and scorpions and over the power of the enemy, and nothing shall by any means hurt me (Luke 10:19). I am covered by the Blood of Jesus Christ of Nazareth and protected by the angels. I am covered by the Shadows of God Almighty. I trust in His name; some trust in horses, some trust in chariots, but I trust in the name of the LORD the maker of heaven and the earth. I am a child of God redeemed by the Blood of His son Jesus Christ (Hebrews 9). Therefore no weapon formed against me shall prosper, I shall condemn in Jesus's name Amen! Have a blessed day Brother Ross! Amos just minute please; what is the meaning of this? Sir it is to have you covered and ready for your victory in Jesus' name. It is around the corner. Have you not heard an entire congregation's Pastor and Missionary are praying for you? Sir when the children of God come together in unity; it moves God. Brother Ross; the good which you are doing over here, blessing the lives of many, reuniting families together, defeating the hands of the enemy and pointing an entire community to find value within themselves.

My big Brother a man of your caliber is protected and elevated by God. Bobby This is the day to pray for those who give you the most trouble in the natural; bless them and don't curse them lift them up in the name of Jesus Christ of Nazareth. Pray for them that God shall forgive them, love them in Jesus name (Matthew 5:44) Jesus's reason for this is "that you may be sons of your father in heaven (Matthew 5:45)". My brother; don't let any man stop you from going to heaven. Be Christ like.

Paul said for in so doing; ye shall heap coals of fire upon their heads. It is a great thing to be free in the spirit. Therefore let everything go and treat everyone with respect, don't judge for God is in control. Love you and stay with God in Jesus's name. Amos know this; that the truth sets free "God's truth" the only truth, which sets free. "Whom the SON sets free; is free indeed" I am so glad that Jesus lifted me from eternal damnation and degradation. Free from political, social and spiritual derailment. Ideally, this is my redemption and I have no reservation about God's truth and that which has lifted me. Praise God in Jesus's name; there are no residual links to a continuous attachment for derailing the peaceful you and I. I have always known that nothing is impossible with God. Our GOD understands what you are going through right now, He sees your heart, and is about to make your darkness light, and the high places He shall bring down!

David said "The LORD is righteous, He loves justice; upright men shall see His face". Walk with God this day and He shall see you through; for you shall see His face. The Apostle Peter said "Cast all of your cares upon the Lord for He cares for you" Friends today don't rush nothing, anxiety must not be a tool of the enemy in your day. Be self-controlled and alert; Jesus Christ of Nazareth is with you for your protection. His angels are watching over you. Keep your relationships in God's control. We have been praying that God grants you the desire of your heart. We have all come to reasoned by faith that your wife shall be Melinda. We have understanding that Melinda's entry into Sisterhood was a mistake on her part. It was not her calling or else she would not look back. Bobby yes Melinda is a wonderful person, but that did not means she was called to nunnery. She was called to be you wife and the meeting of the both of you; were by not mistakes. God had everything in His designed for your lives. Bobby there is something I considered the preliminary you!

Preliminary you!

The preliminary you is the inner person who is feeling his own way within regular grace or the common grace of God whereby all man is given time and chances to survive; (Ecclesiastes 9:11) meaning being in the right place at the right time. Under God's influences over our lives we are permitted to move from stages of graces to greater levels, and this is based upon how well a person draws closer to God. When a person draws closer to God in prayer and fasting; that individual moves from spiritual maturity levels in relationship and dependence upon the creator for greater works, rewards and benefits. Brother Ross you have come to this place with God. You are no longer at the level of common grace of

God where by you only rely on the forgivingness of sins, but you have moved on to maturity level 2 Acceptance of God. Bobby God has accepted the works of your hands and the many paths you have laid for the benefits of many. You are now in the accepted relationship with God. You have drawn closer to God and this relationship has brought God closer to you (Romans 5). You have also reached a level 3 grace in the presence of God "*If they obey and serve him, they will spend the rest of their days in prosperity and their years in contentment (Job 36:11)."* Bobby God relates to you well when you are consistently and currently at this level and always in His presence. It is recorded in the Holy Scriptures "4 One thing have I desired of the Lord, that will I seek after; that I may dwell in the house of the Lord all the days of my life, to behold the beauty of the Lord, and to enquire in his temple (Psalm 27:4)".

My Brother once you are at this point in relationship with God; nothing can hinder your desires nor stand in the way of your destiny. God has enabled you for a time such as this. You are experiencing the maturity level of what is known to be level 4 Spiritual enablement; God's eyes locate us and place us into services for fulfilling a particular good for His good will pleasure. Consequently, to this kind of grace Bobby; you are here in Africa fulfilling God's answers to the many prayers of the many families who without Divine intervention through your work of sacrifices would have ordinarily drifted apart; on accounts of satanic influences through resentments and disdained. God heard the cries of those families and today they have received value added principles to make them better; Bobby this is the greater work Jesus spoke of in the Holy Scriptures:

> "*Truly, truly, I say to you, he who believes in Me, the works that I do, he will do also; and greater works than these he will do; because I go to the Father. 13"Whatever you ask in My name, that will I do, so that the Father may be glorified in the Son (St. John 14:11-13).*

God has enabled you and has blessed the works of your hands. We can also thank God for His freedom, which He has given unto us through His son Jesus Christ. We can all feel free and delivered once we have a closer relationship with God., and this is a maturity level birth in the Holy Spirit; for whom the Son of God sets free is indeed free **(John 8:36) declares.** Walking with God brings a person into greater **Freedom a level 5 maturity** and at this level of grace maturity in the Lord; we can feel free to make all desires and requests known unto the Lord, and by this expect positive answers from the Kingdom of God. Bobby God is not a man that He should lie; whatever God promised that shall He do (Numbers 23:19).

Brother Ross as I have seen from all of the sessions and heard the cries of many of your clients; I saw that most and if not all were missing a part of God's grace. Sir being complete in the Lord is a greater desire of all those who walk upright and are called according to the purpose of God. Sir I find you at level **6** spiritual maturity and in my cleared vision, it is a greater yearning of yours. God saw that Adam was created well but lacked completion. He knew that the responsibilities given to Adam was vast; and thus created a help meet for Adam. Sir when God provides you the necessary help meet He makes not mistakes. So in all of our struggles and torments with life's disappointments'; we can find solace in God's manifold graces for us. Brother Ross; He who begun a good work in you shall perform it to completion. Sir you shall be fulfilled in the spirit, socially, and psychosocially within your soul. This is where God's Amazing love is greatly expressed within the genre of truthful

~Completion and God's Divine will ~

Completion. I know by His grace this shall be achieved in the blessed Name of our Lord and Savior Jesus Christ of Nazareth. Brother Ross it is one thing living under God's permissive will. God permissive will is that God permit us to go on our own volitions, without His guidance and only our desires. We can accomplish and feel it is God's doing, but we are not protected for the guided level successes. The guided level successes are those maturity levels in which every matured believer acknowledges God for every purpose or thing of a task for accomplishment and realizations of the projective desire. This control is the reflection of God's directives in placing His children into providence divinely structured for the guided results. The Divine will of God for our lives are those adherences, which are adhered to with expectations from God. For example God told the children of Israel (Deuteronomy 28:1-14) that if they followed Him and adhered to His ways for them; then all the blessings in the book shall overtake them and they shall be blessed, in cities, fields, in kinds and in time. The only requirement was for that they (Israel) harken or adhered to His ways. In God's Divine will you are blessed in territories and where ever you are located you are to lift up the name of Jehovah God and bless the area for in so doing; when the location prosper; you shall also prospered.

Consequently, your cities shall be bless, you shall experience increased possessions and long lives and that is increasing in time. Bobby Melinda walked according to feelings and projected her desires as that of God. It was a wonderful thing for Melinda and it represented her faithfulness, but she interfered with

God's plans. Sir your meeting Melinda was in God's divine plans for the both of you, however what we have now has to be revisited and undone. In my honest opinion no convicted woman who has vowed and pledged an oath; would be after you as she is. I am of the conviction that she rushed the situation and not being careful; she is in God's permissive will. God shall still approve of her and the beauty of it all; two people of faith shall find greater completion in God Almighty.

~Bobby tells Amos of His gratefulness~

O magnify the Lord with me, and come let us exalt His Name together. I will blessed the Lord at all times and His praises shall continually be in my mouth. O taste and see that the Lord is good; for He has given His angels charge to watch over me. I was young and now I am old, and I have never seen the righteous forsaken nor his seed begging bread. God is King of kings, He is LORD of lords. I am so grateful that He brought me from a mighty long way, and the song says "He took my burden in the heat of the day and I know that God shall make a way" Father God what shall I give unto You for all the benefits; which You have bestowed upon me. I am so gratefully grateful; that through many danger toils and snares; your grace brought me through. I escaped and shall escape all the enemy's traps (Psalm 124:7). I am thankful in Jesus's name Amen. Glory! Glory to God almighty;

I got happy reading Luke 17 about sin, Faith and Duty. I understood that; I have to be on duty believing in the promises of the Father, and serve in every capacity because it is my duty, without complaints (Luke 17:5-10). What made me happy! Glory to God Almighty; was that because of my faithfulness in performing my duties not with eye services; oh yes! When the Master returns; He shall recline me at the table, be please with my work and feed me, but if men could only see that God is pleased with us; when we are faithful to Him in serving Him. Read (Luke 12:35-38) God shall recline you at the table and serve you and your desires in Him. God shall provide you the menu. Amos mountains in our lives have to be spoken to; therefore (Matthew 17:20) Speak to your problems and don't let them trouble you. They must go for you are a purchased possession of God (Eph.1). The power is in you; the Word of Faith.

It is in your heart (Romans 10:8). Tell the mountain or mountains they must come down in the name of Jesus Christ of Nazareth. Say to yourself; today in the name of Jesus, I rebuke darkness, sickness, I rebuke loneliness, I am in the presence of the Lord God Almighty and my life is filled with joy. The word of

God declared that in the presence of the Lord there is the fullness of joy. Get your joy, get your peace and send up some praise for this mountain is coming down in Jesus's name Amen! Call on Jesus for the difficult problems; He wants to hear from you to perform your request (Jeremiah 1:12)"God watches over His words to perform them". To sealed this "if you have faith as the size of a mustard seed; you can say to this mountain move". Tell them to move in Jesus's name. We are saved by Grace; through faith in Jesus Christ of Nazareth by whom this building of mine is shaped and framed according to His good will pleasure. I am a purchased possession of God and I am being built together into a dwelling place for God by the Spirit. And this means that God is working on this building (Ephesians 2:20-22). Oh Amos; ow Great "IS" GOD in your life?

IS represents the third person singular attribute. The description of a personal connect between a noun and the exact purpose. King David in all his splendor said "Oh magnify the LORD with me" Come and let us exalt His Name together " He also said that God is a Careful CREATOR! My friends I want to start telling about God's GREATNESS; I am leaving room for you..... Wow my God, Jehovah IS wonderful, He IS my peace! IN darkness; HE is my light! HE also IS my BRIDGE; over troubled waters; HE IS my DEFENSE, HE IS my Great HOPE, glory to HIS matchless NAME; my strong TOWER; for there is nothing that can be compared to HIM. My friends God IS so WONDERFUL AND AWESOME; my delight IS HE; FAVOR is always settled for His words are sure "FOREVER OH LORD THOU WORDS IS settled" in Heaven THEY are settled! In the earth they are settled.This morning realize Who and What He IS to you and magnify His doings and His favor shall increase for your benefits and sustainable victory. Walk in Jesus's name Amen! I sealed this with (Jeremiah 29:11) God's good thoughts for you!

~Acknowledge God!~

God wants us to acknowledge Him. It really does not matter what situation you might find yourselves; be it up, or down, rich or poor, well or sick, happy or sad, righteous or unrighteous; God wants to be acknowledged in every situation by you. My friends God wants to meet you where you are; He wants to be a part of your situations! It does not matter if you were rejected or accepted; God wants you to acknowledge Him. Hosea 6:2-6; tells us that no matter what the changes, trials and gloomy moments are; God comes as soon as we acknowledge Him. Recognize God in your day "for I desire mercy, and not sacrifice, and acknowledgement of God rather than burnt offerings "(Hosea 6:6). Therefore, for starters; lift up your hands and praise God for all His wonderful works in your life. After all you are the praise of God's glory and His purchased possession. (Ephesians 1) Amen in Jesus's name.

You see those of you out there God knows your trouble, God knows why you are feeling the way you do; right now rid yourself of self- pity, stop complaining and use the name of Jesus. Tell the awkward feeling to step aside for you are covered by the Blood of Jesus. In Jesus's name declare that every deal with Satan is broken; known and unknown can no longer steal your day joy, bad spirits must leave now; so that the Holy Ghost can come. Fill your day with (Psalm 34:4) everything shall line up for you. Sing songs of Zion and make melodies in your hearts. Command the devil in the name of Jesus to lay down his weapon and flee, tell him to flee for God through His son Jesus has given you authority over the enemy(Mark 16:17-19). Exalt the name of Jesus Christ of Nazareth and declare that the weapons of the wicked one are powerless; Jesus has set you free and whom the SON sets free is free indeed. God grace and Mercy are with you this morning and they are with you throughout the day. Keep Jesus in your heart and your deliverance is complete in Jesus's name

~Bobby Ross Answered back

Destroying the works of the devil~

My friends don't think it strange; when struggles in your lives intensify, when projects and other related matters for success seemed almost not possible. Know this that the more you pray; the more Satan attacks, but don't give up or give in you are under attack but JESUS is with you and you shall overcome.(I John 3:8) "Jesus came to destroy the works of the devil". Therefore the more you draw closer to God the more the forces of Satan intensify. Apply to your life constantly and consistently these words of King David "every morning I will put to silence all the wicked in the land, I will cut off every evildoers from the city of the Lord " Psalm 101:8. My friends we have to pray for breakthrough; our weapons to victory are not carnal, but are mighty through God to the pulling down of Strongholds. So when it is tougher; you are in battle, therefore pray for the battle; it is not yours it is the LORD'S; don't be amazed you shall sing a new song in Jesus's name Amen! "Thank God I made it". Circumstances in the world are of great concern: I said I would keep quiet, but I cannot

All of these people are gone mad, and are extremely out of control. Jesus never hated sinners, but was determined that sinners came to repentance. Some of these assumptions and surmising around spiritual faith and its flexibility are in total disarray to the stern hold for moral responsibilities. Are we saying that God's standard for morality is subject to change and acceptance; by will of the majority? My young brother is this an issue and merit based legality; which is totally off base, and the fact remains; sin is sin and living for the rest of one's life in sin; is out of God's desire for humanity. The Bible states "...8But do not let this one fact escape your notice, beloved, that with the Lord one day is like a thousand years, and a thousand years like one day. 9The Lord is not slow about His promise, as some count slowness, but is patient toward you, not wishing for any to perish but for all to come to repentance (2 Peter 3:9). If people blatantly refused to rid themselves of sin and follow a normal life; come to God for renewal from the old ways; God shall accept them. If they do not do such; then by all means there is hell fire! Now how can we change this true of the gospel for the lie for accommodating satanic kingdom.

The soul that sins; and do not repent until death comes; that soul shall die in hell, and if a man sins and confesses his faults; God is faithful and just to forgive everyone and cleanse them from unrighteousness. The soul, which does not accept responsibilities for its actions and thus make it fashionable by legal means shall die as well. Majority rule is not baseline for establishing equity on the base of spiritual morality; it is only an affront to what is proper and just. Christian Believers live in a world control by the Spiritual standards govern; by the Holy Scriptures. Those who does not transformed, conformed are by themselves making a choice; Christian do not relegate to this but instead; lives by example as according to the standard of faith.

Paul Before the Areopagus Acts 17:29-31

...29"Being then the children of God, we ought not to think that the Divine Nature is like gold or silver or stone, an image formed by the art and thought of man. 30"Therefore having overlooked the times of ignorance, God is now declaring to men that all people everywhere should repent, 31because He has fixed a day in which He will judge the world in righteousness through a Man whom He has appointed, having furnished proof to all men by raising Him from the dead."

Something is wrong with the people, the political system, the judicial system, educational system and the moral fabric of societies all over the world. Christian must live in this world as we sojourn! Give God the praise and convert, transform; get conformed by choice and not peer influence, and when you do the light of God shall make a difference for you. I needed to understand this that "From a child thou has known the Holy scriptures; which are able to make thee wise unto salvation; through faith in Christ Jesus" (2 Timothy 3:15)

Our choice of serving God is a blessing; which our parents saw and molded us to this end. It is the greatest choice of life made wisely, and I don't regret it at all; for accepting the advice of my parents and grandmother "follow Jesus; make Him your ruler and your life would be better" Just look at yourselves today and see where God has brought you from. You are better off today than you were 20 years ago. Oh when I only think of the love of Jesus and all He (God) has done for me; where He has brought me from down through the years to my current position; it makes me cry, dance and gratefully grateful for God's grace. Thank God for the choice made on account of knowing the Holy Scriptures - it made me wise in Jesus's name Amen! Love you all! Bobby I 3 John

I pray that all goes well with you and that God keeps you in the best of health. John talks about faithfulness to the truth. You see Jesus said it is useless to be rich with this world's goods and not rich in God. we are the riches people on earth because we are rich towards God. (Luke 12:13-21). If God is always treasured in your hearts; searching for inner peace would be found always on the inside of you. (LUKE 12:34) "for where your treasure is; there you heart will be also" keep God within and stay well in Jesus's name. You have done well over here in Africa and God wants you to be healed 3 John 2 ; God wants you to be in good health even as your soul prosper. If sickness is up against you; step in the name of Jesus Christ of Nazareth and command that your conditions are healed, blood pressure comes down, cholesterol is coming down; blood sugar under control in Jesus's name. Refuse and reject the weapon of sickness; in the name of Jesus Christ of Nazareth by whose stripes you are healed. May the LORD bless your bread and water and take sickness away (Exodus 23:25) from you in the name of Jesus Christ of Nazareth; Amen! I pray that your circulatory system improves in Jesus's name, I pray that the nerve pains subside in Jesus's name; I pray that your days for hospital visits be few and by the power of God only scheduled. I pray that the LIGHT OF GOD meets you right now for healing you in Jesus's name Amen! God is in control be blessed in Jesus's name. Bobby you can ease the storms as you have done for us.

~Easing the storm~

"Win-Win"
Matthew 18:16-18
Searching for perfections; searching for who is right in a group; without assessing the problems leads us to the bad sides of towns and cross roads; the end result is only a sets up for: "Winners - & - Losers". The Children of God

find themselves in a "Win-Win" situation, and by the love of God through the power of godly reconciliations and spiritual agreement, we can all win and become partners and not opponents in the things of God. For there is only one faith; one hope, not many hopes and different faith. There is only One God Jehovah God who loves us all. If your brother offends you, the bible made it clear that you find common grounds by having a good referee; like your Pastor, an Elder or someone who is impartial in the Lord. Carefully (I Corinthians 13: 4-7) can become alive and active if you are truly born again. God is able to ease the storms in every situation. There is nothing so intricate, which God cannot do. Of all the chaos, which we have encountered as people; God has found a way to resolve them and bring about ease into troubled moments. We can always agree one with another Amos in prayers for easing the confusions, which bring about chaos.

We can offer someone needs to know this: wickedness has tracked you down but cannot touch you, it has trapped you, but cannot capture you; before you are awaken; God's Holy angels exposed their plans. God shall rise up in your favor to confront them, they shall be confused and turn their backs to you, and by no means can darkness hurt you for you are in the light and path of God Almighty. Today the presence of God is even more with you to guide you. I sealed it with these words; the written word " And I in righteousness I will see your (God's) face; when I awake I will be satisfied with seeing your (God's) likeness (Psalm 17). In chaos you can lift up your hands and say: O LORD when I think of your goodness and all YOUR benefits towards me; I just want to dance and dance all morning!

For in your presence is the fullness of joy. My soul is overwhelmed in your presence; I want to lose it all; just praising you for my tough times, my sad times, my weak time, my deliverance from sin and shame, and most of all; overcoming the strong enemies. Father God I am so grateful; I have the understanding that apart from you I am nothing; therefore I humble myself always; just to be in Your presence. Lord you are worthy; O LORD of all the praises in earth and heaven above. Amos I was Pondering; and I had to speak into your soul this morning so that you do well; shame the enemy and put your energy into planting the truth of God into your heart for it is God's will that you silenced the ignorance of the foolish man. Anger and assumptions consume the very elect be mindful we cannot go to hell on anyone's account. Be steadfast put your hope in God. I am simple and if my simplicity vex you oh well; God is love, lift Him up stop wasting your time. Reach for the best as you know it to be. God is good and all the times He is good.

△ △ △

~These Are the last Day Amos~

Your focus has to always be on the things of God because, These are the last days and we are living in prophetic times (II Timothy 3:1-4) when the truth shall become lies and righteousness is consider wrong. These are times when the opposites have the appearance of the actual. But Jesus said, "Take heed that you be not deceived by false teachings and doctrines (Matthew 24)." (I Peter 1:13) said, "Therefore prepare your minds for action; be self-controlled, set your hope fully on the grace to be given you when Jesus Christ is revealed" we cannot live in ignorance and fear; just desire God the most and He shall load you with benefits. In this age apply Philippians 4:8 " Finally my brothers whatever is true, whatever is noble, whatever is right, whatever is pure, whatever is lovely, whatever is admirable - if anything is excellent or praiseworthy- think about such things."

May your day be blessed in Jesus's name. You see son, We don't need to set ourselves on fire nor do we need to be surprised; for the Word declared that these are the last days, and perilous times shall come when pleasure lovers shall be more and lovers of themselves (majority) (II Timothy 3:1-5) people shall have all forms of godliness with no Spiritual authority. Jesus is coming because these are signs of the times. Evil people shall be more than those who love God. Therefore, Christians we are in a war not against flesh and blood but against evil, wickedness, and satanic possession as you saw in the Supreme Court. It confused the righteous jurisprudence and give victory to ugliness. Don't fret this is the fulfillment of a prophetic era; just stay with God and hold on to your faith. II Corinthians 4:4 tells us that Satan is the god of this age and he has blinded the eyes of the political system of unbelievers who sit in the seats of law. I Corinthians 4:5-6 we must preach Jesus and not ourselves, we must pray and never tired for there are better days ahead. We are the salt of the earth therefore let us season it.

Bring out the best for God; stand on His promises they shall see you through in Jesus's name Amen! Read (Eph. 6:12, I Corinthians 2:8, 1 Peter 4:12) we are living in prophetic times and they are being fulfilled. Evil shall increase and the love of many shall wax cold. Stay strong in the Lord my friends. People make mockery of other people lives and when this is done; there is a vindicator. God rules are just and He understands the limits of any system, people, places and any realm of the spirits. God sees you, understand the rules; He slower to anger. We all may not understand the merits of the mundane. Nevertheless, you or any system cannot be too far from the eyes of God. So people don't count it strange when evil is rewarded evil for evil. Christians God is in control; He is not blind nor is He a man who does not see! HIS EYES IS ON THE SPARROW AND I KNOW HE WATCHES OVER ME. The relegating facts here are trusting in God not leaning unto ones' own understanding you have to bring all of your weakness to the front so that all left behind you are the directives of God; guiding you to a better you.

Chapter 19

Bobby tells His story to encourage Amos

had my experience and I took it me to understanding that when we praise God anytime and humble ourselves before Him; in His presence our souls take delight. My friend and family out here in this world caution yourself that you do not permit the unrighteousness of others to derail our faith in God. Matthew Chapter 24 tells us that right would become wrong and wrong right for these are signs of the times. People would do wrong in the name of God, justices would appear correct for societal purposes even when wrong, but we cannot lose heart. Jeremiah saw wickedness increasing daily and he asked God why the wicked do what they do? However, he said in all of this "You are always righteous O LORD; when I bring a case before you. Yet I would speak with you about your justice why the wicked prosper? (Jeremiah chapter12).

Friends and family in this we can say as for me and my house we shall serve the Lord. Stay right with God and keep your faith alive. Jesus is coming again indeed! There shall be many events of situations in life, which would make you press forward. Situation cannot make you quit. Not even when it is down to your last home run. I am so determined more than ever that I shall have the beautiful Melinda as my wife. I believe this and I know so. It was early January two years ago exactly today when I arrived here heart broken and torn apart. My heart could not console me; I could not locate any spark from inside of me by which I could have been consoled. I was flabbergasted and greatly perturbed. Wondering why love could be so cruel? I internally refused solace, and subjected myself to an internal regressive attitude. I traveled over and over just to convince myself that I was actually a victim of love. I concluded that distance would suffice and vindicate from this emotional malady. Instead, I ran into a bunch of social dysfunctional individuals. They considered me the fixer.

They didn't know my pains; nevertheless when they spoke; they all expected something or some kind of resolution. I prayed and turn the situation over to God. At times I would listen and then the spirit of god would speak to my heart, and whatever my good conscience told me that I did, and every time this happened; the people followed the instructions and it helped them. I was confused, but it was God. I remembered Father Peter saying "You are lights of the world illuminated by the Blood of Jesus Christ of Nazareth for a purpose; therefore shine for Jesus so that someone sees the way through you and to their promised land. For your presence of light is for them. Speak this into your day "I release the fire of God into my day so that every evil plan of the visible or invisible evil is burned up in Jesus's name Amen! Now declare this "in Jesus name I command my morning to shape into place all my victories of breakthrough in the name of Jesus and I am shining so that I am a blessing to someone in Jesus's name Amen!

Now rebuke distractions and confusions from your day say " in Jesus's name I release peace into my day, and I rebuke evil distractions and confusions from my day" now speak into the atmosphere your desires: In Jesus I command the east wind to flow peace and great love into my day so that all of my desires for...... I release them into the atmosphere and I await my expectations in the name of Jesus. I thank you Jesus for this day of essential blessings in Jesus's Name. Father Peter also said, "A great man once said it is not what you say but it is what you are not saying, and that is what matters."

Assumptions can consume you and it just might affect the people around you. So have good quality judgement, have peace with yourself be sincere in what you are doing never mind what is going on the outside of you; only control your Spirit, your inner man and then your soul man shall aligned with you. The real you ; needs spiritual satisfactions which relinquish you from that inner conflict, not knowing what to do, what to say you find yourself assuming, prejudging and extremely self-deceived, and most of all; at war with yourself. That is the real warfare and you don't need Facebook for this; my good Bishop Bonner in his Book the "Uncontrollable emotions" said that is when you need prayers.

The weapons of our warfare are not carnal but mighty through God to the pulling down of Strongholds. Please Read Matthew 12. We got to fight strongholds, and stop the assumptions of who likes you, dislikes you must live now in Jesus's name! Truthfully tomorrow is really not promised if you permit mere man to drive you into hell. My friends of Liberia it is not worth it. Amos this is my testimony; feel that I should testify that I really love the Lord, He woke me up this morning, and I have send up my petition and I am awaiting my expectation. At night my soul desires my Lord and at morning my spirit searches for Him. God is good to me so good to me.

I may not be where I want to be but I am far very far from what I used to be. I have renounced those easily upsetting events, and have find a better way with Jesus, never mind if I am offensive; I am only enjoying my own space in the Lord and it is my right to do. So down with Satan and up with Jesus. Bobby called the workers and Amos together and said, "My fellow Christians, keep calling on the name of the Lord. Keep trusting in His Name for the Bible declares that this Shall happened to you as you lift up the Name of the Lord. Your heart shall understand knowledge, your tongue shall speak clearly, the wind shall serve as your delivery man, your words shall reach the heart of God, and for you it has been declared that the Spirit of God shall pour upon you more blessings from on high. Stay with God, trust in God be not dismayed, your wilderness shall be fertile, your seed shall grow, and those who take of your plenty shall be stop and quieted in Jesus's name; I have prayed for you and applied Isaiah 32 to sealed these words in Jesus's name"

Bobby Ross begins speaking about His return to the United States

It sounds like I am preaching, I guess I am and equally so, I am about to return to the United States. My Friends and family, I declare victory for you and your family in Jesus's name, my prayers this morning is that you see your way and not only that but that your breakthrough comes by the word of God from your heart. GOD is waiting for you to speak your desires into the atmosphere and His angels are ready to deliver your prayers therefore on this foundation speak your breakthrough, support it by the word of God; Jeremiah 1: 12 assures us that God watches over His words to perform it. Therefore pour out you heart to God; He awaits your request. I sealed these words with (Jeremiah 23:29) God's word is like a hammer that breaks the rocks in pieces. Today is breakthrough day in the name of Jesus Christ of Nazareth; use the hammer and stand on Christ the solid ROCK. AMEN!

Bobby Plans to return to America.

Knowing their thoughts and desires for him to stay and spend additional time doing missionary work; Bobby commenced defusing this aspect of their relationship for his two years of services was over and in the main time Mother Crawford and the Church were constant and consistent in praying. Melinda called and hinted that she would love to see him soon. Cautiously he readied the clients and encouraged Amos to get his documents together. He believed God for their trip together to the United States.

He encouraged them

He said to the people: Yes we are temples of the living God, containers for the Holy Ghost. Paul said "don't you know that you yourselves are God's temple and that God's Spirit dwells in you (I Corinthians 3:16)" therefore my friends God is returning His anointing to His temple but it has to be tested for quality. God knows you; who you are, but you have to be shaken, stripped of excess weight in other to be filled with God's glory; lift up your heads; for today as Jesus said, "Salvation is returning to your house" in Jesus's name Amen!

I don't know what trials shall come your way, but I know that you shall come forth as a vessel tried and ready for the Master's use (I Corinthians 3:12-15).Wherever you are right now find a moment and praise God for two minutes, lift Him up for today joy shall fill your hearts, and you shall overcome in Jesus's name. I also understand that it would not be perfect but Temples you are and Temples shall you always be. Love one another, respect, give honor and it shall be reciprocated. Everybody would not love you, nor would everybody agree with you, but you can be the difference which everybody sees. Do not do what everyone does, do not give back bad vibes for things you do not understand trust your guts feelings and be kind to everyone even when they disapprove of you and you walk with God. Eleanor Roosevelt said "Do what you feel in your heart is right- for you'll be criticized anyway".

Press forward, believe in God and increase from within the inner man. Jesus said the Kingdom of God is within you (Luke 17:21) therefore enlarge the kingdom within with greater compassion. May the peace of God rule your day, may His loving kindness brings you comfort and security. All your good plans in Jesus's name; shall follow you and evil shall not overcome you. May your day become delightful.

To help you along the way I have prayed (Psalm 64:2) that God shall "hide you from the secret counsel of the wicked" and I have bind and rebuke every spirit of Sanballat and Tobia (Nehemiah 6:1-6) in the name of Jesus Christ of Nazareth. Every evil plan against you is scatter in Jesus's name. Pondering couldn't feel any less better when Jesus warns that a man's worst enemy would be that of his household, I thought about this and the word came to me again glorify God and He shall lift you up, acknowledge Him and He shall acknowledge you, draw near to Him and He shall lift you up. Jesus can set us on fire and we have to keep the flame ignited. Don't turn the flame out in your lives. Matthew 10. LEV. 6: You have to work harder at your relationships and keep the flame going. It is good being in the Lord's presence. Understand that His words are His will for us. Therefore use the word of God as tools for salvation, as power and authority for healing and deliverance as protection from the unseen evil (Matthew 10:1), and as light to your path out of darkness. Use God's words wisely and it shall shake your spirit and set your soul on fire. Use it to defeat spiritual stagnation and release in you a glorious joyful, sweet presence into your day. I sealed this with (Jeremiah 29:11). God wants to prosper you. He has good thoughts and peace designed just for you in Jesus's name!

In this I pray that Goodness and Mercy follow you on the left and right side of you and before and behind you; Love and Peace to protect you in Jesus's name. I have to run after my life and some day we shall meet again. I am just saying this or now but this is a reality which must come to fruition. Therefore magnify the Lord with me come and let us exalt His name together, let us make mention of His excellent greatness. Oh praise Him for grace given unto us in Jesus's name Amen! Christians let the praises of God be on your lips and from your hearts let the mention of Jesus be increased in the precious Name of Jesus Christ of Nazareth. Today use the weapons of praise to defeat the nay Sayers and unwanted presence. Let us today glorify the Lord together, let us also lift up His name together. Today whatever you are doing stop for a moment and give praises to God for He woke you up this morning and He has placed blessings into your day. The word of God declares that "those who look to Him (God) are radiant: their faces are never covered with shame"(Psalm 34). You are covered and protected; for an angel of the LORD has been assigned to you to bear you in their hands in the time of trouble. Have a blessed day and have peace with your fellow man and then with God and in this; your day shall be filled with joy. I just want to leave this little confession of faith; which I recite every day for getting me started.

△ △ △

Bobby's Affirming Confessions

I am a child of God; birth by the blood of Jesus' Christ; by His death on the cross my sins and shame were taken away. I am the child of God joint heir with Jesus Christ on account of adoption; a family of God. I am empowered by the spirit of Christ to release into my life peace, love and good Christian reciprocity. I am the Child of God; follow daily by Grace and Mercy. I am not afraid to take chances with God; I am saved, I depend and trust only on the Name of Jesus. I do not trust the will of man nor their hope for me, for they are insincerely designed filled with let downs.

For the word of God declares "Thus says the LORD, Cursed is the man who trusts in mankind and makes flesh his strength, and whose heart turns away from the LORD (Jeremiah 17:5)." I know in my heart that no weapon formed against me can prosper; I know in my heart that every tongue which comes up against me shall be condemned in judgment. I do not have any regrets of who I am and whose I am. I am walking in the fulfillment of my destiny; I renounce daily the hidden works of darkness; I am not afraid of the shadow of death; for God is with me (Psalm 23). I am filled with joy and desire daily the steadfast love of God for me it is New every morning. In Jesus name my enemies shall come in one way and run out in seven different ways. I declare as the word of God says; the Weapons of my warfare are not carnal but mighty through God for the pulling down of strongholds. I pull down evil every plan of darkness against my life; my family life, my Church family, and return every curse visible or invisible to the sender or senders! So shall this be in Jesus' Name! Remember to use these words and recite them daily; they work for me.

Chapter 20

The Intrinsic Values Counseled – unconditional love

These are values which are deep down within, it is inherent and deeply seated within the individual. They are innate and to the core of an individual. This is extremely fundamental to the individual's make up. Any man or woman who is able to view and constructively acquire genuinely a foundational structure for a relationship on these grounds; is resolved within godly directives. To get a wife a man would have to work at it, if he would want his domain of paradise to become a reality.

Marriage is no rush, and many men have made deep mistakes when marriages were rushed and missing the fundamental ingredients for success as desired. Stick with the words of the scriptures and project as the scriptures have said, "As in water face reflects face, so the heart of man reflects man (Proverb 27:29)" When godly values are within a man's heart; it would also reflect that quality he wishes to cohabit within a godly and blessed union (marriage). Adding to this laundry list is the fact that Scriptures admonished all men to possess certain qualities, which are examples of Christ love for the church. Jesus died for the Church. He loves the Church unconditionally. Therefore, the Christian man ought to love, cherish, and appreciate his wife. The bible says, that "So husbands ought also to love their own wives as their own bodies. He who loves his own wife loves himself; for no one ever hated his own flesh, but nourishes and cherishes it, just as Christ also does the church (Ephesians 5:28-29)". Brother Ross leaned against the door and said to Moses, these things equip a man for finding the right woman.

He later said women are precious and must be love; they cannot be left alone and unattended; they must be given the opportunity to realize their worth and in turn they would love you and care for you. This I find in Melinda and to tell you the truth she fits all of such qualities. She is the best a man can have in a wife and I pledge to keep her to myself, honor her and respect her for she is the epitome of love, and I mean a complete personification of love, peace, joy and righteousness packaged in one body. This is my life and I am going after it. I have asked and I believe that I shall have the desire of my heart. No man can take away love felt deeply from the heart. No man can obstruct a deep inner yearning which God has positioned in the heart.

You see Amos, I was in love with a young woman back in my high school days, however she was involved with another young man; she had the liking for me but could not manage the situation and she moved on. She married this man and died not soon after that. It was hurtful but life had to continue. I could not get a grip of myself and ventured into a continuous schooling. I found some sort of satisfaction in education and vowed to help others with my skills, knowledge an abilities given by God Almighty.

I am in love today, this time the fire burns deep within, and I know that this is the will of God. Melinda is God's will for me not any Convent. I speak those things, which aren't as though they are. This is my conviction and I stand by it. We have to stand by our beliefs or else we would stand by the definitions of others. You see the joy of life is having an assurance that God is a present help in the time of need. God is my stronghold and my salvation; He is the delivering force behind the righteous and help from the wicked. Amos I stand today to say to you son in the Mighty Name of Jesus Christ of Nazareth; I claim all of my desires in the Lord. I am reminded that if I delight myself in God; He shall give me the desires of my heart. I shall behold the desires of my heart in my face.

Not soon after this discussion Bobby's phone rang; he heard it ringing, but the phone was in his office; he ran and got to the office just in time. Melinda was on the phone. Hello Bobby and where have you been honey? Bobby quickly jumped in and said what did you say Melinda? She replied oh mine I am so sorry. Bobby reminded her that it was not a slip, but rather a prophetic utterance. You see God would cause prophetic words concerning our lives to come through our mouths. God shall put the fruit of our lives within our hearts and we shall be able by the aid the Holy Ghost to speak them forth. The oracles of God are spoken out the mouths of God's children as derived from the Holy Scriptures (I Peter chapter 4).

Melinda listen to this I love you sister and you have to let us make this real; I know deep in my heart that you love me as well. Miss Yates hear this; I trust in God and I know He cares for me, though billows row, God shall keep me safely sure and I know that God watches over me. "Cast all you cares upon the Lord for He cares for you (1 Peter 5:7)" it is a faithful saying that those who put their trust in the Lord shall be as mount Zion. God is our Refuge and Strength a very present Help in the time of trouble. God is the Stronghold of our salvation and He delivers the righteous from all troubles in the Mighty Name of Jesus Christ of Nazareth Amen! Father I thank you for help, health and strength in the Mighty Name of Jesus Christ Amen. I know that dependence on God brings the answer to everything we desire in Him and Melinda I desire you in God. I may not be the best of the best but I know that I love Jesus and can make you happier for the rest of your life. Bobby! Bobby! I am in tears right now; tell you the truth I love you and want to be your wife and the mother of your children. However, I have to do things the right way. I am deciding leaving the nunnery. Mother Crawford met with my parents and they have agreed that it is best to be with you! I am a bit confused but I am certain that this is for my good. Only one thing Bobby breaking this vow with the Catholic Church seems difficult but the benefits outweighs this obligation. I am a believer, and I am a child of God; I am convinced that this vow was a choice of mine and not the will of God. I read the scriptures and the purpose for my existence. I am made to love and to be appreciated! I am to be the beginning from which another generation of professionals originate. I am supposed to be committed to the principles of godliness and not my choice of celibacy. I can be a devote mother, an appreciated wife and yet still in love with Holiness and the will of God. I have read the lives of so many others after whom I came and how they found love, life and marriage. Today they are happy and are committed members of the Church. Bobby this I have chosen, and can feel and taste the wondrous of God in this entire process. So what do you think Mr. Professional Ross?

Melinda consider yourself bless and an ordinary person chosen by God. God loves rejected, cast down ordinary people so that He can transform them into royalties and priests. God has chosen you for blessings and honor, therefore see yourselves as a precious possessions of God Almighty. The Bible says "But you are a chosen people, a royal priesthood, a holy nation, a people belonging to God, that you may declare the praises of Him who called you out of darkness into this wonderful light (I Peter 2:9). Friends the Lord has chosen you to praise Him; And He has called you to be precious to Him in the Mighty Name of Jesus Christ of Nazareth Amen! Father I am thankful that You have chosen me to be bless and no man can curse me. I thank you in Jesus Name Amen! Melinda God has selected us and have called us into favor so that we may praise Him. God honors you and He has crowned you with glory and honor. The scripture says

"What is man that Thou are so mindful of him and visits him, You have made him a little lower than the angels and yet You crowned him with glory and honor (Psalm 8:4-5)" My friends consider yourselves blessed by God to make a difference in this world on account of His grace and mercy toward You. See yourselves as set apart people of God to show forth His praise in the Mighty Name of Jesus Christ of Nazareth Amen! Father I thank you for grace, glory and honor in Jesus' Name Amen! This is no ordinary situation but God is in control. What I think is the fact in knowing that miracles come from God Almighty. Melinda what if God selects you and your success is based on your commitment to the assigned tasks, your actions are the reason to bless others what would you do? I was selected for a time such as this.

JEHOVAH GOD ALMIGHTY SAID TO MOSES

"If you do these things and God so command you, you shall be able to endure and all these people shall go to their place (Exodus 18:23)" we have to fight always to stand in the gap for others, taking all of the upsets and pains. Jesus offered Himself for us so that we can have a place of comfort in Him. Take a stand for God and bless someone in the Mighty Name of Jesus Christ of Nazareth Amen! We are called to be selflessness in the Lord! You got the power! Jesus said, "I give you power to trample over snakes and scorpions and the power of the enemy and none shall by any means hurt you (Luke 10:19)." Know this, no voodoo, witchcraft, jealous mind, resentment nor traps planned schemes against you can prosper; you 've got the power use it and hammer all over the enemy of progress and stop fear and move forward in Jesus 'Name towards the prize of your high calling in victory in the Mighty Name of Jesus Christ of Nazareth Amen! This is your destiny Melinda move on and let us be what is intended for us in Jesus' Name. God rewards His children for keeping His commandments (Law) in their hearts. God rewards you when you take precious His ordinance. David said "The Law of LORD is perfect reviving the soul, the statutes of the LORD are trustworthy, making wise the simple, the precepts of the LORD are right giving joy to the heart (Psalm 19:7-8). God told Moses tell Israel "see what I did to Egypt. I carried you on Eagles wings and brought you to My Self, now if you obey ME and keep My covenant out of all nations ye shall be My treasured possession (Exodus 19:4-5). We can get the blessings today; stay with God and become His treasured possessions in the Mighty Name of Jesus Christ of Nazareth Amen! Father I thank You for the light of Your words which give entrance and access to You in Jesus Name Amen!

△ △ △

God's sufficient Grace.

I can understand what you might be going through and also what experience or trials you may have now, but no matter what God is working behind the scenes for you. The scriptures let us to know that eye have not seen nor ear heard the great things the Lord has in store for those who love Him. You have to hold on don't let go and put your trust in God always no matter what. If you have prayed and yet no answer, if you have fasted and yet no answer don't give up God is still in control. (2 Corinthians 12:9) the Apostle Paul was sick and three times he asked God to take away his problem, it did not happen, however God told the Apostle "My Grace is sufficient for you and my strength made perfect in your weaknesses" you may be going through and I am telling you that God is behind the scenes working it out for us!

Melinda spoke back

In this life of which we speak, I am confronted with the question as to why so many Priests of the faith engaging in sexual relationships behind closed doors and accept the confession. This has confused me and the Church has spent millions upon millions to resolve many of these cases. I have seen these over and over again. A young lady stopped me; she said Sister Melinda kindly assist me into understanding this; it is almost trivia, priest that I am supposed to look up to would try to engage in relationships with boys, little girls and some adults male and female why? I was almost flabbergast, and I mean totally dumbfounded! This bothered my spirit and I realized the Scriptures which states "8But I say to the unmarried and to widows that it is good for them if they remain even as I. 9But if they do not have self-control, let them marry; for it is better to marry than to burn with passion (I Corinthians 7:8-9)".

Self-Control

Bobby self-control has to be of God. It has to be God given and a called. No one of himself can out of some form frustration practice celibacy. If God calls a man or woman to Ministry; He enables them have self-control prior to marriage and or commitment to ministry. Man people enter the faith knowing their conditions and yet subvert and suppressed their emotional cravings which are not aligned with the faith. These are the individuals who end up into acts against their faith. A person has to be truthful to his call, trust God and keep focused. It is better to marry than to burn with passion which runs out of control. So many priests have shamed the faith and have caused the Church a great deal. The Church normally transfer some of these emotional run away priest to remote areas in the world. When this happens the rouge priest take with them the same perverted attitudes.

I have self-control and I believe in my call, but there are moments in my life in ministry when my emotions have driven me into questioning my called. I have seen Starr, Molly and the rest of them interacting with children, exhibiting loving motherhoods, and these have become my struggles night after night.

It is better to marry than to burn and tell you the truth; the burning when not controlled it can become an allusive phenomenon, and also a defining you. God has never made a mistake nor has He spoken and did not mean what He said. If God said be fruitful and multiply; then it was what He meant. My mother had me and she is a mighty and wonderful Christian woman. My father likewise; well respected and a good family leader and husband. Had they not come together where would I have been? In this I too owe a responsibility to the next generation. I cannot abolish the path through which another generation of great godly people should travel.

Bobby all these situations of thoughts brought me top this point of becoming your wife and still remain a great Catholic Church member with my faith in God Almighty. My Parents is aware of a Priest who struggled with his emotions, he suppressed for years his God given passion for the opposite sex. He was sent to Liberia, West Africa up in the country, in a little town called Tappita, he connected well with the congregation and served well the community. He loved children and wanted some of his own, but he church prevented him. The priest was in charge of the orphanage in the city of Virginia, West Africa, there he saw a beautiful young lady. He personally paid attentions to her and send her to the University of Liberia. Not wanting to continuously burn with suppressed passion and confusions at that; the priest a very good man and a wonderful role model, left the faith and married his beautiful African princess. They now live in the United States with their children. I mean Bobby this is God's will and I am in it. I am sorry but my vows would have to be broken and I shall love you until I am no more!

Bobby all that life offers are the tranquil and comfort of been love by God and belonging to a selfless human man. I am hoping that Starr, Molly, Mother Crawford and my parents are ready for this decision. Thank you Bobby I have to go now.

Bobby Spoke

Melinda No need to run from trials, troubles and tribulations. Confront what you do not and cannot see physically, with the power of prayers. Forces would want to contain you and shut you up but be vigilant on the words of God. David felt like escaping when he thought about the wicked and slandering people and this brought him into the chambers of fear; He said "Only if I had wings of a dove, then I would fly away and be at rest (Psalm 55:6). Friends we don't have to desire an escape route but we can hide under the shadow of the Almighty God, and fight back with prayers. Today I pray that all forces against you become powerless and confused in the Mighty Name of Jesus Christ of Nazareth Amen! I know that meeting the superiors at the convent would not be easy, but this is our victory.

I trust in God and I know He cares for me, though billows row, God shall keep me safely sure and I know that God watches over me. "Cast all you cares upon the Lord for He cares for you (1 Peter 5:7)". It is a faithful saying that those who put their trust in the Lord shall be as mount Zion. God is our Refuge and Strength a very present Help in the time of trouble. God is the Stronghold of our salvation and He delivers the righteous from all troubles in the Mighty Name of Jesus Christ of Nazareth Amen! Father I thank you for help, health and strength in the Mighty Name You are honored by God and He has crowned you with glory and honor. The scripture says "What is man that Thou are so mindful of him and visits him, You have made him a little lower than the angels and yet You crowned him with glory and honor (Psalm 8:4-5)" Melinda consider yourself blessed by God to make a difference in this world on account of His grace and mercy toward you. Just consider yourself set apart child of God to show forth His praise in the Mighty Name of Jesus Christ of Nazareth Amen!

My Dear what if God selects you and your success is based on your commitment to the assigned tasks , your actions are the reason to bless others what shall you do? JEHOVAH GOD ALMIGHTY said to Moses

"If you do these things and God so command you, you shall be able to endure and all these people shall go to their place (Exodus 18:23)" we have to fight always to stand in the gap for others, taking all of the upsets and pains, once

It is the means by which many people are blessed. Jesus offer Himself for us so that we can have a place of comfort in Him. Take a stand for God and bless someone in the Mighty Name of Jesus Christ of Nazareth Amen!

In my closing I leave these words with you; God rewards His children for keeping His commandments (Law) in their hearts. God rewards you when you take precious His ordinance. David said "The Law of LORD is perfect reviving the soul, the statutes of the LORD are trustworthy, making wise the simple, the precepts of the LORD are right giving joy to the heart (Psalm 19:7-8). God told Moses tell Israel "see what I did to Egypt. I carried you on Eagles wings and brought you to My Self, now if you obey Me and keep My covenant out of all nations ye shall be My treasured possession (Exodus 19:4-5). Melinda get the blessings today stay with God and become His treasured possessions in the Mighty Name of Jesus Christ of Nazareth Amen!

$$\triangle \ \triangle \ \triangle$$

Bobby's testimonies of God's Greatness experience and personal counsels

I want you to know that your circumstances are not strange to God and what is happening to you now; it has happened to someone before and Jehovah brought them through also. By the way if you are a righteous person in the LORD your afflictions are many, but God delivers out of them all. You must understand that everything gained from God comes with a period of testing for quality and abilities to remain steadfast. God knows your needs and the things you are going through; your help is coming from the sanctuary of God Almighty (Psalm 20). God has all the skills and experiences for resolving your particular circumstantial conditions; do not lean on your own understandings invite God into your particular situation; trust me He listens to you and secures your tears in Heaven within a special bottle. (Psalm 56:7-8). Your precious tears are always before God Almighty and His Son Jesus Christ of Nazareth is Advocating in your behalf. Do not give up God is in control of you in Jesus' Name Amen!

I just want to say no one is perfect, but everyone who calls on the Name of the LORD must be committed in living for God! Certain things we have to be honest about and come straight with God. Tell God about the things which easily upset you, things which easily take you off balance and off guard. Tell God that somethings are just too difficult for you and that you need His help! Stop trying to figure out what is wrong but instead give what is wrong and broken to God; He can mend them. I have stopped walking around with guilt and instead relied on God to help me in my weakness! I also discover this Scripture to come handy and by this I measure my position with God; it reads "2 But have renounced the hidden things of dishonesty, not walking in craftiness, nor handling the word of God deceitfully; but by manifestation of the truth commending ourselves to every man's conscience in the sight of God (II Corinthians 4:2)" Today I am hoping that this also becomes a focus of yours in the Mighty Name Jesus Christ of Nazareth Amen! Stay Blessed in Jesus' Name!

Pray! Pray! Say many prayers and patiently wait on the LORD! There is not a pit nor mud God cannot get you out of. There is not a valley so vast and a mountain so high that God cannot locate you when you pray! PRAY! PRAY God answers prayers. He may not come when you want HIM to but He shall be right on time! "Then Jesus, again groaning in Himself, came to the tomb (John 11:38) Friends Jesus shall also groan in your situation and command the stubborn tomb to be roll away from your life. Only Prayers can keep you alive form principalities which attack you in the heavenliest. Pray and wait on God He may not come when you want Him to but He is always on time. David said "I patiently waited LORD for You to hear my prayer. You listened and pulled me from a lonely pit, full of mud and mire. You let me stand on a rock with firm feet (Psalm 40:1-2). Friends you shall also stand firm on your rock of deliverance in the Mighty Name of Jesus Christ of Nazareth Amen! Wait for God and let them see your praise in Jesus Name Amen!

God Is On My Side

Listen God is on my side, on your side do not fear what man may do to you. If someone wants to walk away from you let them go maybe they need a better focus but as for you stay with God and make the best of your current location and position in God. Dare not trust the sweetest fame but wholly lean on the name of Jesus Christ of Nazareth Amen! Make the best of your worship service today and get the praises going for God!

When situations run out of hand and you think the hope of managing them is lost; just stop and remember your creator. There are somethings in your life which might seem overwhelming; don't quit turn to God with praise!

II Chronicles 20:12 - Put your trust in God
"We have no power against the great multitude that is coming against us, nor do we know what to do but our eyes are upon YOU"

In everything put your trust in God, depend on Him and stand upon His promises; sing songs of praises, and songs of deliverance in the Mighty Name of Jesus Christ of Nazareth Amen; and they can put any problem, any opinion, any bad situation to flight. Read II Chronicles 20. Peace and blessings in Jesus Name Amen!

My little expressions

You are so real to me Lord, and I thank you for your loving kindness, Your tender mercies; for they are so real to me! You have defended and protected me from behind and before me; Heavenly Father. Now I confess and profess that my head shall be lifted up in praise and worship of You! LORD for you have never failed me yet. All that I have wanted and needed you have given. I praise and bless your matchless Name Amen! Satan has no power over God's Children (Luke 10:19)

Struggles - Struggling

Maybe this is not you or you might be struggling with restless conditions and troubling situations; have you ever thought of casting some extra baggage away? I was reading Ezekiel 18:31 and it states "Cast away from you all your transgressions which you have committed and make yourselves a new heart and a new spirit! For why will you die, O house of Israel?" I thought this was necessary for me as well and I decided to live and therefore I cast away my transgression and then I started a new relationship with Jesus Christ! Today I am free not perfect but now I depend on Jesus Christ for peace and it passes all understandings. Why don't you try? Why don't you lay aside those things which are easily pulling you down, and cast them away in the Mighty Name of Jesus Christ of Nazareth! Get a New Heart! Get a New thought and walk with God not as others but as yourself in Jesus' Mighty Name Amen!

Struggles struggling may hold you down but break free today with the greatest breakthrough of praise in the Mighty Name of Jesus Christ of Nazareth Amen. Let not that pain, let not that neglect nor rejections steal your praise. Lift up thy hands and keep God ahead of you for this is your time to come out and shine in Jesus's Name Amen

Jesus cancels all dead situations even funerals

Jesus cancelled a perfectly good funeral, turning mourning into joy, terminated brokenhearted and delivered life to a broken-down mother. Luke 7:11-17 holds an account of a small town Nain- pleasant as it is meant. Christ the Savior stopped the funeral procession, spoke to the dead and commanded that life returned to that lifeless body. Friends there are many dead situations in our lives today, but God through His Son is well able to bring life into your dead moments. Seek God more and your sadness shall be turn to joy, your emptiness shall be filled and strong enemy shall turn their backs on account that God is greater in you than in the world. Have a blessed day in the Mighty Name of Jesus Christ of Nazareth Amen!

Take it back God's plans are greater than the plans of man

Take it back! Know your creator and understand that His plans for you are greater than the mere words of man. God said those who trust in Him shall not be ashamed (Psalm 9). You don't need to turn to man after you have boasted of the greatness of God Almighty! Demand that any obstacle hindering you; to get out in the Name of Jesus. Refuse and reject any negative words against you in the Mighty Name of Jesus Christ of Nazareth Amen; evil must be returned to the sender in the Mighty Name of Jesus Christ of Nazareth Amen!

JOB 10:12 " You have granted me life and favor, and Your providence has preserved my spirit " God is with you repeat this

I am not under the control of any negative force against my destiny; every evil plan hindering my peace and blessing must die at the roots and be aborted in the Mighty Name of Jesus Christ of Nazareth Amen! Spirit of the living God I take courage and refuge in your Holy and matchless Name Amen in Jesus Name!

When God changes you; you go from a Beggar to a Beautiful Soul

When Satan signal you out for degradation, he attacks you from the womb also and from a dream or something within the natural realm. Hitting you with limbs problems, eye sights trouble, mental illness and many other conditions. Maybe you may not have come across this before but there was a man in the book of Acts 3:1-10 His entire life was turned into bondage from birth to a bagger, he was limbed and depended on others for sustenance. Friends God can make a way when there seems to be no way. The man met Peter at the gate of called beautiful. I found this very strange in contrast to this man's life where he sat did not described his condition, his condition was far from beauty. God can change the ugly condition to one of beautiful once you meet Him. Friends reach out to God and get a change condition today God is able caused you to leap to a new you just like the man in the story; in the mighty name of Jesus Christ of Nazareth Amen!

Father I thank you for the change in condition and position today in Jesus' name and for the furnace of afflictions to be tried, polished for greater things (Isaiah 48:10). Sometimes evil men tried to hurt you because God has made you different that is also okay; only seek God and don't be bitter soon they shall have their rewards. Wickedness is temporary but Good last forever Psalm 92. So let them laugh now evil never goes unpunished. Your time is coming out wicked man amen!

This one is for you

I don't know who you are or your situation right now, but I am inclined to let you know that God shall see you through. You may be rejected, forsaken, confused or hurting don't give up your case or cases is/are in the hands of God Almighty. God shall heal your hurts, your pains and settle you out of the confusions. He promised in (Psalm 147:3) to heal you wound, and your brokenness. I call on you today to break your heart before God Almighty and you shall be comforted in the Mighty Name of Jesus Christ of Nazareth Amen. For you Jesus Christ of Nazareth came to anoint, set you free and mend your broken situations. Just hold on your help is coming from the sanctuary of God Almighty with victory and praise in the Mighty Name of Jesus Christ of Nazareth Amen!(Psalm 20, and 30) seals this just for you in Jesus's Name Amen!

△ △ △

Your Destiny is in God's hands

Your destiny is in the hands of God! Your life is protected by God. Like Job they may have slowed the progression of your flesh, but your spirt is heighten by the love of God Almighty. Your steps are completely ordered by God and there are three which bear records of your position with God in heaven (The Father, The Word and The Holy Spirit) They testify of you and your place in God (1 John 5:7). In the earth (The Spirit, The Water and The Blood (John 5:8). These records in heaven and on earth keep you alive in the perfect will of God, and when you are broken; the Word declares "He heals the brokenhearted and binds up their wounds. Psalm 147:3) God is in control. I am thankful for multiple struggles for; without them I would not have known the keeping powers of God. (Psalm 119:50) The word of God is the comfort in your affliction in the Mighty Name of Jesus Christ of Nazareth!

Just a little Spiritual warfare plan

Woke up to pray this morning, first confession was the weapons of warfare; they are not carnal but Mighty through God so that evil strongholds are pulled down. I realized that I have to first *"LOCATE and IDENTIFY"* the source of the evil one to apply my Spiritual Weaponry!

I said what are they Lord?

1. I Corinthians 6:19 the Holy Ghost indwells us; not the building. Great weapon - no Christ; no spirit, no Holy Spirit No joy.

2. The Blood of Jesus Christ of Nazareth

3. Our testimonies Revelation 12- helps you to overcome every battles - Confessing grace, deliverance from sin and shame

4. Philippines 4:8 meditate on things that are praise worthy- the fruit of the Holy Ghost, which indwells you, are pure, kind, of good report, lovely with virtues -Psalm 19. Grace and peace in the Mighty Name of Jesus Christ of Nazareth Amen!

I realized how thankfully thankful I am! Woke up this morning by the kindness and power of God Almighty with victory of the day already in my heart because of the blood of the Lamb of God. Father I am grateful for the blood which you have caused running warm in my body! I thank You O Mighty God for the beautiful lives You have created to praise You! Thank You for distracting the haters with shame and embarrassed positions. Thank You for lifting up my head and saying to me "this is the way; walk in it" in the Mighty Name of Jesus Christ of Nazareth Amen!

What God Promised Trust me; It shall Be a Reality

What God promised is what He does (Numbers 23:19). If God promised to protect you; you are protected! Wicked people want you to believe that God can become a liar and so they attack, but Jehovah God promised to rescue those who love Him and knows His name (Psalm 91:14-16). Wicked people wants you to believe that this is not possible and so they have tried and try. You don't worry because every impossible moment in your life is God's possibility. God has promised deliverance in the time of trouble for those who love Him and those who put their trust in Jehovah God; shall never be ashamed (Psalm 9). Father I thank You for stopping the hands of the evil ones in the Mighty Name of Jesus Christ of Nazareth Amen!

God shall see you through family

I don't know who you are or your situation right now, but I am inclined to let you know that God shall see you through. You may be rejected, forsaken, confused or hurting don't give up your case or cases is/are in the hands of God Almighty. God shall heal your hurts, your pains and settle you out of the confusions. He promised in (Psalm 147:3) to heal you wound, and your brokenness. I call on you today to break your heart before God Almighty and you shall be comforted in the Mighty Name of Jesus Christ of Nazareth Amen. For you Jesus Christ of Nazareth came to anoint, set you free and mend your broken situations. Just hold on your help is coming from the sanctuary of God Almighty with victory and praise in the Mighty Name of Jesus Christ of Nazareth Amen!(Psalm 20, and 30) seals this just for you in Jesus's Name Amen

△ △ △

Godly Adorations in prayer

My God! My Father! What a wonder You are? You have been a way maker before there was a way! YOU LORD have made all impossibilities the various steps to my growth and reasons for trust in You! Father God I am grateful that you have not permitted my embarrassed moments to be my downfall, but You O God have heard my cry, and You have delivered me from the noisome pestilence in the Mighty Name of Jesus Christ of Nazareth Amen! Today I walk in victory for You LORD have hedged me in with a wall of fire and have covered me with the blood of the Lamb of God. I thank You today that no weapon formed against me shall prosper in Jesus's Name Amen!

Lift up your hands and shout to God with gladness, do not hold back press forward with praise and let this worship bring down upon you a freedom of praise in the Mighty Name of Jesus Christ of Nazareth Amen!

Hear this and this might be for you

I don't know your pains or your positions today, I don't know what you are going through; I don't know how well you have emptied out yourselves in prayers and yet you are going through! Lamentations 3 teaches that " it is good that one should hope and wait quietly. For Salvation is of the LORD" the indication here is that your deliverance is in God's hands and it brings glory to God's precious Name; when in trials we can still look back and appreciate Him for His goodness. Christians; blessed quietness and Holy quietness bring joy and strength through the Holy Ghost. Hold on; it won't be long, better days are yet ahead in Name of Jesus Christ of Nazareth Amen!

When Situation make you stone cold?

God is in the business of retrieving the coldest of hearts and making them new and warm.

God wants you to turn to Him and He can resolve your stone cold heart with a new heart of flesh and give you a new outlook. God love Israel but when they turn away from Him to a new way; He also turned from them with greater recompense. But those who knew God He delivered and rebuild. Friends God can set you free! GOD can lift you up with a new heart, a new outlook and mind filled with mercy, grace and love (Ezekiel 11:18-20). Remember God is able to resolve your stone cold situation and make it a fountain of living waters in the Mighty Name of Jesus Christ of Nazareth!

When Situation makes you stone cold just do me a favor; erase fear and press forward; give it to the Lord; He is in control; If God is for you who can be against you? Who can subdue you; if God is on your side? Look just draw closer to God and they shall move distance apart from you. You are an overcomer, and the BLOOD OF JESUS CHRIST OF NAZARETH,

AMEN; has sealed you. (Revelation 12, Psalm 56:9)

"WHAT THEN SHALL WE SAY IF GOD IS FOR US; WHO CAN BE AGAINST US; IF GOD IS ON OUR SIDE (Romans 8:31, Psalm 118:6) So friends in Jesus ' Name Amen move forward!

If you have a situation, a condition or something that won't go away, then you have a strong enemy which must be turn over to JEHOVAH SHAMMAH (Ezekiel 48:35). David prayed, "Father deliver me from my strong enemy and from them that hate us, for they are too strong for me." (I Samuel 24:19) Ezra prayed, "God, help me against the enemy that would stand "in the way." (Ezra 8:22)

Overcome every strong force by your testimony and by the blood of the Lamb of God. JESUS NAME IS A STRONG AND HIGH TOWER run into it for you are saved. Peace and blessings in the Mighty Name of Jesus Christ of Nazareth Amen!

When God directs you from the right side to the left side. "This the way; walk in it"

God is so good! No one knows these benefits until he tastes and sees the goodness of the LORD. We could have been overtaken by a storm which tossed from left to right without a compass, but God, in His wisdom, call unto us in the scripture (Isaiah 30:21). When you turn form left to right, the voice of the LORD shall sound from behind you saying, "This is the way walk in it" Friends, it is time to hear the voice of God in directing your every move. The Bible tells us that in everything we do; we must acknowledge God and He shall direct our paths. I pray today that you acknowledge God for what-ever you are about to do; so that you also hear "this is the way walk in it" in the Mighty Name of Jesus Christ of Nazareth Amen!

Another day that the Lord has bless us! Another day to show forth His loving kindness; another day to be grateful, another day of struggle but not without Jesus. Another day to be fearless and trusting in the Mighty Name of Jesus Christ of Nazareth. Remember that this day God is with you and you need not be dismay for the same God who saw you through yesterday is the same God who shall see you through today in Jesus Name Amen.

Through Jesus, walk in the ways He has directed you. Fret not thou self because of evil doers only put your trust in God and lean not on to your own merits. Today, acknowledge God and you shall make it through every situation, in Jesus's Name Amen. (Psalm 9) sealed this Amen!

When we walk in the light of God's gospel, He keeps us constant in the right path to go whether to the left or to the right; He God keeps us constant in His records.

God is keeping records of you and His Witnesses are following you

See the Word below which declares this to be true!

- 1 John 5:7-9 King James Version (KJV)
- 7 For there are three that bear record in heaven, **the Father**, **the Word**, and the **Holy Ghost**: and these three are one.
- 8 And there are three that bear witness in earth, **the Spirit**, and **the water**, and **the blood**: and these three agree in one.
- 9 If we receive the witness of men, the witness of God is greater: for this is the witness of God which he hath testified of his Son.
- God's witnesses are always around us to bring us to a good conscience state in relation to Jehovah God. Keep alert God is in control!

Always use the Word of God – it is power and life

Always give thanks unto the Lord for He is good and His mercy endure forever. Today speak the word, use it, it is your power and it is life for you in the Mighty Name of Jesus Christ of Nazareth

> "Then he said to me, "This is the word of the LORD to Zerubbabel saying, Not by might nor by power, but by My Spirit,' says the LORD of hosts.. (Zechariah 4:6) "

> "The Spirit gives life; the flesh profits nothing. The words I have spoken to you are spirit and they are life (John 6:63)".

Don't hold back break out in praise and let the blessings of the LORD come down. Make no room for the devil he is not your friend. Your only friend is Jesus therefore show Him more love and praises in worship today and always. Have a blessed Sunday in Jesus Name Amen! God's word is your life and fulfillment!

~Easy Assessed Views and unknown experience~

Bobby Later added more words of comforts and encouragement. As you continue in your journey, the focus must always be placed on what is ahead not on what is in your easy assessed views. The easy assessed views are those conditions, which are repeated from the past, and you can easily predict the outcome. What makes a journey in life worth the while; are the unknowns. The unknown are the not experience situations which can teach you something new as oppose to the easy assessed views. The easy assessed views destroy maneuverability and limit the scope of innovative adorations and faith dependence. Faith dependence is trusting only in the merits of the blessed Holy Spirit of God with hope of achieving the impossible. An instant replay allows the view an extra assessed analysis of the predicated outcome; whereas the case of the unknown experiences there are full dependence on the mercy of God and what He provides as His desired results for anyone who depends on Him.

When people choose to go after the unknown experience, they are applying faith. Faith is what is not seen, unassessed and unknown. It is not Hope it is positively trusting God for the impossible desired of greater results. What makes a believer of Christ different or unique from other believes is the unified focused on the things of God and His perfect will for man. Walking in faith is not hoping it is believing that all request made in the name of Jesus Christ of Nazareth are pleasant and answerable by God the Father. In God's will we are encouraged to make our request known to God and that He is able to supply our every needs and good desires in Him. Notice that I said good desires in Him; not all desires are necessarily in Him. Some desires are purely self-centered and not God focused and they are destructive. Knowing God's will for oneself enables you to operate within God's divine will for your life. Therefore trusting in God is the step to being in position to become the hands, ears, eyes of God in services for a period and time. God might need you to fulfill a promise in the lives of others and so He works things to aligned you up with His plans for helping and fixing the lives of those who are in dire need of His intervention. He makes situations present themselves so that His perfect will and desires are accomplished in the lives of others.

Amos it was never my desire to work in Africa, but unlike Jonah; I was willing to travel the distance to do God's will, and I am glad that my pursuit of Melinda enabled me to see the will of God in my personal life for pleasing and satisfying Him. Whenever a person willed himself to the divine will of God that person benefits are beyond measure. God is pleased with the outcome of the services and thus rewards more graces for that obedient man or woman. Today I am pleased to say that because of my rejections and distresses; I found a clearer relationship with God the Father. Today families are blessed and the joy of marriage and truthful appreciative apparatus for sustainable union were constructed in good faith in God. Amos nothing happens for nothing; in the will of God there are causes and impacts. Some folks may call these impacts; effect.

God took my bad and despondent, hopeless and downhearted self and made it a blessing for many. What I thought was a punishment for me was actually a design of God for answering prayers of those families under attacks, and I mean deeply psycho-social and spiritual attacks would have stripped them off their dignities and would have destroyed their developmental stages for successes in living godly with refined happiness in the Lord. It is the design of the enemy to steal, kill or destroy. However once an opportunity relegated to godly chance, time and trust in the Master (Jehovah God Almighty) will; the abundance of life become visible in the purest of relationship with God.

Amos heed to this, it is time that your desires and inner yearnings for peace; knowledge and wisdom be set towards God. The more your affections for godliness increase and your heart draws closer to God; the more your affections are towards God. The Bible wants us to set our affections on things about the Kingdoms of Heaven and of God, for they are eternal and permanent. The things which are visible are only temporal and more troubling; therefore draw near to God and He shall be closer to you in the Mighty Name of Jesus Christ of Nazareth Amen! (JAMES 4:8 II Corinthians 4:18) Praise the Lord Jesus Christ of Nazareth Amen!

~Given Authority to live victoriously~

God has given us authority over the enemies of our souls, and JEHOVAH GOD ALMIGHTY Son Amen; has defeated these enemies and placed back into our hands authority and power to deal with any strong man in our lives. Therefore, your cleaned house must stay in your possession, you must take back your joy, your peace, and all other victories in the Mighty Name of Jesus Christ of Nazareth for it is your heritage. You cannot toy with bad spirits for they are not your friends; they only lurk around to steal, kill or destroy. You must stay with God and accept the abundant life through Jesus Christ the Lord (John 10:10, Matthew 12) Think of the goodness of Jesus in every worship; contemplate all that He has done for you, and permit your soul to cry out the hallelujah praise in the Mighty Name of Jesus Christ of Nazareth. Become the sheep that you are; see everything and everyone around you as pure. The word of God declares that to the pure, all things are pure, but to the defiled, there are criticisms for everything (Titus1:15).

Have a pure heart for everything today and praise God mightily in service; let your joy break forth in praises for God is good and His truth is everlasting Amen! Amos my son working through the unknown brings you closer to God and this dependence is appreciated. Joseph while in the dungeons of Pharaoh's prison; knew that God could work things out as promised. God can never lie and He fulfills whatever He says. I am not concern about what the outcome would be right now I am relying and trusting only in the merits of Jesus Christ my Savior. All that I need Christ shall provide for me. God wants you to be amazingly focused and inspired. Choose Holiness and go after it." One thing have I desired of the LORD that's what I seek; that I may dwell in the house of the LORD all the days of my life, and to inquire about the beauty of the LORD and to seek Him in His temple " My friends without respect, honoring one another and Holiness; no one can see God. (Hebrew 12, Psalm 27). To see God you got to seek holiness you have got to treat one another with respect, love and honor in Jesus' name!

~ It is Human nature~

Is it true that the Facebook attitudes are the same as it is in the real world? Smile with everyone at all times; stand up and tell the truth about your feelings and they avoid you so well; even the praying folks they do this so well and yet want to cause fire to come down from heaven; is this possible? I get confused with this but then again it is human nature to be fake and conditional. Listen if you can be my friend or acquaintance when I agree with you then you should always be my friend when I disagree with you. Preachers, lay people and others practice human nature and call it faith! We have to get real by having good knowledge of the truth; pretense would not get anyone into heaven! My view what do you say? I wanted to see how folks would respond to such an open ended question; some folks were stoic, and while others were verbal and expressively focused on refuting the concept of blaming things on nature as oppose to sin and the distracting influences it has on the flesh. The works of the flesh is a paralyzing tool skillfully utilize over and over again by the enemies. Funny how it is always the same tricks which are utilized every time when the opportunity surfaces. One would think that the principles of the Easy assessed views are the experience of the very near with quality of wife / husband; which takes into account how people from different areas in life come to meet each other, get connected well and then circumstances interfered.

This interference is not to be ignore, it is a test for quality and sustenance. The most we get in life are the experiences we are fortunate to encounter. Our human pride sometimes derail what life affords. How do we know that we would not have been the source of a Doctor, Prophet, Lawyer, Nurse and civil individual? Life oh life what disdainful feeling thrown to the unknown which we negate chances relevant for the good of us, only to wallop in the myopic of the unknown. Today I rid myself and hold on to what experience and people God permitted in my life. In total absent of tomorrow; I wished that my yesterday was accommodated by today's sights. Nevertheless to this fact; I am grateful!

Getting A Wife; And Not Just A Woman

A wife is a blessing! People find each other and know this is truth when the results are lasting, good and trustworthy. We appreciate the time for getting to understand one another, and the good uplifting which comes with this opportune moment of truth and joy. It is a blessing to have a wife not just a woman. Any man can have just a woman, and not a wife, but this never last. The outcome for such a relationship can be brutal, abusive and demeaning, however the good word is that: "He who finds a wife finds a good thing,

And obtains favor from the Lord (Proverb 18:22)" . A wife is not a thing but the scripture is comparing the joy which comes with locating the best, and once a man finds the best it brings him joy, great happiness and security. An awful wife is a woman and she brings no favor to her husband. When a man finds the good wife she becomes a path to greater favor. Not all women who fits the biological requirements are necessarily wife material, and not all women would ever become a wife. Nevertheless if a woman finds God and forms a relationship with Him that woman increases her chances of been discovered for her good value and deportment and the potential of becoming the great good for a godly man seeking a respectful, committed and trustworthy woman. Therefore any woman who finds a place with God is due for discovery as the price above rubies. It is clear that a woman or man who is content in faith, is resolved peacefully in all matters. The reason for this is that they have located the Object of faith and are resolute by His awesome favor.

Getting a woman of favor has to be derived by discernment and not postures. Postures can be deceiving and completely disillusioning. Many men have gotten themselves duped by the observations of mere posterior and by this enveloped a relationship only to find out that its soul mates were mere fantasies; Nevertheless, a good and godly relationship would base all its value on the principles of the Holy Scriptures and love from a pure heart without regrets. Disillusioned relationships are the ones Satan seeks to protect. His business is to keep the persons involve in sin and later an ultimate destructive end. Getting a

wife has to be by prayers and diligence. It is not wise to base your criterion on what is seen by the eye, but rather base your criterion on the values which are intrinsic.

△ △ △

Life and fulfillment

The God of the hill is also God in the valley. You see folks can easily find words to talk about faith when things are going well. They talk about how good God is when they have not been tested. Oh how things change when there is a shift in position form up to down, pains and rejections. Friends; good faith in God gets tested by fire, it gets tried when things are not at their best. I have learned to call Him God when there is no way out, when folks turn their backs on you, when you are looked down upon. Know that God is God regardless of your state of positions be it up or down, hill or Valley; God is God all the time, everywhere in every circumstance. Please read I Kings 20:28. In the Mighty Name of Jesus Christ of Nazareth Amen. To be fulfilled is to know your relationship with God and measure how well you are in your Christian deportments.

It is a truthful saying that all perfect and beautiful things come from God. God gives the best and He only requires that we honor and respect Him as the creator. The enemy has no fulfilling place for us, but to temporally dupe people with false bliss and later require the soul of them. This is in the reverse order to God. Jehovah place for us is His good will pleasure in Heaven.

Even as we sojourn in this universe, we can reach a zenith with Christ in control of all of our ideals and ideological perspectives. Idealistically we were created to be in control of our choices and to delve into a bliss with God's care when praises of Him is released into His presence. This is why we have to confess Christ openly; everywhere and then our joy shall be fulfilled. A good life is spiritually connected within a Spirit domain. A living link in every sphere of life; be it on a hill, a mountain top or a valley; life is fulfilled wherever the Spirit of the Lord is. In every location God can locate you when you pray and He is always just a prayer away. If God connects with you and you with Him there is not less for you but being fulfilled to a full life. Therefore When Christ is on the vessel no ship sinks! No storm or man or demon sinks this ship while God is in control! Listen your life maybe located within a seesaw moments of great turbulence, nevertheless do not let the violent rage loosen your grip! Hold on and become louder in prayers; calling on the name of Jesus Christ of Nazareth until your voice is heard as in the case of blind Bartimaeus (Mark 10:46-52).

You may need to recognize that Jesus Christ the Savior is on board with you (Isaiah 43:2); therefore no matter how hard tossed you may be just remind yourself that this ship is not sinking, and wait for the calm as it comes from the Sanctuary of God (Psalm 20) "God shall send you help from His Sanctuary" in the Mighty Name of Jesus Christ of Nazareth Amen. Father thank You for the help and I am holding on in Jesus Name Amen!

Amos Interrupts Bobby Ross

Bobby Sir; you speak with such assurance and deliberate attitude affirming your position with God. I have relegated this entire journey to God's plan for man's fulfilled lives. Truly God gives the desires of everyone's heart and in my opinion He has granted thee the good which you have sought in Him. I see you talk like you are on the verge of a breakthrough therefore follow these points

1. Don't listen to what people are saying, they cannot help you. (Job 5)

2. Pray until God recognizes your voice and bottles your tears. (Mark 10:46-52). Cry out louder.

3. Do not attack man; attack the Spirit behind the scenes (Ephesians 6:12)

4. Know that God is in the struggle with you and is applying all the weapons to protect your soul from evil (Isaiah 43:2-3)

5. Understand that you are the clay and God is forming you for His glory and praise. (Isaiah 43:24)

6. Rejoice in the Lord always no matter the situation in which you find yourself. For in everything give thanks it is God's will concerning you in the Mighty Name of Jesus. Delight yourself always in the LORD and you shall see your Mighty breakthrough in Jesus's Name Amen!

Bobby my good Sir. This is your time and I think you should make a call to Melinda. However, before you do Sir. I like to leave these words with you and that I am hoping that they would become pointers for your new journey. Here it goes.

When you at a low circumstance or low point?

Just think this; we all need low points or situation in which we are hard pressed into position for appreciating the Divine Providence of God! God is moved when the broken hearted; the contrite heart, the poor in spirit, the needy and the outcasts seek His assistance. When we are full of our selves; God cannot filled us, but when we are emptied of ourselves God can use His ever flowing fountain grace and mercy to fill us to an over flowing point. Today there are great men filled of themselves and have come to positions in time where they compare themselves with enticing words full of man's wisdom thus hypothesizing the Divine Providence of God to fit their presuppositions; whereas the simple and the down trodden consistently and constantly seeks the Divine mercies of almighty God with complete devotion while invocating! In lamenting the innocence and the offending persons genuinely cry for the mercies of God, and seek restoration and deliverance, but the already filled has already much and are constantly judging and casting blame on account of their would be self-righteous selves. The contrite always ask for God's mercy "Be merciful to me oh God" take me to where you want me to be in time; towards Your (God) favoring positions. Ludie D. Pickett said "; My Savior helps me to carry, My cross when heavy to bear. Though all around me is darkness, Earthly joys all flown; My Savior whispers His promise, "I never will leave thee alone." There is an adage "empty barrel makes the most noise" and that is true within the natural sense as they do, but in the spiritual sense; God seeks the empty barrel making the most noise in godly lamentation! When a heart is broken it must cry to God! When in need of help from an emotional drained; cry to God! When confused and cannot figure out why?

Cry to God; make the most noise in the spirit and invite the presence of God into your situation. At your low points seek God first; rid yourselves of the reasons why you are where you are and be filled by the invited presences of the most High God. He would not despise the broken hearted; nor would He reject the one contrite in spirit; if we call on God; when we are in lowly situations or at the upper heights in Him; He abundantly pardons. No matter what your circumstances are God wants to fill you with His presence and flow within you joy so that you are strengthen from within and out. Once our moments meet the conditions of God; without the self-righteous attitude; He raises us from the low to the upper and He fills up the emptiness.

Friends and Family Remember you have to call on God in the time of trouble; seek His mercy in the time of need, Christ came to this earth on account of our lowly moments and for this very reason to rescue us from those who would pressed us down.

Once we empty ourselves of all of the issues tying us down and present them to God, He is certainly able to mount us up on wings of eagles. Today let the peace of God rule the day; and I declare for you in the name of Jesus of Nazareth that there would be no bad feeling of rejection or guile of bad spirit of emotional drain; keeping you down. I nullify the enemy plans and declare by fire that they are defeated in Jesus' Name! AMEN!

Most of all know this that the secret to life is trusting in the Name of Jesus Christ of Nazareth and the ability to adjust to circumstances positive approach having God in control. You see the word of God is alive and it directs our steps so that iniquity is less effective at keeping you down. Your prudent attitude as a child of God defeats every evil plan formed and directed at you. It keeps you humble and in the presence of God ALMIGHTY. Therefore, the arrows which flies at day or the terror that comes at cannot move you. Your trust is under the shadow of the Almighty God. Today stand in faith after doing all you can stand and positively, be adjustable, do not fret; God is with you in the Mighty Name of Jesus Christ of Nazareth Amen! (Psalm 91, Psalm 149, Proverb 1)

Amos changed the focus and directed it to Melinda

Bobby for as it seems Melinda just might leave the convent; I think Sister Yates were not purposed for celibacy, in my imaginable view; she was slated for decency in the position as a mother and a beautiful professional wife. The essential facts remained glaring in that all roads lead to a beautiful family in God Almighty. I have had so many thoughts as to what it would be like? How beautiful and intelligent the fruits of your bodies would be? Bobby just the thought of Melinda becoming your wife I am wholesomely affixed on the end of nunnery to the start of a bliss made in heaven for earth angles such as yourselves. Interestingly, Bobby interrupted the younger man Amos with a startle remark.

Amos he said, "What makes you profess such prophetic reality of which many prayers have been geared towards. I believe this is an answer to a new beginning, and I have no time to wait. Son hope is never lost once what you hope is permissible in accordance with the acts of God Almighty; who is the maker of heaven and earth and He rules all things here and above. He has great plans for those who have compassion for others and trust in God Almighty with all their hearts and souls. When a man desires a woman and I mean a woman of God; he desires a precious ornament. Melinda in my view is that precious ornament and like Jacob the son of Isaac; I have paid my bride price and this time I am getting my Rebecca. I am speaking this into been as if it was meant to be, and this I know that nothing beats God's giving. Amos let us get ready for travel. Brother Ross what do you mean travel? Are we going to America to meet Melinda? Amos you have well spoken; yes to meet Melinda!

△ △ △

When the truth of all men hearts touches happiness

Just in time the telephone rang and Bobby picked up the phone and He begin speaking; it was Melinda after all, but she would not speak but instead broke down in tears. She was caught in between two opinions. She felt she had disappointed the Clergy and the host of others by disavowing celibacy. She had just resigned from the ministry. She was over taken by an emotional upheaval and this relegated her to tears of disappointment and an inner disdained. Melinda could not utter a word; her sobbing had Bobby frantic and flabbergasted. As he listened carefully; his professional analytic skills kicked; comparatively he could sense an idealistic cadence. He deduced an exhilarating garth impregnated by a grand euphoria with blissful origins; concaved in the heart of freedom; Melinda had disavowed, and now wishes to return to Christian normalcy.

Friends we cannot predict when the acts of love would arrest you and profoundly subject you to a path of joy. However when it happens nothing can keep a man heart from searching until he is satisfied. True love would make you happy! True love would bring the ocean into your backyard. True love would make you do things beyond your imaginable view. True love propels you even when running on empty. True love shall satisfy your empty soul and equip you to keep on keeping on. Melinda Yates has find true love; Bobby Ross.

△ △ △

About the Author

TKBphoto 2012

Bishop **Emerson Deline** is the head of the United Christian Assembly Church Inc.

In his maiden book, he writes about VOWS, an important aspect of any relationship.

He and his family reside in the United States. He is working on his second book, which should be out sometime in 2018.

www.ingramcontent.com/pod-product-compliance
Lightning Source LLC
Chambersburg PA
CBHW060834110426
R18122100001BA/R181221PG42736CBX00028BA/29